> *We are all wanderers on this earth*
> *Our hearts are full of wonder and*
> *Our Souls deep with dreams*
>
> —Romani Gypsy Saying

Jakob Smith was a wild and reckless youth whose passion in life was to travel to new countries. Wherever he went, he was interested in the local history, daily life and culture of the people. During the daylight hours, he enjoyed visiting museums, religious sites, zoos and national parks. At night, contrary to his daytime wanderings, he would enjoy drinking beer and mixing with the local people in neighbourhood bars or restaurants. He would attempt to talk with anyone despite sometimes language difficulties. Frequently these conversations took place in places of ill repute where hookers and petty criminals made up the numbers. They conned him relentlessly but their stories, true or otherwise were often amusing and worth the few drinks they cost. Now somewhat more mature, Jakob looks back on such times with fond memories. So many people met only once for just a few, sometimes drunken moments, but never forgotten. Despite the odd-black eye and a couple of nights spent in lock-up, was it worth it? Must say yes, as if he had his youth over, he would probably go down the same path. The few bad times fade into obscurity, and the many good times, prone to exaggeration, just seem to get better with age.

A travel story different from most; entertaining, informative at times, Jakob quite simply loves travelling to new places and meeting new people is his life.

For my loving wife, Rachada, who puts up with me; my daughters, Rikki and Kara-Xica, and not to be forgotten my grandson, Somshai-Fabian, who is the real-life image of Jake in *They call me Jake*.

Jakob Smith

THEY CALL ME JAKE

Life on the Ocean Waves and
Other Stories

AUSTIN MACAULEY PUBLISHERS™
LONDON * CAMBRIDGE * NEW YORK * SHARJAH

Copyright © Jakob Smith 2023

The right of Jakob Smith to be identified as author of this work has been asserted by the author in accordance with sections 77 and 78 of the Copyright, Designs and Patents Act 1988.

All rights reserved. No part of this publication may be reproduced, stored in a retrieval system, or transmitted in any form or by any means, electronic, mechanical, photocopying, recording, or otherwise, without the prior permission of the publishers.

Any person who commits any unauthorised act in relation to this publication may be liable to criminal prosecution and civil claims for damages.

All of the events in this memoir are true to the best of author's memory. The views expressed in this memoir are solely those of the author.

A CIP catalogue record for this title is available from the British Library.

ISBN 9781035831562 (Paperback)
ISBN 9781035831555 (ePub e-book)
ISBN 9781035831579 (Audiobook)

www.austinmacauley.com

First Published 2023
Austin Macauley Publishers Ltd®
1 Canada Square
Canary Wharf
London
E14 5AA

Table of Content

Sydney The Early Days	12
However, the Tale Unfolds	13
A New Life Was About to Begin	16
First Stop—Colon, Republic of Panama	18
Colon And the Fun Begins	20
We Discover Stowaways	24
Well, Hello USA Charleston, South Carolina	26
Highlights of Our Stay in Charleston	29
Brooklyn, New York	33
Boston	37
Canada	39
New York Take 2	43
West Africa	49
Ecuador	52
Newark, New Jersey	53
Guayaquil, Ecuador	56
Haifa, Israel, and My 21st Birthday	59
Argentina	61
Brazil	68
Paranagua	74

Fortaleza, Brazil	76
Rio de Janeiro	78
And I Decide to Become a Deck Officer	80
Life as a Student in London	83
I Join the *Bernard* as 3rd Mate	89
The Mighty Amazon	91
Manaus	94
Belem	100
Liverpool	104
I Take a Sabbatical	106
Life in an Israeli Kibbutz Ramat Yochanan	109
Eilat, Israel's Red Sea Port in the Gulf of Akaba	121
Au Revoir, Eilat Hopefully, A Job Beckons	128
Gaza	130
The Missing Submarine	132
Orli	136
"Uncle Bar-Lev"	138
Logs and Plywood from Africa	145
Encounter with a Warship	150
A New Career Change	152
Introducing 'Curly King'	158
My Apartment in Tel Aviv "Home Is What You Make It"	161
Bar Life in Tel Aviv Bernie's	167
My Humble Apartment	171
Returning Home After a Night on the Town	173
All Good Times Must Come to an End	174
Saint John's Newfoundland	179

The Isolated Township of Cartwright, Labrador	185
Hope to See You Again, St John's	194
Israel Again	196
I Lose My Passport	199
A Pickpocket Strikes	204
A Spell as Relief Manager	211
The Territory of Amapa A Jungle Wilderness	224
Jaguars and Ocelots	230
Same Job but with a New Employer	235
Wonderful Copenhagen	244
Gabon, Port Gentil Take 2	249
We Run Aground	252
Luderitz, Namibia	254

I'm Jakob Smith, known simply as Jake.

Came into this wonderful world just outside the small country city of Wrexham in North Wales.

My father was a builder's labourer. At the time, employment in the building trade was hard to find and after long late-night discussions with my mother, they made the difficult decision to leave their extended families and friends and apply for emigration to either Canada or Australia.

Australia won out and, as the only child at the tender age of 2, we left the green hills of Wales for sunny Australia.

Sydney
The Early Days

We settled in the western suburbs of Sydney, Australia's largest city, and home to many other newly arrived immigrants. Our neighbourhood was very cosmopolitan with large numbers of people from the UK, Holland, Greece and Southeast Asia.

We generally got on well with the native-born Aussies, though our parents tended to mix mostly with those from their former countries. My father quickly found work and for the first time, the family did not have to worry about where the money for the next week was coming from.

By the time I had completed my kindergarten years, I had become a typical young Australian, though my mother and father never let me forget that I had been born in Wales. To this day, as a middle-aged man, I am still very proud of my Welsh heritage.

Primary school followed kindergarten, and despite a poor academic record, I duly graduated to the local high school. As a group, my close friends and I disliked school and hated the very minor discipline that was imposed in that era. In short, we became problem students for whom the cane and detentions after school became a regular occurrence.

Street gangs were on the rise in our suburb. It was almost inevitable that my next step was to be initiated into one of the two gangs in our area. At the age of fifteen, I became a junior member of the Purple Gang. Marijuana and LSD were available everywhere and we indulged whenever the opportunity arose.

Heavy drugs were just starting to become available, and thankfully, by the time they became commonplace, I was long gone. Sadly, in the following years, one of my friends was to overdose on heroin and a number had spent varying periods in state prisons.

However, the Tale Unfolds

A cold, heavily overcast morning seemed appropriate for what lay ahead as escorted by my parents, I made my way to the Juvenile Court. My three best friends with similarly stony-faced parents were already in the courtroom. We were not even allowed to greet each other.

Like most late teenage boys in Australia, we were obsessed with cars. Through an older gang member, we had pooled funds and illegally bought an old, post-World War 2 Chevrolet.

The car was a green and black monster almost identical to the mafia mob cars prominent in prohibition era of the 1930s in the US. A four-door model complete with running boards, wooden spoked wheels and surprisingly, the leather interior seats were still in good shape.

It had been sitting in a far corner of a giant used car yard seemingly forever and forgotten. It was covered with layers of dust, jacked up and sitting on cement building blocks. The wheels had been removed and dumped on the back seat inside the car. Any visitors to the yard would never have given it a passing glance.

The yard was probably glad to get rid of it, sold it for just twenty Australian pounds. Four of us each contributed five pounds and one of our elder brothers purchased it for us. It was the dream of all young men to own a car and even though it was jointly owned, it became our pride and joy

As the minimum age to own a car was 18 and we were 16-year-old teenagers, the purchase had to be kept secret from our parents. Only one of us held a driving licence and we had to park it in neighbourhood streets not frequented by our parents.

On most nights, we would go for drives through the back streets of the suburb; the car crammed with as many of our friends as could squeeze in. 14 jam-packed bodies were our record.

All went well until rival gang members jacked it up one night and stole all four wheels. They were bitter enemies, and we were quick to hear that the wheels were lost and gone forever. The fact that we no longer had a car now presented a problem as driving somewhat recklessly through our local area had become almost an addiction.

Logically, the next step was bound to happen. No longer having our own car we took to 'borrowing' those belonging to others and so our joyriding escapades began.

Again having illegal wheels, there was no shortage of teenage girls eager to join us, the very fact that they were now joyriding in a stolen car turned them on even more. They would wait at a local sleazy Greek owned cafe until our 'limo' for the night showed up.

Little did any of their parents know that none of their darling daughters were innocent virgins. It was all teenage boys could wish for, cars, sex, pot and booze; life just did not get any better!

And then, to use the popular expression, 'the shit hit the fan big time'.

Friday night was the one night of the week that the shops stayed open late until 9pm. Lots of people and families took advantage of this, the mall car parks were full and security almost non-existent. In those days, it was so easy to hotwire any of the standard production cars after initial entry being made via the quarter glass ventilation window on the driver's door.

It was on our third consecutive Friday evening that we were caught. As usual, we started by buying beer from contacts behind the local pub. This night, we were flush with cash and bought more than usual. It was perhaps as well that for once, none of our various girlfriends were with us.

After making inroads into the beer, we stole a car and headed to a dirt track just out of town. It ran through a government planted pine forest and was a favourite place for cornering at speed sliding about on the loose surface. Just as we turned into the track, Simon hollered that we were being followed and it was a cop car.

All drunk, we thought it was hilarious and that he was having us on. Seconds later, Joe who was driving lost control and we slammed sideways into a big gum tree. None of us were hurt and as there was some damage to the driver's side, we all piled out from the passenger side.

Simon had not been joking and the police car arrived to catch all four of us standing by the side of the road, peeing into the scrub. It had never occurred to us the regular Friday night car thefts had alerted the cops, and they were just waiting to apprehend the culprits.

And back to the Juvenile Court.

The presiding lady judge labelled us hooligans and a disgrace to our respective families. She decided not to send us to a juvenile detention centre on the grounds that our parents had covered all repair costs to the owners of the stolen vehicle and that this family who were staunch churchgoers did not want to press any further charges.

Any repetition of any anti-social or criminal behaviour would however guarantee lock-up. The whole proceeding was over in 20 minutes with her final warning that the four of us were not to associate socially and that our parents were to monitor this.

My father was quick to react. In less than two weeks, he lined up a friend of his who was a shipping agent and had arranged for me to join a Swedish freighter that was presently docked in Sydney.

And so with a newly acquired passport and vaccination card in hand, I met up with my dad's friend and was taken on board the ship *Baltic Sea*.

A New Life Was About to Begin

After being accepted by the ship's Chief Mate as a new crew member, I had to go to the Swedish Consulate where Jakob Smith was officially signed on the vessel as a deck boy. My new, totally unexpected and hopefully trouble-free life had begun.

The ship had almost completed loading a full cargo of Australian frozen meat destined for the US Navy, to be discharged at several ports on the US East Coast. Those navy boys would eat well!

We sailed from Sydney to Brisbane where a small, final consignment of meat was loaded, the ship's cargo gear was all secured and we departed on the long Pacific Ocean transit to the Panama Canal in route to the mighty USA, 'Capital City Hollywood'.

I had also become a member of the Swedish Seaman's Union, and even as a deck boy, the most junior rating, my monthly wages, when converted into Australian dollars, were more than I had expected. The crossing of the vast Pacific Ocean provided the 'hands-on' experience of life as a junior seaman.

Swedish ships used a lot of relatively inexperienced young men, working under the supervision of a handful of professional seamen. They in turn received their instructions from the Bosun, a company dedicated man, who in turn reported daily to the Chief Mate.

To us youngsters, the Bosun was 'God', was our mutual enemy, and who was quick to give us a swift kick in the backside if we screwed up. We had no social contact with the ship's officers, and it was doubtful if some of them even knew our name. If they wanted our attention, it was always, "Hey, you!"

In addition to the cargo we carried, we also took on up to six passengers. These were older, wealthier folk who preferred the quieter, less organised life on a cargo ship as opposed to regular passenger ships. They enjoyed the longer spells in the different ports and actually paid higher fares than on the classy passenger liners.

My day's work was divided into two periods, each of four hours, which I learnt to call sea watches. I worked from midday to four in the afternoon and again from midnight until four in the morning.

In daytime, my work consisted of endless cleaning, washing exterior paintwork, and then painting over the clean areas. At night, I went to the very front of the ship, the bow, and kept lookout duties. My task was to report any light I spotted to the officer in charge on the bridge. It would invariably be another ship and if necessary, he would take any evasive action required to avoid a possible collision.

Like all new deck boys, I mistakenly reported stars low on the horizon as possible ships, which at least let the officer know I was not asleep. For our off-duty hours, we had a well-equipped recreation room with gym equipment, a table tennis table, dartboard and a library of books.

Saturday was a special day as all of us junior ratings could buy two cans of beer at very cheap duty-free prices. Yep, just two miserable cans! We all decided to save up our two cans weekly allowance for the three weeks plus Pacific Ocean crossing and then celebrate by drinking the lot just before we reached Panama.

Despite the best of intentions, it never happened! The senior seamen, old guys to us youngsters, were each allowed one bottle of spirits when we received our beer issue. When, and not if, they polished off their bottle, they could then report to the Captain and request a second bottle.

Incredible as it sounded, he would have them walk down a line on his carpet, which if they stayed on course would then entitle them to another bottle. Being semi hardened alcoholics, they always scored a second bottle. I guess it was just a game the Captain played.

Mind you, Captains and Chief Engineers were themselves quite often heavy drinkers.

First Stop—Colon, Republic of Panama

We arrived off the Pacific side of the Panama Canal early morning after a 27-day Pacific Ocean crossing from Brisbane. Almost immediately, a Panama Canal pilot came out in a small boat, boarded and we headed into the first of the locks.

It was a mind-boggling experience for me as less than two months previously, I had been in court with the possibility of being locked-up and here I was on a ship, preparing to enter the Panama Canal.

The Panama Canal was built in the early 1900s to provide a short route for ships to go from the Pacific Ocean to the Caribbean Sea/Atlantic Ocean. Prior to this, they had to sail down to the bottom of South America to achieve this transit, adding thousands of miles onto their voyage.

The Canal is some 80km long and we were entering it from the Pacific Ocean side. In the Canal, there are a series of three separate locks whose function is to control the water level difference between the two great oceans.

The passage of a ship thru the locks is controlled by electric locomotives running on railroad lines on each side of the lock. The locomotives are called 'Mules', as though they were electric powered donkeys. Mule crew sent wire ropes up to the bow and stern of the ship which the ship's crew then had to make fast. The ship used its engine to move slowly into the lock while the mules kept it straight and could also be used to act as a brake if needed.

As the ship approached the lock, a huge gate at the far end of the lock was closed. Once inside the lock and in the correct position determined by the mules, another massive gate behind the ship was closed.

The water level in the lock was then adjusted as necessary to be identical to that at the exit gate, which was then opened. The mule lines were released, and the ship sailed out towards the next set of locks.

We deck boys worked in pairs and our job was simply to make fast and then later release the mule lines. Even two inexperienced deck boys couldn't screw up a job that easy. As we had to stay there for the whole transit, we saw all the locks.

First lock was 'Mira Flores', which I was told meant 'look flowers', although all we could see in the background was jungle, no flowers.

The second lock had a person's name 'Pedro Miguel', guess at some time he must have been a VIP while the third and final set of locks was called 'Gatun Locks', no doubt after the lake we had just crossed.

Shortly after clearing Gatun Locks, we arrived at, and tied up in Colon. The ship was to take on fuel and we boys were going to hit the town.

Colon
And the Fun Begins

As soon as we had tied the ship up in Colon, those of us who had finished their work for the day were free to go ashore. We had all taken a cash advance on our wages from the ship's radio officer and the money was burning a hole in our pockets.

Four of us headed quickly out the port gates and into the teeming streets and alleyways of downtown Colon. It was my first ever visit to a foreign country and I had entered another world.

The noise created by the traffic was deafening as cars, buses and trucks cleared a path down the narrow streets with their horns blaring incessantly. Couldn't drive like this in Australia, but here in Panama it seemed to work just fine.

The footpaths were choked with people dodging around endless sidewalk vendors and all to a background of high-volume Latin music. Being all new to me, it was exciting. We had originally decided to wander around the crowded shops and buy some souvenirs as mementos of our first stop in Latin America.

However, two of the guys had been in Colon before and all they had talked about for days prior to our arrival was the Zam-Zam bar, a place we just had to visit. By all accounts, the bar was a lonely seaman's dream, a perfect place to relax after a long sea passage. With cheap drinks, beautiful young Colombian women chasing a dollar and with short time rooms upstairs, it sounded too good to be true.

Still full of good intentions, and reluctant to split up from our buddies, we decided to go with them to Zam-Zam, just for one drink, check out the girls, then take care of our shopping before returning to the bar.

We found it easily enough as despite the noisy street, we heard the bar before we actually saw it. Turning a corner, the latest hit songs boomed out, seemingly from the heavens. Zam-Zam was on the second story accessed by a narrow staircase.

When we went in, it turned out to be quite a place. Centre piece was a well-lit horseshoe shaped bar surrounded by bar stools. There was a mini dance floor, and the remaining area was in clothed in semi darkness with small booths along the walls, cosily designed for couples.

A magnificent juke box was in one of the corners. Apart from two very drunk guys arguing loudly at the bar, there were only a couple of girls in the place, but seemingly, in less than a heartbeat, as if by magic, more women appeared.

Young men were prone to boasting or straight out lying. Our shipmates had told us the girls were young, many of them very good looking and were a lot of fun. They had not been bullshitting us, the girls were everything they had said.

The juke box had 'died' so first up, we were hit for the twenty-five cent coins needed to bring it back to life. It turned out that when there were no paying customers, the girls operated the jukebox without coins, however when 'punters' entered, the barman did whatever so that it only worked when fed with money. Smart business!

In a few minutes, we had cold bottles of beer in front of us, arms around gorgeous hookers, and all thoughts of souvenir shopping rapidly fading away. The girls, despite their tender years were seasoned pros and quickly paired us off. In no time and still with just the first drink in hand, our newfound partners shepherded us off to the more intimate, dark and semi-private booths.

The seats were comfortable and small, so we really snuggled up together. To the young man from western Sydney, this was as close to paradise as he could get. The girls would ask for a drink, which was probably nothing stronger than soft drinks or cold tea and which on our wages were a little expensive.

They got a percentage from the drink payments but of course, their main income was derived from sex. The bar was simply an elegant facade for a brothel. You had your drinks in the bar and danced on the small floor alongside the bar if you were in the mood. Then when you felt the urge and still had money remaining, it was but a short trip up the stairs to the next floor.

We had decided that the first guy to go upstairs for a short time would have the room paid for by the rest of us. Nils caught us by surprise, rushing off with his girl before even finishing his beer. To be sure, he, like the rest of us was horny, but a Norwegian not finishing his drink was almost unheard of. Within minutes, all of us had followed.

Until now, my only experience with prostitutes had been doing the schoolboy thing of walking the narrow backstreets of King's Cross in Sydney, checking out the women in their small rooms, daring each other to have a 'quickie'.

Here, the girls had their individual little rooms where they both entertained clients and also lived when not actively 'working'. Main feature was a large comfortable double bed, the remaining furniture being very basic.

The girls were by no means shy and very quickly knew how to arouse young seamen. They had no inhibitions at all, and despite the business arrangement, really looked after their customers and were, as we had been told, a lot of fun.

The first trip upstairs was invariably 'over in a heartbeat' as being young men in their late teens and early twenties, in the hands of young, sensual and very experienced women, at best a few strokes with 'wee willy' and we would shoot our load.

I was embarrassed until I found out my friends had all had the same experience. The girls thought this was hilarious and in broken Spanish, assured us that the second time around would be much better.

The bar then had a custom when after sex, the girl would place her panties on the guy's head, and he then had to return to the bar. We had a good laugh over this but none of us took the panties off as our new partners were now bottomless and braless, wearing just their light cotton dresses.

A few more drinks and round two up the stairs was a foregone conclusion. And yes, it was better! The girls, ok to use the less polite term, whores, were all from Colombia, the country immediately to the south of Panama. According to a notice posted in the bar, they were officially eighteen years old, which may have been true though none of them could have been more than in her early twenties.

They were probably specially chosen as they were without exception very good looking. Typically slim, with excellent figures and varying from a light creamy skin colour to dark brown, they had the looks to cater for all clients. There wasn't an ugly one amongst them.

We organised a topless competition where each of the girls had to show her boobs, the winner getting a cash reward. The participants were eager, and we dragged out the final judging decision as long as possible.

None of the girls spoke more than the few English phrases necessary for their trade, so we were able to pick up our first Spanish words, words no doubt best not repeated in respectable company.

They told us they came to Panama for a month at a time. Goodness only knows how much sex they had in a month, then returning home with some money for their families who were all poor. We were taking turns to pay for rounds, trying to keep an eye on our rapidly diminishing bank notes.

It was probably as well that our precious shore leave time was all too soon coming to an end, so with the inevitable call of 'one for the road', we paid the bar bill, gave small tips to the girls and with fond farewells, navigated somewhat unsteadily back down the stairs and out into the street.

They had won our hearts and of course, we promised to be back next trip, promises they must have heard a thousand times over. Collectively, we had just enough cash for the taxi back to the ship, so in place of the souvenir shopping, we had fucked our brains out, drank a skin full of booze and had a million laughs with the girls.

After all, who really needed souvenirs to remind them of Colon, memories of Zam-Zam would endure long after any souvenirs had been lost or trashed.

We arrived back on the ship, in varying conditions of sobriety. Feeling no pain whatsoever and happy, happy, happy, we departed Colon. After a cursory inspection from our boss, the Bosun, we assisted with the unmooring of the ship's tie-up ropes and waved goodbye as Colon faded into the distance.

One thing for sure, we had plenty of stories to tell at future coffee-smoke breaks, stories that would surely only get better with passing time.

We Discover Stowaways

Our next port of call, and our first in the USA was to be Charleston, South Carolina. We sailed out of Panama with our full crew of 29 on board. Two days later, much to the annoyance and dismay of the Captain, two extra bodies appeared. Yes, we had stowaways!

They claimed to be from the Central American Country of Nicaragua, which at the time was politically very unstable. For whatever reason, they had fled their homeland and found their way to Panama with the sole intention of finding some ship on route to the USA.

To shipping companies, stowaways presented huge problems in that it was very difficult to get rid of them. The fact that they were able to successfully stowaway was directly blamed on the ship.

Company and International Security Regulations required the ship's crew to make a thorough search of the vessel before departing from any port. Object being to locate unauthorised persons, or any suspicious items not previously noticed. Records of such searches must be kept by the ship. According to the deck officer on duty at the time, this search had, at least on paper, been done.

The stowaways conveniently had no identification whatever, spoke no English and their Nicaraguan nationality was a 'maybe'. One of our senior deck seamen was Spanish and he assisted the Captain in questioning the pair of them. From their accent, he confirmed they were definitely Central Americans but could not identify their nationality beyond that.

No doubt after consultation with the company head office in Sweden, the Captain assigned them a two-berth cabin and informed them they were to work with the crew. And so, we now had two additional cleaner-helpers.

When cleaning with us, they would take off their shirts, revealing chests and backs covered with crudely done tattoos, which were apparently politically motivated.

Despite all but total language barrier, we got along well with them. They joined us for all meals. The poor buggers were starving and for the first few meals, really tucked into the very good Scandinavian food.

Through our Spanish seaman, they asked the Captain if they could remain on the ship and receive wages.

He had to tell them this was not going to happen, and that when we got a day out of Charleston, they would have to be locked in their cabin while we made landfall and until US Immigration had come on the ship.

Well, Hello USA
Charleston, South Carolina

It was a brisk, sunny morning when we tied up just after daylight in Charleston Port. A cool 45 degrees according to the radio someone had turned on in the accommodation. No doubt it was the USA as we were in the land where weather temperatures were measured in degrees Fahrenheit.

It was a pop music station with all the latest Top-100 hits interrupted constantly with road traffic reports from around town. The DJ's accent intrigued me, and not only me, as soon several of us were trying to imitate the rich US southern drawl; we must really have sounded like idiots.

Immigration came and did their thing. All newcomers like myself had to be fingerprinted and have our mug shots taken, complete with an ID number on the photo. Purpose of this was that we would receive a US Landing Card, which we were to always carry in lieu of our passport when we left the ship.

The immigration had come prepared and had the fingerprint equipment and a special camera with them. I now realised authorities had my prints and photo on their records in 2 countries, Australia and again in the USA. Wow, I was starting to make my mark on the world!

Two days later, our new ID cards were brought to the ship. I now found out that not only were our new cards for trips off the ship, but if we requested to sign off the ship in the USA, this card would allow us to do that.

As for our newfound stowaway friends, they did not receive a red-carpet welcome to the 'Land of the Free'. For time being, they had to remain on the ship and were shifted to a cabin which had toilet facilities. Immigration posted an armed guard at the ship's gangway. He had to come onto the ship and escort us whenever we took food to the guys while we unlocked and opened their door.

They remained for almost three weeks when suddenly they were no more. Asked the security what had happened and all he knew was that they had been taken off by immigration in the early hours of the morning and that he would leave us as well, as soon as his shift was up.

He laughed and told us he was paid for 8 hours, and even though there were no stowaways to guard, he had to still put in his 8 hours. Meanwhile, the very day we tied up in Charleston, the workers who load and unload ships, longshoremen as they were called in the US, went on strike in several ports along the US East Coast.

After four days with no work in the port, our local agent decided he would try and bring in non-union labour to discharge our meat cargo. We had a consignment of just 88 tonnes for Charleston.

The longshoremen in Charleston were most, if not all, African Americans, and there were some huge dudes amongst them. Their organisers had anticipated such action by agents and had formed a picket line around the entrance to the port. Big and mean looking as they were, the longshoremen were also carrying baseball bats and left no doubt that they would use them if pushed.

The agents' attempt to use non-union labour evaporated. After two weeks in port with still no discharge, a decision was made for the ship to go to Philadelphia and discharge the Charleston cargo there along with the much larger consignment destined for that port.

That plan also fell in a heap when the longshoremen in Philadelphia backed their brothers' picket action in Charleston. So here we remained in the delightful city of Charleston/South Carolina. We were free to leave the ship whenever our daily duties were completed and had plenty of time to wander around the city.

We were greeted on a friendly basis by the guys manning picket lines and in the neighbourhood bordering the dock area, which was also very much African American. On my first trip out of the port confines, my initial experience of America was somewhat bizarre.

I had written a letter to my family in Sydney, had purchased postage stamps from one of the security watchman assigned to the ship, and was looking for a post box to drop my letter.

Suddenly, a police car pulled up right behind me. Busy looking for a post box, I hadn't seen it come. One of the two white cops in the car rolled down his window and called me over. He asked me what I was up to. I told him and he said, you are kidding, what are you here for?

I thought my accent would have told him I was a foreigner but maybe not. Again, I told him I was from a Swedish ship in the port and wanted to post this letter.

He pointed and said, "Well, go ahead, that's a post box right over there."

I looked and said, "Where? I don't see one." He gave me a strange look, like he was dealing with some imbecile and pointed again.

I said, "I can see a blue box, but post boxes are always red." The cops laughed and then set me straight by telling me that in the USA, post boxes are always blue.

They asked me if I was going back to the ship and told them I was on my way into town. The driver said, "Go post your letter and we will give you a lift into town."

I jumped in and off we went, the city centre was not very distant.

The cop that had first called me told me they had stopped because they thought I was looking for drugs. They told me this was a 'nigger' part of town, was unsafe, and that white people only came here to buy drugs.

I had heard racist stories about the Klu Klux Klan in the deep south of the US but thought these were simply a part of an unsavoury history which took place in the years following American Civil War.

Now in the squad car were a couple of cops who certainly did not like African Americans. Just before they dropped me in town, they told me never to walk through that port area but always take a taxi. I thanked them for the ride.

I had a quiet chuckle to myself when I realised what a great story this would make when I got back to Sydney and met up with my friends. Jake, being given a lift in a police car for no other reason than the officers concerned being helpful and friendly.

Such things never happened in Sydney's West, at least not to any of my friends! The strike went on for 31 days and the ship stayed firmly tied up to the wharf.

My first trip to the great USA and here I was getting to spend a whole month in my first port instead of just the one day which was the original schedule when we docked.

Highlights of Our Stay in Charleston

As deck boys, we worked just eight hours a day so had plenty of free time much of which we spent going out as a group. Young men were always on the lookout for young women and Charleston had more than its fair share of these, and again they had that accent 'to die for'.

However, this was not Panama and to get anywhere with the local girls, we were faced with problems. While the girls may have been willing for a flutter with seaman speaking a very different English from them, they all had steady boyfriends who were not impressed and kept an eagle eye on them.

Nevertheless, we made friends with quite a number of these couples at a ten-pin bowling rink in the centre of the city and we would go there often. Somehow our new friends got us 'student rates', which were quite cheap.

Before long, when we realised that trying to hit on these girls was not the way to go, we ended up having mixed teams of us and the locals. We really did make friends, which was just as well as, without exception, they were far better bowlers than any of us.

We visited a museum. Big factor was that entrance was free and we were watching our dollars. In my wildest dreams, I had never imagined I would ever do this; museums were just not my scene. However, as it cost nothing, we all trooped in.

I hated history when I was at school, but to my surprise, I found it interesting to learn a little of the city of Charleston and the State of South Carolina, which is one of the oldest of the American States.

The American Civil War played an important part in the history of the state. In 1861, Abraham Lincoln was elected President of the USA and one of his strongest election platforms was to abolish slavery throughout the country. Most of the slaves worked on big farming plantations in the thirteen Confederate Southern States of which South Carolina was one.

The Southern States were opposed to freeing the slaves as they made up their vast agricultural labour force. Following the election of President Lincoln, South Carolina was the first state to break away or to use the correct term, to secede from the Union. This was in 1861.

In Charleston Harbour there was a Fortress, Fort Sumter, garrisoned by soldiers from the Union government supporting President Lincoln. Shortly after seceding from the Union cadets from The Citadel, a military academy in Charleston, bombarded Fort Sumter with cannon fire. Fort Sumter, lacking military support, surrendered.

These were the first shots fired in what became a horrific and bloody civil war that was to claim enormous casualties on both sides. After initial battle successes for the Southern or Confederate Armies, the tide slowly turned and the Union forces, backed by the industrial supremacy of the Northern States, got the upper hand. The war ended in 1865, leaving a shattered nation, but once again a nation, to begin the slow task of rebuilding.

In many of the southern cities, it was payback time for the victorious Union armies. In Charleston where the first shots had been fired, Northern or Yankee soldiers as they were known, set fire to the old city, burning two thirds of it to the ground.

One Sunday morning, with a day off from duty, another deck boy and I decided to go for a walk through the port neighbourhood. Despite the early warning from the cops not to walk through this area, we never took taxis, or cabs as they were called, and had never felt any aggression at all. It was indeed much safer than parts of my old stomping ground in western Sydney.

We saw a smallish wooden church some distance ahead and could hear beautiful music coming from it. We ventured closer and could see into the church as it had large, fully open double doors facing the street. This was an African American neighbourhood, and the congregants were all black people.

All were singing and swaying to the music. From the sound and out of our sight, there had to be a choir hidden away somewhere, probably up in the front of the church.

We were a bit scared and did not want to go closer but moved off to one side where we could not be seen from those inside. We sat and had a cigarette while listening to the music. So, it dawned on me that this was what Gospel music was all about. From that day on, occasionally, I liked to sit by myself and listen to this music performed by African American or indeed African choirs. It just seemed that they put something into their singing, what I don't know, that made them special.

I had my first taste of 'moonshine' whisky one night with the security watchman at the ship's gangway. I was passing time chatting to him when he took out a hipflask and had a swig. It was a cold night and I asked him what it was. He told me it was the very best illegal moonshine that could be found in the state of South Carolina and would I like a sip.

Told him, "Sure, why not," in my newly acquired Charleston accent. It was OK, burnt my throat a bit but was no doubt strong as my body immediately felt warmer. He then asked me if I would like him to show me how to test moonshine to see if it was of good quality.

Again my, "sure, why not." He told me to fetch a spoon from the ship. No sooner said than done and I was back with a spoon.

He poured a little of the liquor into the spoon, took his cigarette lighter and held it under the spoon. The moonshine lit up, burning with a steady blue flame. He told me that if the flame was at all discoloured or smoky then the hooch was not the best quality.

So now I knew how to buy illegal moonshine whisky of the best quality, yet another important thing every young person should know, especially if visiting the deep south of the USA.

Shared a few more swigs from the hipflask, and really could feel its impact. After the second sip it tasted so much better, my throat muscles probably partially numb.

Told him I'd better not have any more as he still had some hours to work, and it was cold at the gangway. His quick reply, "I have a bottle in my car so can top up the flask. So why not have a few more swigs?"

By now, my standard reply, "sure, why not."

I finally headed back on board to the warmth of my cabin and a good sleep. His parting words, "I forgot to tell you when the whisky burns with a blue flame, you will never have a hangover, you'll just feel thirsty when you wake." Again, he was so right, no hangover at all, but yes thirsty. Asked him to score a few bottles for my friends and me before we left Charleston. This was done, to the delight of my fellow workers. Happy days loomed ahead!

There was a small bar a couple of hundred metres from the port entrance and two or three times a week, we would drop by for a few beers, usually as we made our way back to the boat. On our wages it was somewhat of a luxury, so calls were limited. The attraction was a real honey of a barmaid, who like the owner of the bar, hailed from Puerto Rico.

She was gorgeous and loved the attention three or four young guys showered on her, but steadfastly refused our pleas to 'come on, show us your boobs'. The owner was a surly miserable sod whose place behind the bar was at the cash register, with, as he showed us one time, a .38 pistol hidden close by.

All good things must come to an end and after the port had been idle for exactly one month, the labour dispute was resolved and the longshoreman, minus their baseball bats, turned up ready to resume work.

Two days later, our Charleston cargo had been finally offloaded and we sailed. Our unofficial holiday was over.

Brooklyn, New York

To complete discharge of our cargo of Australian meat, we now had to make calls to Baltimore/Philadelphia/New York (Brooklyn) and finally, Boston.

After Charleston, our wallets were pretty much empty as we had already drawn maximum permissible limits from our ship wages. This put an effective damper on our social life but we were still able to get off the ship at such times as we had completed our duty hours.

We all followed sports but none of us were familiar with either baseball or basketball, which were so popular throughout the USA and drew huge crowds. Our longest stay in port after Charleston was in Brooklyn, New York and we were able to take a trip to Shea Stadium in the borough of Queens to take in a baseball game.

In the baseball season, Queens is the home for the New York Mets and when winter comes around, the New York Jets football team take over the stadium for their home games. From time to time, it was also the venue for rock concerts and several groups, at the height of their popularity, had performed there.

We went to Shea via the New York Mass Rapid Transit system, which was an experience. The different stations were none too clean. Many of the train carriages were covered with graffiti, some of which were a blaze of colour and the actual work artistic. I didn't know whether the artists operated within the law or whether the transit authorities had simply given up trying to stop them.

The result was that it lent a certain character to what would be just another mundane big city metro rail system and we thought it great. We picked our baseball venture on a day when the New York Mets were up against a team from Los Angeles and there was a big crowd. We got seats high up and just off to one side behind the guy batting, so the view was excellent.

It was a real American experience. Vendors selling beer and hotdogs moved constantly around the stands and did a roaring trade. About halfway through the game, everybody got to their feet as a woman vocalist sang 'God Bless America'.

A lot of the spectators stood with their right arm across their chest and over their heart. A simple way of showing their pride in their country, while on a giant screen where all could see, the American flag, the 'Star Spangled Banner' appeared to flutter in the breeze.

The crowd around us were friendly especially when they found out that an Australian, two Swedes and a Chilean were seeing their first ever baseball game. They constantly told us what was going on and we picked up a whole new vocabulary of baseball sayings.

In the end, the New York team lost by 5 runs to 3 but nobody seemed too disappointed. On the way out of the stadium, I bought a blue and orange NY Mets baseball cap and the other guys bought Mets T-shirts. Some of the things the fellow spectators told us were surprising. I had no idea just how big baseball was in the US, and how highly organised the sport had become.

Most of the larger cities had a baseball team participating in one of the two established leagues, namely the American League and the National League. Some cities, such as New York had two 'franchises' as they were called.

In New York, the Mets were in the National league and their great cross-town rivals, the New York Yankees were in the American League. Anyone wanting to buy a franchise would be set back hundreds of millions of dollars.

All teams played an incredible 162 games during the season, stretching from April through to September. After a series of playoffs, the top team in each league then played off for the prestigious title of World Champion. It was all about money and lots of it.

Players could be extremely highly paid, the top guys earning millions a year. In the subway on the way back to Brooklyn, we all agreed it had been a great day's entertainment and worth the hard-earned bucks we had parted with.

New York is widely known under its nickname, 'the Big Apple'. This kind of weird name for a city really fascinated me but when I tried to find out how it got its origin, I got widely diverse answers.

According to some, it was named after an infamous city brothel, an African American nightclub in Harlem, was a name coined by jazz musicians in the 1930s, or was somehow related to the sport of racing, where the prize for a horse winning a race was termed 'the Big Apple'.

Take your pick, the brothel suggestion was colourful, but perhaps lacking in respect to the USA's best known city, so I'd go for the jazz musicians' choice. Then again, it could have been a combination of all the above. Whatever, it was a popular term which persisted until today and native New Yorkers seemed quite proud to relate to their city as 'The Big Apple'.

For the trivia freaks, New York is made up of five separate big suburbs or boroughs as they are called. These being Manhattan, Brooklyn, The Bronx, Staten Island and lastly Queens, the borough made famous by the hilarious comedy movie *Coming to America*, starring Eddie Murphy. If you haven't watched it, do so, OK it's a bit dated, but is a great movie and most probably, like me, you'd love it.

It's obvious I'm an Eddie Murphy fan so if you like *Coming to America*, back it up with another of his comedies *Trading Places*, another oldie but goodie.

Before coming to New York, we had calls in both Baltimore and Philadelphia. By now, our funds were mostly the kind that jingle in your pockets when you walked, but we still had a few 'Abe Lincolns' or $5 notes remaining with a handful of $1 bills.

It was enough for one visit in each port for a highlight of our first trip to America, a breakfast meal in a diner, or what we would call a worker's cafe. Americans would probably find this amusing as to them a diner was a diner, but to us, they were something special.

There were always diners near the entrance to the port and they offered huge helpings of the best breakfasts at very reasonable prices. The breakfast menu offered many choices starting with a good-sized glass of real orange juice, a choice of eggs, bacon or sausage, hash browns, waffles and pancakes coming with maple syrup. The more choices you made, the more you paid, but even being a bit greedy, the cost was still reasonable. Most breakfasts seemed to include 'eggs sunny side up'.

It was the first time I had heard this expression, thought it funny until I realised what an apt description it was. My favourite were the pancakes which came with a very generous little jug of maple syrup, enough to not only cover the pancakes but to practically drown them.

Because of the locality, customers were always working-class men and women, many of whom knew each other, and we found the atmosphere both light-hearted and friendly. Coming with the breakfast of your choosing was a mug of coffee.

Of course, coffee, this was the USA, was there any family in the country who did not kick start the day with a scalding cup of coffee?

In the diners we visited, we found that there was a standard bonus offer in that if you ordered breakfast accompanied with the obligatory coffee, you could then have a second coffee for free if you so wished. We never turned down anything free.

Boston

Our final port of call to complete the unloading of our cargo was Boston. With a special pilot on board, we approached this 'so historically Irish' immigrant city through the scenic Cape Cod Canal.

America as such did not have hereditary aristocrats, but they do have distinguished families, who by virtue of their great wealth, have acquired a social status akin to an aristocracy of sorts.

Cape Cod with its huge luxury mansions was home to such families, the Kennedy Clan being a well-known example. We spent four days in Boston. Only left the ship once but it was special.

Together with my Chilean friend, I was able to go to the Boston TB Gardens and see the famous Boston Celtics basketball team in winning action. We were lucky to get in as apparently for most of their home games in Boston, all tickets were sold out, sometimes well before the actual game day.

I had watched them on TV before and was familiar with their green uniforms with the Leprechaun Mascot, a real touch of the old Ireland there! The atmosphere at the game had to be experienced to be believed, the Boston fans loved their team, make no mistake.

Nearly all of the US professional basketball stars, or for that matter players, were close to two meters tall or even taller. The athleticism of such giants was quite incredible, as some were not merely tall but heavily built as well. We were told that when the basketball season was over, then ice hockey took its place; The Gardens then becoming the home of the Boston Bruins.

Boston people were definitely a sport minded lot as in addition to the basketball and hockey franchises, they were also home to one of the oldest established baseball teams in the American League, the Boston Red Sox.

Some years ago, there was a TV sitcom called *Cheers* named after and centred on a local Boston neighbourhood bar. It was funny, made good watching and went on for many seasons.

Didn't get to see very much of Boston, but four days just flew by and then it was time to head to Canada. While we had been discharging our meat cargo in the different ports, we were, at the same time, loading cargo for the trip back to Australia.

With the frozen meat all discharged, the company now needed to complete loading the ship for the return voyage back to Australia. There was cargo lined up in Canada in the ports of Three Rivers and Montreal and more in the Great Lakes US port of Detroit.

Canada

We now headed for Canada, steaming north after leaving Boston towards the mouth of the Saint Lawrence River. I was on lookout duty on the bow of the ship as we approached the entrance to the Saint Lawrence. We were sailing in darkness through dense fog at reduced speed with the ship's foghorn sounding at intervals to warn other ships of our presence.

Because of the fog, and even though it was still supposedly summer, I was shivering, it was so cold and damp. I kept looking at my watch as if urging the minutes to tick off so that my relief would appear out of the gloom and my one hour's lookout duty would be over.

And then the duty navigation officer called me on the radio. He told me to keep a very good lookout ahead as he had a ship target on the radar within a half mile of our vessel. This ship was not making the internationally required fog signals.

Less than a minute later, I saw the silhouette of a ship and immediately reported it. The Captain was with the junior officer who gave me an abrupt thanks and confirmed they could also now see the other vessel. The vessel was at anchor, showing very few lights, not giving the prescribed foghorn signals and not replying to our radio calls.

We passed very close and were able to identify it as a Russian ship, possibly a large fishing trawler, though it had a far more antennas and dishes on top of the accommodation than would normally be found on a fishing boat. Why it was acting in defiance of International Rules was anybody's guess. We later found out that our Captain had reported the ship's position to the US and Canadian authorities, who must have known the ship was there.

Excitement over, my relief appeared, and I rapidly disappeared. We duly entered the Saint Lawrence Seaway. The river passing through the Canadian Province of Quebec. As we steamed further upriver, we came to Lake Ontario, the first of the Great Lakes. Now we had Canada on one side and the USA on the other.

The Seaway System, stretching a massive 3700km, connected the Atlantic Ocean to the central interior of North America. There were many locks and canals throughout the system as the water level fell some 180 metres from the Atlantic Ocean to the final ports in the western most Lake Superior.

There were many ports along the Seaway and into the Great Lakes on both the US and Canadian sides. The international boundary between Canada and the USA pretty much bisected the various lakes with the sole exception of Lake Michigan, which was totally within the USA.

Winters in these northern latitudes could be bitterly cold and the Seaway was iced up and closed from late December to April. Our first scheduled port was Three Rivers in the Canadian province of Quebec.

I got off to an embarrassing start while we were still tying the ship up when I yelled at one of the linesmen on the dock asking him to speak English. He was pissed off and yelled back in French.

I'm sure he was not saying welcome to my city, more likely telling me to get fucked, whatever that was in French. I should have paid attention as it was a handy saying in any language.

I ended up feeling being kind of embarrassed as until that morning I had no idea that Canada was a bilingual country with both English and French being the official languages.

Proof again that I should have paid more attention in school, though couldn't remember ever being taught anything about Canada. And to think that when my parents decided to leave Wales, it was a toss of a coin as to whether they went to Australia or Canada.

Wow, had their choice been Canada I would now be a Canadian, and although it would have been most unlikely that my parents would have settled in a French speaking part of the country, but then again who knew!

We spent just one day in Three Rivers, by which time I had learnt that the city's official name was Trois Rivieres, so if nothing else I had learnt my first two words in French.

Did go for a walk around the town with no less than four guys, safety in numbers, keeping a wary eye open in case we bumped into the linesman I'd apparently insulted.

Saw some high school girls who looked just great, ever so sexy, even though they were just wearing their school uniforms. We were all late teenagers, and they would have been at most only a couple of years younger than us.

We said a friendly, "Hello" and were totally ignored. No smiles, no cheeky backchat, just straight out ignored by a bunch of beautiful young women. As one, our respective male egos nose-dived.

Feeling a bit downhearted, we headed back to the ship where the loading of huge rolls of paper was all but completed.

Trois Rivieres probably had a lot going for it, maybe we just went to the wrong places at the wrong time. Mind you, a weekday mid-afternoon in a city centre was not exactly the right place for four young foreigners hoping to hit on some local girls. A late-night disco, on a weekend, might have been a much better option.

Back on the ship, we asked a guy why the high school girls so totally ignored us, was it because we spoke no French? He burst out laughing and said that for sure they all could speak English, probably better than us.

It was time to say a sad farewell, take in the mooring ropes and head for our next port Montreal. Montreal, as with Trois Rivieres, was also in Quebec Province, and as such a part of French speaking Canada. The difference here was that the people we came across also spoke English.

The city dates back a long time as it was founded by the French way back in 1608. After a long war against the English, the French militias were defeated, both Quebec City and Montreal surrendered and New France, as the French called their colony was gone forever.

Just after berthing in Montreal, we were told by the Captain that the ship would have calls in Hamilton, Ontario and then in Detroit USA to pick up cargo waiting for us. It would then return to New York to top up with final cargo for the return to Australia.

Myself and two of my shipmates decided we would give notice that we wanted to leave the ship, when it arrived back in New York. This being the new plan, money or rather our wages now became important, as we would have to have cash for New York.

As such, we jointly decided on no more trips off the ship until New York. The joys of Montreal, Hamilton and Detroit would have to wait until another day. In just over two weeks, the impressive New York skyline hove into view and soon after we tied up, our shipping agent came on board.

He told us to be ready to go off with him as soon as he had completed the necessary paperwork to clear the ship into the USA. Bags packed, we were ready and waiting.

New York
Take 2

Leaving the ship or 'paying off', the correct 'sailor' terminology, was straightforward and easy. The Crew Landing Card that US Immigration had prepared and given us many weeks ago in Charleston now came into play.

At this time, the various Scandinavian countries had large fleets of ships calling constantly in US ports. Many of these ships rarely returned to their home countries and as such had to engage crews when they visited American ports. The Norwegians, Swedes and Danes maintained joint crewing offices in both New York and San Francisco.

The Landing Card entitled us to spend a total of 28 days in the USA while we waited for another ship. To satisfy US Immigration authorities, our employment within this period was guaranteed by the Scandinavian crewing offices.

First step was to the Swedish Consulate in Manhattan as our vessel *Baltic Sea* flew the Swedish flag. Here we signed the release or discharge slip from the ship and had to show our final wages statement. A seaman leaving a vessel had to have a certain minimum cash balance before the Consulate concerned would permit him to sign off.

The Consulate was nicely furnished, all expensive pine furniture, quality art pictures mounted on the walls and a plush beige wall to wall carpet.

When we entered, there were two older Norwegian seaman waiting to sign on a Swedish ship as both leaving and joining vessels had to be done in front of the respective consular staff. They were drunk, obviously short or out of funds, and desperately in need of a cigarette. In those days, you could still smoke in some offices.

They had upended the ashtrays on the plush carpet and were sorting through the discarded butts. They would then break open the butts and deposit the remaining tobacco in a small pile on the carpet, produce a pack of cigarette papers and roll a couple of smokes.

Task completed they lit up, sat down again and did not even replace the ashtrays on the tables, never mind try and clean the mess on the carpet. The surprise was not so much what they were doing but more that the two lady secretaries paid absolutely no attention to what was happening. It was almost as if this was normal sailor behaviour, perhaps it was!

Consulate business completed, the agent then took us and dropped us at the Norwegian Seaman's Home in Brooklyn. It was a fourteen-story building, and the small rooms came at a very modest cost. Payment of your room also entitled you to a breakfast the following morning.

There was a large foyer at reception and apparently in winter, which could be bitterly cold, seaman who had run out of money were allowed to sleep on the floor in the foyer until 7am.

The shipping office was a small building adjacent to the home. As soon as you left a ship, you then had to report to this office. Your union book was checked to see you were financial, and you were registered as available for your next ship.

There were notice boards around the walls with cards showing the jobs available on that day. The cards listed the name of the ship, flag, the trade the ship was in and a breakdown of the positions available.

My Chilean friend wanted a ship to South America, and I was prepared to go anywhere in the wide, wide world. I was also hoping to spend a couple of weeks in New York until finances demanded I find another job.

The hostel was in Hansen Place in the borough of Brooklyn. This part of the borough had experienced major cultural changes with different ethnic groups over the years. It had successively been home to the Irish followed by Jewish immigrants from Eastern Europe, then Italians, to where it was now largely Puerto Rican with an ever increasing number of African Americans or black people from the Caribbean moving in.

As each of the ethnic groups prospered, they tended to move out almost collectively to better quality neighbourhoods.

The hostel worked closely with the Norwegian Seaman's Church although I never met any sailor who had actually attended any of their religious services. What they did offer once a week was a dance where all guests of the hostel were welcome. A fair sprinkling of Norwegian American ladies would show up and provide the necessary female partners.

There were never any 'Miss Brooklyn' candidates amongst them and there was no doubt some were out to either score, or hope for an ongoing relationship, with a man from the old country. A notice in the hostel required all guys fronting up for the dance to be clean, well dressed and the final huge stumbling block- sober!

As there were always seamen in the hostel, there were several bars in the immediate vicinity to cater for their 'needs'. Lots of 'buy me a drink' girls who if they scored would then sit on the guy's lap and gyrate their mini skirted ass around, a move guaranteed to get another drink from a fully aroused customer.

Speaking from experience, it was easy to blow your hard-earned dollars ever so quickly. The bad part about it was that these girls were not prostitutes and even though we all knew this, we all succumbed to their looks and dirty talk.

The bar owners would not allow their girls to have steady boyfriends come into the bar, apparently this was a known invitation to trouble, but come closing time, the boyfriends would be waiting outside to take them home. No matter how much cash you had parted with and how many promises you'd been given, there was no way you were going to get laid that night with that girl.

And the girls were very attractive. Young and sexily dressed, their looks were to die for! Some claimed to be university students simply supplementing the rather meagre allowance their parents gave them. This may well have been true because some were very well spoken.

But if it was sex you were after, it was right outside the bar. There were very few women that I'd seen who were better looking than young Puerto Rican chicks. Slim, generally coffee coloured skin, black hair and eyes, these with a handful of African American girls, were our local whores. They were strictly short time only girls, and they were relatively cheap.

There were several dodgy hotels with rooms available by the half hour also just meters away. The downside, many of the girls were young, probably not eighteen and therefore legally considered underage, though their looks defied this.

VD was not uncommon, and HIV was already making the rounds in New York. Even worse, all the girls used drugs. Mind you nothing wrong with cannabis, a joint now and then, and then and then, a great way to relax, but unfortunately many of these women were crack or heroin addicts.

I was told they were introduced to hard drugs by their boyfriend, also their 'pimp', as a means of both controlling them and providing his drug needs as well.

Looking at these strikingly beautiful young women, I could not help but think of them as cute at 16, potential catwalk models at 20, then dead from a drug overdose late 20s when their looks and bodies were nothing more than memories.

Took advantage of the excellent subway system to take trips around the city, trying to catch at least some of the well-known tourist spots. Duly saw the UN, Times Square, The Stature of Liberty and Madison Square Garden where I went to watch a middleweight world title fight. Went there, yes, but did not get to see the fight. All tickets had been sold so back to the subway and back to Brooklyn.

Became an avid movie buff and as New York always had the latest releases, I went to a different show almost every day. And a 'one-off'. I was walking in Atlantic Avenue in Brooklyn when I saw a sign in a window 'Rumanian Gypsy Fortune Teller'. Well, I thought, why not.

The apartment door which opened out onto the footpath, sidewalk (am learning these American expressions) was ajar. I knocked and a young girl appeared. I asked her if her mother was the fortune teller, and she said no that was her Granny.

She hollered and Grandma appeared. The obvious question, "how much?" As I didn't have much money. She replied normally $25 but for me $15. She would not budge from this amount, so OK this could be interesting. And so it was. I asked her if she had one of these crystal balls, but she said no, she would use a kind of playing cards.

She told me I was from a country far away and travelled a lot. Really nothing amazing about this and then things started to get better. I would have a long life, enjoy good health, and would be considered financially well off by most people. Obviously if it's about you, then you want to believe it, but even in my naive state, I thought she was just giving me the standard $15 reading.

And then came the surprise when she said I would meet a very attractive young woman whose father was some sort of a religious leader in his country. We would both fall deeply in love but on no condition was I to marry this woman. When I met this woman, I was never to forget the old gypsy's prophecy, and although apparently blinded by love, I had to break off the relationship at once.

This kind of shook me up and the appointment ended shortly after, but as I went out the front door, she repeated, "don't forget what the cards have told you."

Walking back down Atlantic, I tried to make fun of her message saying to myself, "In future, I must ask every nice girl I meet if her father is a religious leader," but no inward laughter; it just was not funny, totally non-suspicious Jake believed the old lady.

Money was starting to run short, partly to blame on a stop in the lap dance bar and it was time I became serious in looking for another ship. I had been glancing at the notice boards each day but not too interested as had things to do and still had some dollars to play with.

One last Brooklyn experience I would never forget. I had taken a wrong turn on my way back to the hostel and was a bit lost, when I saw a cop in the street. It was the first time I had seen a police officer on foot, usually you would just see them drive by in their squad cars.

Anyway he could point me in the right direction to Hansen Place. His back was towards me, and he was near an intersection watching the traffic. I walked up behind him and tapped him on the shoulder, a big, big mistake. He stepped forward, spun around and jerked his .45 revolver out in one fluid movement. Now, I'm looking squarely down the barrel of this huge gun only two meters away from me.

I spoke first, worried that this dude might really panic and blow me away. I said, "Officer, I'm sorry. I did not mean to alarm you." He was a very pissed off cop, but he did at least recognise that from my accent, highlighted no doubt by fear, that I was a harmless, and surely in his mind, a very dumb foreigner who intended no harm.

He told me in no uncertain terms that nobody approached a cop from behind and then touched him. I was lucky he had not instinctively shot me. I mumbled apologies and walked off, having forgotten to ask him the directions to Hansen Place and certainly not about to go back. Earlier I had taken a crap before leaving the hostel, if not, I'm sure I would have shit myself when he pulled the gun on me.

My rent would be due in the hostel tomorrow so decided to take a serious look at the job notice boards. There were several jobs for deck boys, and I decided it was time for a first-hand look at West Africa.

The job(s) were in a Norwegian Ship, the *Titania* owned by one of the largest shipping lines in Norway. Took my union book to the desk, they OK'd it and with two other guys was told to wait for a bus which would take us to our new ship. There we would have to report to the Chief Mate and if he was satisfied, we would then be taken to the Norwegian Consulate for the official signing on the ship.

Said my goodbyes to the hostel for the first and last time as it was due to be closed, or moved elsewhere in the near future

Instead of the Chief Mate, we found the Captain himself waiting at the gangway. He spoke to us in Norwegian, and when he got blank stares in return, he tried English. He was faced with an Aussie, a black guy from the Cape Verde Islands in the Atlantic and a Nicaraguan.

The Captain's first question was, "do any of you play football?" And he meant European soccer.

Through the Norwegian Seaman's Church, all Scandinavian ships in port were asked to put up a soccer team and social games were then arranged between the different vessels. Our new to-be-Captain was football mad. The Cape Verde guy said he had played in competitions as a younger lad, the Nicaraguan replied that all his countrymen played football and the Aussie, me, lied and said he had played a bit as a defender. I had no idea what a defender was supposed to do, but I guess defend, what else.

The Captain must have thought, well two out of three isn't bad and he agreed to sign on the three of us. A couple of hours later, we were through at the Consulate and ready to start work on our new ship.

West Africa

The ship was on a line service to various ports on the West African coast. We would call into Liberia, Sierra Leone, The Ivory Coast, Ghana and Nigeria. This was my first trip to Africa, and I was really looking forward to it.

In many ways, each port we visited was like the previous one. Witnessing poverty, and in some cases, extreme poverty was a totally new experience for me and it was a real eye opener to see where and how some of these people lived.

The city centres or built-up areas were holdovers from whichever colonial government had been in power before independence. Buildings and offices, once rather grand, tended to be very run down and invariably in need of a coat of paint.

But one very noticeable thing was that people, the ordinary folk in the street, be they young or old, would often give you a smile and a greeting. Take note, New York, a smile and a greeting cost nothing! However, there were some highpoints in the trip.

I found out that the country of Liberia was actually founded by the USA in the 19th century as a home for former African slaves who had been freed after the American Civil War ended in 1865. These African Americans were then offered a return to the continent where, either they, or their forbears had departed as slaves in the not-so-distant past.

In Monrovia, I purchased a Liberian Silver Dollar for a souvenir. A simple, and in a way, a kind of unique reminder of my visit. In Ghana I was just wandering around town when I came on a bunch of little boys and girls playing in potholes on the road. The potholes were full of water and the kids were splashing one another.

When I came close, they ran up to me and laughing all the while, reached out, tentatively touched me, then quickly jumped back. They thought this was hilarious, each one seemingly daring the others to do the same. I wished I had my camera to catch the moment as it was so completely impromptu.

Parted giving them each a small coin, in retrospect probably not a good thing to do, as now whenever they see a European, they'd be expecting money.

In Nigeria, I stopped by the side of a street to watch a group of Muslim traders conducting one of their daily ritual prayers. They stood in a line, some five or six men, with their leader a few paces in front of them. I understood they faced their holy city of Mecca whenever they knelt in prayer.

Prayers over, I approached one of the men and was pleased to hear he spoke some English. He told me they were from the far north of Nigeria and regularly came to Lagos to sell their carvings.

I bought two small, but quite heavy wooden heads. They were finely carved and shiny black. The wood itself was not black but a result of repetitive coats of black shoe polish. The man told me this was not only to give the carvings their shiny black appearance but that the polish would prevent the wood from cracking, particularly if taken to a cold climate.

It was noticeable that there was a big difference between the Northern Nigerians and those from the Southern regions of the country. The north was predominantly Islamic with the largest ethnic group, the Hausa people while the south was mainly Christian. Tribal Chiefs still exercised enormous power over their people although increasing western influence from TV and movies was impacting on this.

My work all along the West African coast and ports was normally to act as a watchman in the cargo holds of the ship to prevent the workers from stealing whatever they could lay their hands on. They would jemmy the lock off a container in an instant and spill the contents out. They seemed to know which containers had 'goodies' inside, be they electronic goods, cigarettes or liquor.

Rather than act like cops which could have been dangerous, we all elected to let them take a little, just asking them not to damage more than one or two packages as these all had to be documented for insurance reasons. To them, stealing from the cargo was a job-related privilege and there was nothing wrong in doing this. A part of their ill-gotten gains would then be given to the Port Security on their way out. It was a proven and successful system.

Had a surprising experience in Ghana. Our Captain had been on the USA/West Africa line for years and had made friends in most of the ports, to where he was usually the first off the ship when we tied up.

In Tema, one of his good friends was the Australian Ambassador. A car with diplomatic plates would arrive at the ship's gangway specially to pick up the

Captain. He would have his dress uniform on, four gold bars gleaming on his shoulder epaulettes, naval type cap with the company logo the front centrepiece and the black uniform pressed as though he was off to a military parade.

On his return from one of these visits, I was summoned to his cabin, something that was just not supposed to happen with deck boys. I was trying to think where I had screwed up, and decided it had to be in our last football game against a Swedish ship where I had given the Swedes a gift goal, which turned out to be, for them, the winning goal.

But no, this was not the case. Captain Johnny Bye, with a grin on his face presented me with a case of genuine Australian Beer. During his visit, he had mentioned that he had a young Australian from Sydney on board and the ambassador had responded with a most typical Aussie gesture.

The worthy gentleman had no idea how much this gesture was appreciated, or in all probability, how fast the case was emptied. It was hot thirsty weather in Ghana. The ports followed in quick succession. Our last loading port was in Abidjan, the capital city of the Ivory Coast, a former French Colony better known by its French name 'Cote D'Ivoire'.

Crew members who had been on the ship for some time told us first time visitors that Abidjan was a real fun city, and that the red-light district of Treichville was a must to visit.

None of us had been partying so far on the trip and were really looking forward to checking out this Treichville. However, our hopes were dashed when the Captain, advised by the agent, told us there would be no shore leave as there was some ongoing politically inspired violence in the city.

Having had my first visit to West Africa, I decided to quit when we got back to New York and look for another ship as there was still a whole lot of worlds I wanted to see.

Ecuador

As luck would have it, I found a new ship almost at once. On the notice boards in the shipping office, I saw there were jobs available on a Danish ship running between Newark, New Jersey and Guayaquil, Ecuador. I applied and was accepted.

The ship was called the *Brazilian Reefer* and was a refrigerated vessel, chartered by a big US company to carry one cargo only; bananas, from Ecuador to the USA. The voyages were short, the round trip taking just 3 weeks. I had just qualified for promotion to ordinary seaman from deck boy, which didn't alter my duties a lot but did put a few more dollars in my monthly wages.

A part of the enjoyment of the trips was that we now passed through the Panama Canal twice every three weeks. Repetition of anything could become boring but for me, the Canal was fascinating and I really enjoyed the transits, more so as following my promotion, I now got to actually steer the ship.

The Panama Canal pilot would give me an order, I would repeat it back, and then do what he required, the Captain and one of the deck officers keeping an eye on things in general and on the new ordinary seaman in particular.

The unfortunate part was that we did not stop in Colon so further visits to the Zam-Zam bar were out. But in its place, we had our time ashore in Guayaquil, which was just as good.

Newark, New Jersey

In all truth, the less said about the port terminal in Newark the better. The area surrounding the wharves and outside the gates was at best drab. It was a purely industrial area, roads busy during the day and all but deserted at night. The walk back from the main traffic thoroughfare and nearest subway was only a kilometre or so but a bit scary if you were alone.

There was a good diner near the gate, so a repeat of my favourite breakfast was available. Next door was a port workers bar, which featured a large screen TV permanently tuned to sport. Once a trip, several of us would pop into the bar after work, watch some TV and relax with a few beers.

One evening when we were sitting along the bar, a young guy started chatting to us. He told us had come to the USA from Puerto Rico in the Caribbean with his parents when he was very young. We couldn't help but notice his left arm was heavily scarred, nothing special, but it looked like he had suffered some very bad injury.

Anyway in due course he left and there was just three of us from the ship in the bar. The old barkeep asked us how we knew this guy who had been talking to us. We told him we had never seen him before, and the barman said I'm going to tell you a sad story about him. When they were not busy bar workers, men or women, were always good for a story or two.

The young man was a local and since very young had been crazy about boxing. He watched all the boxing movies and trained in a local gym with other young enthusiasts. The owner of the gym had been a fighter in his day and had several second-rate pugs in training.

It turned out that the Puerto Rican had real talent. The gym entered him in various amateur contests, gradually taking on better and better opponents as his skills improved. The barman said, "The kid was lightning fast, had a lethal right hand, was tall with a long reach and most importantly he could take a punch."

While telling us this, the old boy was dancing around behind the bar, throwing punches in quick succession. Visible scar tissue over his left eye left no doubt he had been a fighter in his day, whether in the ring or on the streets not important.

Anyway the Puerto Rican, who fought as a lightweight, had now reached a level to where the gym entered him in the State of New Jersey Golden Gloves Championship.

The Golden Gloves Tournament was run every year for amateur boxers in most, if not all, states of the nation. State winners compete against each other, in each weight division until only two remain and of course, the winner is the US amateur champion. What next? Well, if the Olympics were not too far away, they were automatic selections to represent the United States.

Most however become professional boxers. The lure of big money with all its side benefits, glamour lifestyle, fast cars and even faster women, too much to resist. Our bar acquaintance won the state lightweight title for New Jersey and his name went into the national draw to determine his next opponent. And then fate stepped in.

He had been a member of a street gang and had stepped aside to continue his boxing and to avoid trouble with the police. Some gang members bitterly resented this and a bunch of them attacked him with crow bars. The damage to his arm had occurred when he was trying to protect his head.

No police report was ever made, and it took a series of operations before he could use his much-weakened arm again. He would retire as lightweight golden gloves champion of New Jersey and never fight again.

The barman ended by saying, "we would never know just how good he might have been, guys, you just had to watch him box, he had world champ written all over him."

A sad, but I'm sure, a true story.

One of the real bonus' we picked up every trip to Newark was cleaning the cargo holds once the bananas had been discharged. This was supposedly a job that should have been done by the longshoremen who unloaded the ship, but they did not want to do it and our agent got permission from their local union to use ship's crew to do this work.

The union insisted however that the agent pay us at the same rate as their members. This was a huge bonus for us as their wages were much higher than ours. The job would take two days, firstly cleaning the banana debris, then sweeping the smaller bits and finally washing down the whole loading bay with some sort of chemical product. It was easy work and the extra money, paid in cash, provided our spending money for the next call in Guayaquil.

Guayaquil, Ecuador

Bananas, bananas and yet more bananas was probably the best way to describe our time in Guayaquil. All the loading was done while the ship was at anchor, the fruit being brought out in big barges. We had access doors in the side of the ship with a portable ramp leading down to the barge from the door.

In each hatch, the entire loading space was divided into wooden framed pens each about 3 meters x 3 meters. The bananas were loaded in complete stalks, which were placed upright in the pens.

Each stem of bananas was carried up the ramp and into the ship's hatch on the shoulder of a worker. Quite a backbreaking task as the stems were heavy and the ramp sometimes a bit steep. As the worker reached the top of the ramp and entered the ship, he was given a small plastic disc. At the end of the day, his discs were counted, and he was paid accordingly.

We also had a doctor come with the workers. The bananas were the favourite home of a nasty and very poisonous spider as well as small viper snakes equally as dangerous. At each entry door, a picture poster was placed showing these. If one of the workers was bitten, the doctor would immediately give him an injection of anti-venom.

I never saw either 'nasty' in Guayaquil, and none of our workers suffered any bites. I asked one of the foremen what happened when a worker was bitten. He told me he was taken to a medical centre in the city for observation for several hours, then if OK, was released.

I asked if he received any payment for his day, and with a surprised look on his face, the foreman said he would be paid only for the number of plastic discs he surrendered. Tough luck if the guy was bitten on his first run up the ramp.

Loading would take from two to three days and the social life in the city very much catered to visiting seamen. There were many bars, well supplied with booze and friendly bar girls and we quickly established one of these as our designated 'watering hole'.

The bar was on the second floor of a big old Spanish style house. It had a sort of rundown grandeur about it and in former days might well have been the home of a local dignitary. Now, it was a whorehouse!

Downstairs was where the girls lived, the second floor, the bar, was reached by an outside wooden staircase, while the third floor had several small rooms for the girls to take their customers. There was a toilet and bathroom at one end, and it was usual practice to have a shower before or after, (or both) with your girl. Funnily, some guys were more modest than their sexy young lovers.

It was the outside staircase that nearly resulted in tragic news being relayed to the Smith family way back in Australia. I had just reached the staircase, had one foot on the first step when out of the doorway at the head of the stairs came a juke box in full flight. It whizzed down the stairs as I threw myself off to the side.

With a sickening thud, it finished up in a sorry heap at the foot of the stairs as a bunch of guys ran down, leapt over the jukebox and disappeared down the street. By this time, the bar girls had gathered, all talking nonstop, when a police car pulled up.

Apparently, there had been a fight between guys all from the same ship when one of them had jerked the jukebox away from the wall and propelled it towards their foes table. It had bounced off the table, out the door and down the stairs.

I had a vision of a telegram reaching my parents to tell them their only son Jake had been tragically killed when a jukebox fell on him, following a bar room brawl. It seemed so funny afterwards, but at the time was anything but funny.

I had completed eight round trips when the contract with our charterer came to an end. When we arrived in Newark for what was the final time, we then heard that in addition the ship had been sold to Swedish owners. It would not be continuing the run to Guayaquil.

The new owners advised all crew members that any who wished to stay on the ship could do so. The ship's name was changed from *Brazilian Reefer* to *Dolores*, the Danish flag came down to be replaced by that of Sweden.

We sailed from New York to Bangor, a small port in the northern state of Maine where we loaded a full cargo of potatoes for Genoa in Italy. A few of us went ashore just the one time, as usual on the prowl for any loose women, and as usual with no luck.

Ended up in a bar watching baseball along with some port workers. Americans certainly love their summer baseball, and their endless comments were funny. They wildly cheered every time their team, the Boston Red Sox made a good play, but it was all in vain as they ended up losing.

A billboard outside the bar advertised 'the best pizzas in the state', and sure enough, it was not an idle boast. Washed down with cold draft beer, we said farewell to our newfound baseball buddies, asked the barman to call a taxi when one of the workers said he would drop us off at the port entrance. All in all, an enjoyable afternoon.

We sailed, crossed the North Atlantic, Genoa came, and Genoa went. When we had finished discharging the potatoes, we received instructions to sail empty to Israel to load oranges and grapefruit for Buenos Aires in Argentina.

Before departing from Genoa, we took on an Israeli loading supervisor as the ship's cargo holds had to be carefully cleaned and prepared for loading. It was a lot of work; the Israeli was very specific in what had to be done and even though he was a supervisor, he worked alongside and harder than the rest of us.

Haifa, Israel, and My 21st Birthday

Arriving in Haifa, we were told to anchor up inside the main port area and wait for an available berth. It was here that our Captain excelled. Although he had only been on board since the change of flag, we couldn't help but notice that he really had a drinking problem.

At sea, captains come to the navigational bridge at intervals but especially late each afternoon to write up what is called their night orders. These orders tend to be basically repetitious instructions to the junior officers on what to do and look out for on their watches in the hours of darkness. The orders would invariably end with, "call me at any time if you have any doubts at all."

Our good Captain would often appear decidedly 'under the weather' to scrawl his orders and a couple of times had to be led back to his cabin by the duty officer. This was the man to be called at any time in an emergency! As soon as we dropped anchor in Haifa, the ship's agent invited Captain Willy Johansson go ashore with him as the ship was to remain at anchor until the next day.

The ships gangway was lowered down and a launch came alongside. The agent stepped onto the launch and Willy dressed in his full captains' uniform and cap stepped off the gangway and into Haifa Harbour. Luckily, he was not crushed between the launch and the side of the ship, so maybe there was some truth in the saying, 'the Good Lord looks after drunks'. He was fished out onto the launch who then had to rescue his gold braided cap, which had drifted off.

It was during our stay in Haifa that I celebrated my 21st birthday. The city of Haifa was built on the steep slope of Mount Carmel. We had found a bar about halfway up the mountain, which came with good music and 'buy me a drink' girls. We had decided to celebrate my '21st' in the bar.

The day got off to a good start when at the mid-afternoon coffee break, Captain Willy sent down a case of beer to our mess room. 24 beers meant that each of us got two cans, which was certainly a nice surprise from an unexpected source.

Later, we found out that he would do this on whatever ship he was on whenever a crew member had a birthday. Our Swedish crew members said this was highly unusual but then again, Captain Willy was a somewhat eccentric character.

The party in the bar was a success, highlighted by my birthday photo being taken with my right arm around the waist of the prettiest bar girl, or so I thought! She had snuggled up to me then, in cohorts with one of my friends, had taken my hand off her waist and put it around my friend's waist.

I was blissfully unaware of this until the photos, front and back views, were produced shortly afterwards. Later in the evening, when I tried to talk one of the girls into spending the night with me, she couldn't stop laughing, telling me I obviously preferred my friend just like the photo showed.

Around midnight, the bar owner put a bottle of brandy on the table with some Coca-Cola to act as a mix. We had been jokingly pestering them for a free round of drinks and this turned out to be their birthday gift. The brandy must have been the cheapest on the market and tasted like shit, but it was free, we were all half pissed and in no time, the bottle was empty.

I remember leaving the bar, clutching the empty bottle, which I intended to keep as a memento of my big day, obviously drunk, and when I woke up the next morning in my cabin, I could not remember getting back on board and the bottle had disappeared. You only turn 21 once and I would always remember it, or at least some of it!

The loading of the cargo was completed, and the loading supervisor called a meeting with all the ship's crew. He told us he would give us however many cases of oranges and grapefruit we wanted for our trip but asked us not to take or damage any of the cargo in the ship's holds.

The Chief Steward gave him a figure and shortly after, the cases were delivered. These were all Jaffa brand oranges and grapefruit and were top quality export produce. It was a smart move on the part of the shipper.

Shortly after we sailed from Haifa, a stay memorable for a happy drunken 21st birthday, seeing our Captain fall overboard, having oranges and grapefruit by the case, and finally seeing so many beautiful Israeli girls and not getting laid!

The myth of a sailor having a girl in every port again proving to be a story and nothing more!

Argentina

It was a long voyage, leaving the Mediterranean Sea at Gibraltar and then across the Atlantic towards South America. The sometimes-stormy Atlantic was in a good mood, and we were blessed by unusually fine weather for the entire passage.

Buenos Aires, a city of some two million people was located on southern side of the mouth of the River Plate or Rio Plata to give it the correct Spanish name. Across the river on the northern side was the country of Uruguay and the city of Montevideo.

Our Captain had adjusted his arrival off the Port Pilot Station for daylight and no sooner were we there than the pilot came on board and by breakfast time, we were already tied up alongside our designated berth.

During the course of the Atlantic crossing, I had decided to try and learn at least some basic Spanish, and with this in mind had given notice to the Captain that I would like to pay off the ship once we arrived in port.

The ship *Dolores* was now a Swedish ship and in that era any crew member could leave their vessel, providing the relevant immigration Authorities were given prior notice and had given their consent. This was done by the Captain, contacting the ship's agent in that port, who would then deal with the immigration.

This meant nothing to me, at that time, and I was told that my request had been approved and that I should be ready to receive my wages and leave the ship once the port arrival formalities had been completed.

Bag packed and ready to head off, when surprisingly I was called to the Captain's cabin. This a most unusual occurrence, low life like myself a junior ordinary seaman, just did not face the Captain, unless it was for a disciplinary offence.

He invited me into his cabin, where an old man was sitting on the settee surrounded by papers. This turned out to be the ship's agent, a Norwegian, who had been living in Argentina for forty years. He had duly arranged for my permit to stay in Argentina, and more good news was about to follow. He was kind of frail and was looking for somebody to act as his assistant when he visited the various ships.

Apparently, the job would simply be to carry his briefcase and any other documents he might need. At times, this would involve visiting ships at anchor. For him, this was an issue as he would have to climb off a small launch, bouncing around in the sea, and onto the ship's gangway.

I thanked him and told him I would be happy to work as his assistant, and learnt that I would get paid into the bargain. Having collected my wages, I left the ship with him. He then asked me where I would be staying in Buenos Aires and I confessed I had no idea.

Things were just getting better by the minute when he told me one of his best friends owned a Pension, or boarding house, in the downtown city centre area and he would give him a call if I was interested. Told him please do, he called his friend and there was a room available.

We reached his car. He drove a very dilapidated small French Citroen 2CV, commonly known as 'flying dustbins', probably by virtue of the hood or bonnet which was rippled or corrugated, like the roofing on so many houses in western Sydney.

He told me we would go his friend's Pension, introduce me and drop my one bag before going to his office. He threw the car in reverse, backed up until he hit the car parked behind and off we went. I was soon to find out that was his normal parking procedure, that is, back in until light contact made with the car behind and then move forward and away, apparently, he had never been taken to task for this somewhat unusual way of parking.

Met my new landlord who spoke excellent American English. My room was tiny but all that I needed. He then told me he had a son of my age, and I would meet him when I came back that evening.

At Mr Johansen's office, yep that was his name, he then told me what my work would entail. Basically, nothing more than what I had been told before we left the ship. We would however be busy as he was the agent for several major shipping lines that made scheduled calls in Buenos Aires.

I had a distinct impression it was not only the need for somebody to carry his briefcase and other odds and ends, but that he wanted company while he went about his work. He talked nonstop and I asked him to please use basic Spanish, so I could at least pick up some words and phrases, but inevitably he would lapse quickly back into English.

My salary, wages whatever, were very small so I would need to be careful, but more importantly I would not be dipping into the pay-off I received when I left the ship.

Back at the Pension, I met the landlord's son Carlos. He was in second year university doing a business course with the objective of taking over the running of the Pension when the time was right. Like his dad, he spoke very good English.

His father owned an old two door 1976 Chevrolet Impala convertible. It was immaculate, bright fire engine red body with a white vinyl top and for a finishing touch all white walled tyres. Most importantly, his dad gave him free rein to drive it seemingly as and when he pleased.

Instinctively knew I would get along with Carlos and in no time, he started telling me he would fix me up with an attractive girl from his big circle of friends. I reminded him that I was a seaman with very limited funds, but this did not faze him in the slightest.

I said his girlfriends from university might not be happy going out with a seaman to which he simply said, "don't worry, we won't tell them; I'll just say you are a backpacker who has decided to stay in Argentina."

He was a social member of River Plate, one of the biggest and most supported football teams in Argentina and his membership allowed him to sign in friends to the various social activities at the club. All this had happened within twenty-four hours. I almost had to pinch myself to be sure it was just not one big dream.

The next few weeks seemed to flash by. I really enjoyed working with the old man, though there was quite a bit of night work as not all ships arrived in the daylight hours. Pilotage and berthing could take place at any time and we had to be there the moment the ship had tied up or go out to the anchorage if the vessel was waiting for a berth alongside.

Nonetheless, I did have plenty of free time. Carlos, as good as his word had introduced me to a number of his young women friends, and with one of them, a raven-haired Sophia, things were definitely heating up.

We would always go out as couples usually with at least one younger brother or sister as a chaperone or chaperones in tow in order to comply with the upper-class social requirements of the day. Probably inherited from Spain but from a Spain in the distant past.

The minders could be blackmailed into disappearing for a while giving us some smooching and petting time though to use an 'Americanism', if you got as far as second base, it was a good night.

Sex before marriage was certainly on, and widespread, but these girls were from upper middle-class backgrounds, were invariably strong practicing Catholics, and would come across only when a future marriage was officially confirmed.

In the eyes of the family, their daughter's first encounter with sex was to be on her wedding night, though I'm sure most parents were not that naive. Another inhibiting factor was the use of rubbers, French letters, call them what you will. Yes, all used them but with the knowledge that it was against the church's beliefs.

The confessional booths must have provided some interesting stories, as I was told a person couldn't lie when in the box with the priest. Memoirs of a priest, from the confessional box, of course totally forbidden, would probably make some internet sex sites look tame.

For Carlos, me and our other male friends, even though we boasted of our sexual exploits, quite frankly we weren't getting any from our girlfriends, or if we were, social ethics decreed that we should not admit to it.

To counter this, we did what most, if not all young unmarried Latin American men did, we chased after the whores. As long as you had money, you got laid and some of these women were not only very attractive but amazing lovers who seemed to delight in breaking in willing, if inexperienced, young men.

There were a number of bars between Avenida 25 de Mayo and the nearby docks which were very lively, and once you got to know the different girls, lots of fun with loud music, dancing and a guaranteed sex whenever the urge arose and pesos changed hands. All of us claimed to have received a 'freebee sex' but in truth, I don't think any of us ever did.

Went to two football matches. The first was in Monumental, the River Plate team stadium, where to our delight the home team had a 2-0 win over visitors from the city of Rosario. The second was in the home of River Plate's biggest enemies Boca Juniors and resulted in a hard-fought 1-1 draw.

Argentinean football fans were fanatic, none more so that those from Boca Juniors in their colourful stadium 'Bombora' just off the docks. Fanatic yes and unfortunately prone to crowd violence to the point that rival supporters were strictly separated, sometimes with barbed wire along the separation.

The police presence was enormous both outside and inside the ground. There were signs posted on the pitch before and after the game, imploring people not to resort to violence, signs which all too often were ignored.

When the game ended, the visiting teams' fans had a twenty-minute time window to clear the stadium and surrounding streets before the home team supporters were allowed to leave the ground.

Sophia had found out that I was not a Catholic, but nominally a Protestant who had never graced the inside of a church. This disturbed her as I think the sound of wedding bells, though far in the distance, were starting to chime in her head.

What worried her was what she should tell her parents. I had met them just once and they seemed very nice people though very conservative and set in their ways. Apparently, they accepted me as a suitor for their daughter, but her elder sister was quite openly hostile.

I really liked Sophia and was starting to think of the possibility of becoming a Catholic. I had no idea what was involved, and then the walls of my Buenos Aires castle came crashing down.

I would always remember it was a Wednesday, why this should be relevant I don't know, when I went into the office to find the old man hunched over his desk, handwriting a letter.

It turned out that the Immigration Department, who at that time was run by the Argentinean navy, had sent him a letter stating that his employee's visa, for one Jakob Smith, was not in order. He was busily replying to this letter. He told me not to worry, and that he felt a small payment would resolve the issue.

The following Monday, he was summoned to the immigration Headquarters. To this day, I don't know what the visa problem was. He never told me, but I believe that when he originally applied for my visa/work permit, he may have cut corners somehow and got caught out. Anyway, this was dealing with the navy and one thing you did not do was question their decisions.

The long and short of it was that I was to be deported from Argentina as an illegal entrant in the country and, to make it worse, working without the correct documentation. I was given three days to depart Argentina before which I had to inform the immigration of where I was going and show the associated travel ticketing.

Told immigration I would take the ferry from Buenos Aires to Montevideo, Uruguay, as it was cheap and close. This was rejected on the grounds that I could very easily slip back into Argentina from Uruguay. With this failure, I then proposed going by bus to Asuncion, Paraguay, where at least I could continue learning Spanish. This was rejected for the same reason as Uruguay.

The Immigration Department then told Mr Johansen that I had to depart Argentina by air at least as far as Brazil or further.

The old man purchased me a ticket to Sao Paulo, Brazil, something he did not have to do, presented it to immigration who accepted it. They then told him he must bring me to the immigration a couple of hours before the flight departure, and they would take over from there. I was to be deported from the country and not permitted to re-enter for a period of two years.

There followed a sad farewell to Sophia, assuring her I would keep in touch and return as soon as the two years was up. I think that each of us knew that this was not likely to happen. I could imagine the look on her parents' faces when she told them her boyfriend and possible future fiancé had just been deported.

My newfound friends thought the whole situation hilarious and threw a fabulous going away party at River Plate that ended in the wee hours. Goodbye to Carlos' mother and father then the last ride in the Citroen to the immigration, suffering a horrible hangover, where the old man handed me over to the navy.

Thanked him hugely and then as we shook hands for the last time, he slipped me a $100. He was genuinely sorry to see me go and wished me every success for whatever the future had in store for me.

Amazingly, I was to leave Argentina with a little more cash than when I had stepped down the ship's gangway. The whole Buenos Aires experience had happened in just a bit over two months, memories of which would remain with me forever.

However, there remained the final touch. The US Pan Am aircraft was parked away from the terminal and all the passengers had boarded except for me.

I was taken to the aircraft gangway in a navy jeep but then instead of allowing me to board by myself, I was escorted to my seat in the plane by two navy marines with side arms. When they had seen me seated, could you believe it, they then said a friendly goodbye and departed. God only knows what the other seated passengers must have thought.

The flight was from Buenos Aires to Montevideo. The cities were a stone's throw apart. The aircraft had barely taken off than it was landing in Montevideo. Apparently, the stop was not only to take on passengers but to primarily to refuel at cheaper rates than Argentina.

When we had touched down, there was an announcement over the public address system in both Spanish and English, advising that all passengers except Jakob Smith were to leave the aircraft and proceed to the transit lounge for an expected one hours refuelling.

The situation was becoming more embarrassing by the minute, and I pretended to browse through one of the brochures from the seat pocket while the disembarking passengers filed past. An hour and a half later and all passengers back on board and we took off, destination, Viracopus Airport, Sao Paulo, Brazil.

Once airborne, I got a tap on my shoulder and turned to the row behind me. A Canadian couple excused themselves, saying they did not want to be rude, but they were curious, and would I mind telling them why I was getting such special attention.

I laughed and told them I was not a bad guy, but a person who because of an administration screw-up in Buenos Aires was being deported as an illegal immigrant working with incorrect documentation in Argentina.

The Canadians were retired and on a grand scale tour of Latin America. They had been somewhat shocked by my navy escort when boarding the aircraft, assuming I must have been in big trouble. They were also getting off in Sao Paulo and told me if there was any way they could help me, they would be happy to do so.

I thanked them but said I would possibly have a delayed passage through the Brazilian immigration due to the prominent and unusual exit stamp from Buenos Aires in my passport. We landed, said our goodbyes and parted company.

Brazil

We had arrived at Sao Paulo's Viracopos Airport late in the evening but as there were not many passengers disembarking, I quickly made it to the immigration desks.

The officer attending me was a very Brazilian woman who spoke good English but was either having a bad day or for some reason took an instant dislike to me. In retrospect, the exit stamp from Buenos Aires with the statement 'not permitted to re-enter Argentina for two years' may have had a lot to do with her attitude. She summoned her supervisor who was an older woman.

First question obviously was, "why have you been deported from Argentina?" I went over my story, and she followed up with, "why Brazil, and what are you planning to do here?"

I told her that as a seaman working on Scandinavian ships, I was planning to go to Santos Port and look for a job on any Norwegian, Swedish or Danish vessel in or scheduled to arrive in that port.

It was the truth and she accepted it, but then told me that she would report my arrival to the Federal Police in Santos. Further I was to go to their office shortly after my arrival. I was not sure what to make of this, but the first step was to get to Santos.

Sao Paulo is the capital of the state with the same name, and Santos the busiest port in the state. Airport information told me I could catch a bus to Santos from almost directly in front of the terminal.

As I left the terminal exit, lo and behold, there stood the elderly Canadian couple. They said they were worried about me and would be happy to put me up in their hotel until I found my feet. Again, thanked them and told them I was on my way to Santos where I had to report to the Federal Police. Again, a goodbye to such kind people.

I had changed some Argentinean pesos and had a handful of somewhat 'tatty' Brazilian banknotes. Until then, I had no idea that Brazil was in a period of hyperinflation. Every service or purchase cost literally thousands of cruzeiros, which was what the currency unit was called at the time.

I quickly found the required bus, was told that the trip to Santos took about 4 hours, bought my ticket and once paid, I could sit in the bus in my appointed seat. Sat down and as young unstressed people do, promptly went to sleep.

Still sleeping, the bus took off and three hours later, I woke up. Tried to ask the conductor how much further to Santos? Now he spoke only Portuguese, and I spoke not a word. Brazilians were by nature inquisitive and fellow passengers listening to us chimed in to say we had left the Santos Bus Terminal ten minutes ago.

They told me to get off as we were still within the Santos City local buses. Catch a bus going in the opposite direction and tell the conductor, "centro da cuidade," this would drop me somewhere in the centre of the city itself. Did as I had been told and after a short ride, the conductor indicated I should get off. It certainly seemed like the city centre with offices and shops everywhere.

First step was to find a cheap hotel. Any hotel in the main thoroughfare would certainly be upmarket and therefore likely to be way outside my humble budget, so I decided to check out one of the side streets. And there I found the Hotel George Washington. Impressive name for a not so impressive building.

Entry was from a small door at street level, which led onto a staircase leading to the reception on the first floor. There was a young guy at reception, who spoke some basic English. He looked surprised when I told him I would probably stay for one week, and maybe more. He told me how much this would be, I figured it was reasonable, paid upfront and moved into room 201.

The room key was attached to a large heavy metal plaque, so obviously tenants were not supposed to take the key with them when they went out. The room itself was basic, extremely basic, with a double bed, a toilet with a small hand basin and a single cupboard whose sole occupant was a broken coat hanger. But it was a room and for the time being, I had a base.

I now had to find the Office of the Federal Police to report to them as instructed by the immigration at the airport. While settling in, I had heard what seemed to be high heeled shoes going up and down the stairs to my floor and above.

Small wonder, the receptionist looked a bit surprised when I told him I might stay a week, The Hotel George Washington was a short time hotel or what in

Sydney we called a 'knocking shop', a place where street girls took their customers.

No problem as I would have to watch my budget closely, so for the time being, bars and bar girls were out of the question. But no harm in saying hello to the 'girls' when passing, (many of them much older than me), and this was always good for return greeting and a smile.

Next morning the Federal Police had to happen, but how to find their office. At mention of the word police, the hotel receptionist backed off, really did not want to know. I decided to go to the place the bus had dropped me off and ask in any office around there.

Did not need to ask as for directions as once back in the bigger street, I walked right by a Shipping Agency run by the Blue Star Shipping Company. All shipping agencies had staff who speak English, and this was no exception. I was shown to the manager's office.

Not only did he speak English, but he was also English. He burst out laughing when I told him where I was staying, and then gave me directions to the Federal Police Headquarters, which was quite close.

Ten minutes later I was at the entrance, guarded by a military policeman in an immaculate dark green uniform and carrying an automatic weapon. He stopped me, asked me something, and then realising I had no idea what he was saying, escorted me into the reception.

A lady took over, asked me for my passport, told me to sit down and disappeared. After a long ten or so minutes, I was getting a bit nervous, not knowing what was going on, and of course imagining the worst, thinking that surely, I was legally in Brazil, or was I?

She reappeared and beckoned me to come with her into another office. The man sitting behind his large desk, a desk devoid of any papers, was holding my passport out in front of him, but holding it upside down. Surely this was not a good sign.

I was nervous and my friendly attempt at good morning did not come out right but in any case, he did not answer. He had light brown skin, a giant black moustache, and looked mean. This did nothing for my nerves as to me he looked more like a Mexican bandit than a senior Brazilian Immigration Officer.

However, looks can be deceiving, and fortunately in this instance, this was the case. He motioned me to sit down facing him on a small chair in front of the desk.

Suddenly in very good English, he asked me why I had come to Brazil. Having seen the exit stamp from Argentina, he obviously knew I had been deported. I rehashed the story I had told the immigration when I entered Brazil, about how I would look for a Scandinavian ship that needed crew when I got to Santos.

Then he astounded me by saying, "now you are in Brazil why do you want to leave?" I was dumbfounded as this was the last thing I had expected him to come out with. I guess he thought my silence meant that I really did want to join a ship as opposed to staying in his beautiful country.

He then wished me luck in my search but said his officers boarded ships all the time and he would have them check if any needed crew and I should report back to him in a week's time. Thanked him, told him I would be back in a week, and walked out in a daze.

Spent the next week combing the multitude of bars which were just outside the enclosed Santos Port. My favourite hangout was 'Bar Amsterdam' which, despite the name I don't believe had any connection with Holland. It was however a very popular drinking spot for Scandinavian sailors as some of the girls looked more like models than hookers.

I would go mid-morning, slowly drink a beer, do the same in the mid afternoon and then come in around 9pm and have a couple more beers. By now beer, bread and cheese was my staple diet. Once the girls got to know me, they were friendly and in the afternoons, I was prompted into writing letters for them in English to their sailor boyfriends.

Talk about loving and faithful women. They all had more than one 'true love' and their biggest worry was that more than one of their lovers' ships would arrive in Santos at the same time. Two boyfriends turning up at the same bar at the same time looking for the same woman would have been disastrous for the girl.

They usually managed to avoid this by reading the ship expected arrivals in the local newspaper, as this covered the next few days. If more than one boyfriend was expected in port, the girl would then have had to visit a sick family member. They were smart, these women.

Worried because these guys were giving them money and sometimes quite large amounts in the belief that while they were away at sea, their wives would not be 'moonlighting' on the side.

The guys were genuinely in love with these girls and in all fairness, had they stopped going to sea, settled down in Brazil and found work, some of these same girls might well have made very good wives. However, by the same token it must be said that some of them enjoyed the prostitute lifestyle and would not have been the type of girl you would take home to meet Mum. Whatever, the men would certainly have enjoyed super sexual satisfaction.

The evening before my appointment with the Federal Police, I met a couple of crew members from a Swedish ship the *Itajai,* which had just docked in Santos. According to them, they were needing a couple of junior ratings so first thing the next morning I went to the ship, reported to the Chief Mate and was hired.

Back to the police only to find that he had also found a vacancy for me on an oil tanker running between Santos and the Arabian Gulf. Thanked him and told him I would prefer the Swedish vessel, which was on a fixed line service between several east coast ports of the USA and Brazil.

He offered me a 'cafezinho', a small almost syrupy black coffee loaded with sugar, which was almost a mandatory starter for many Brazilians as they greeted another day. It hit your system with a real jolt, jerking you from the last of the previous night's sleepy moments into instant awareness.

I gratefully accepted the coffee, and parted company. He was a nice guy. Paperwork formalities completed, I was taken back to the ship by the shipping agent and promptly put to work.

On the South American leg of every voyage, the *Itajai* called at four confirmed Brazilian ports; Santos, Paranagua, Itajai and Rio de Janeiro and then at any additional ports subject to inducement. This meaning that if another port, or ports, had sufficient cargo available to make the stop profitable, then the vessel would call in.

Apparently, there were usually one or two extra ports outside of the fixed schedule. In the US, calls were made in Savannah, Charleston, Philadelphia, New York and then the Canadian Port of Montreal subject to season. Again, the term 'inducement' allowed for calls in other ports.

The ship's officers were all Swedes and all of them either married or engaged in Rio de Janeiro. The crew were a real United Nations mix, Europeans, Central and South Americans, a couple from the USA and now an Aussie/ Welshman.

As with many Scandinavian ships, the *Itajai*, rarely if ever returned to Sweden, just running up and down between North and South America. We spent the next four weeks loading and unloading at different ports. My pockets were near enough empty, so I had little choice but to stay on the ship until the cash flow situation improved.

Paranagua

All went well until we docked in Paranagua as the ship was now loading for the return to the USA. Again I had no intentions of going ashore, but one of my newfound shipmates took pity on me. He had picked up a girl from one of the bars and brought her back to the ship. Obviously in a good mood and feeling no pain, he decided to bring a girl back for me as well.

There was just one slight hitch as 'my new girlfriend' had brought her girlfriend back with her. In the early hours of the morning, my cabin door burst open, I heard my friend say, "have fun, Jake," and the door shut. It was not until I turned on the little bed light that I realised that my surprise was not merely a surprise but a double surprise.

The cabin had two bunks or beds, one top, one bottom. The girls were young and pretty. Were there any Brazilian girls who were not pretty? One white and the other very dark, almost black. With no further ado, the dark girl stripped to her knickers and jumped into bed with me, while her friend scaled the little wooden ladder to the top bunk.

When I tried to ask why she had brought her friend, she said, "She have no boyfriend tonight," but then said, "After you can have her too." This was turning into quite a night. We made love and fell asleep. I woke up with a real hard on. It was the need to pee, not a 'must have more of this good pussy' erection.

Toilet over, I came back to the bed, my partner was still sound asleep. And then a wee devil was whispering in my ear, "Go for it, Jake, she said you could." I shot up the ladder like a rat up a drainpipe to find her not only wide awake but eager for the show to go on.

Woke up later still in the top bunk. We were not sailing that day and my new friends decided they would stay on board for the time being. My benefactor from the early hours showed up and his girl joined my two lovers. We got them some breakfast and then left them chatting away as we had to start work.

Scandinavians had a wonderful characteristic in that they were very tolerant people. They had no regulations restricting sailors from bringing their girls on board. In most cases, these would be working girls from the nearby seaman's bars.

It was however insisted upon that the girls stayed in their boyfriends' cabins and did not wander around the ship. We were warned by written notices around the boat to be careful with our possessions as many of these hookers would no doubt pinch any money or valuables if they thought they could get away with it.

The girls stayed with us for a further day, collected their 'pay', waved goodbye and, I so loved them for this, were last sighted going up the gangway of another ship a few hundred meters down the wharf.

The first thing a guy does when getting out of bed in the morning was to take a piss. A few days later, out of bed and into the toilet busting to pee, I found my penis was partially blocked by a sticky discharge. When the urine flow finally cleared it, it felt, as the saying goes, that I was pissing razor blades. One or both young ladies had left me with a parting gift.

Went to the 2nd Officer for the required injections in the buttock, his taciturn, "Smith, you have gonorrhoea, why do you think we leave condom packets at the gangway, in future use them." And then, as I walked out the infirmary door, his parting words, "congratulations, your first dose of the clap Smith, you now qualify as a genuine seaman."

We made a couple more stops on our way north before leaving Brazil on the ocean passage back to our first US port which this trip would be Savannah in Georgia.

Spent nearly a month discharging our cargo from Brazil and loading new for our return. The company must be making money as we were completely full when we left Philadelphia, heading south and back to Brazil.

Fortaleza, Brazil

This time, our first port of call was to be in the northeast of Brazil in Fortaleza. Spent four days in Fortaleza and enjoyed all of my free daytime hours on their beautiful beaches. The beaches were very clean. I am a moderate swimmer; really like body surfing and sometimes wish I had gone in for surfboard riding in Australia. The desire was there but the cost of a board way beyond our family budget.

In Fortaleza when we were there, the average wave height was between one to two meters. This was fine for body surfing and was enough to get a good 'ride' if you caught the wave right.

I was now realising that Brazilians flock to the beaches whenever they have the opportunity. Everybody from the littlest ones, still to get their first bathing suits, to the grandparents. Certain areas of the beach were set aside for soccer, invariably men, and volleyball for mixed sexes.

Photos of sexy Brazilian girls in their bikinis were splashed in magazines around the world and could only say that when seeing these women in real life, they were even 'hotter' than their photos.

The bikinis were small, tiny a better description, covering the absolute minimum. Thongs bisecting the cheeks of their bums and the all-important front so low cut that it was common to see a few pubic hairs peeping out. Sexy and arousing yes, but there was a big downside!

It was just as common to see these delightful girls' mothers and even grandmothers decked out in a mini bikini. The sight of a large mature lady, bulging in all the aging places was not nearly as much a turn on.

I wondered if the guys who swarmed around the young women like bees around a honey pot were at all put off by the formidable figure of Mama. Probably not, their thoughts were focussed on somehow getting this woman into bed, not on what she might look like in years to come.

The nick name for these mini bikinis was both funny, relevant and so Brazilian. They were called 'Fio Dental'. 'Fio Dental' the Brazilian Portuguese term for what we call dental floss, the light cotton fibre string many people use to clean between their teeth. An apt description.

Heard an interesting story about a nudist beach that was supposedly established in Fortaleza a few years ago. If the story is true, then the whole concept was apparently an abject failure. While Brazilians, especially women, were quite happy to wear the most revealing swimwear, they totally rejected full nude beaches, at least in Fortaleza.

From a male point of view, a girl in a sexy bikini gave rise to all sorts of erotic thoughts, the imagination ran riot. Now if women were to go nude then men would have to do likewise. Would women be turned on by the site of a balding, potbellied Don Juan trying to hit on them on the beach, not likely!

At the top of the sand, furthest from the water, enterprising locals had set up ramshackle lean-to shelters from where they sold all sorts of tasty snacks, beer, soft drinks, and boiled crab garnished with chilli sauce. Costs were very reasonable, and they had several small tables and chairs arranged if you wanted to eat right there.

The crab was served on a small wooden board, and you were supplied with a little mallet to crack the shell. Large bottles of ice-cold Brahma beer really went down well with the crabmeat.

Adjustable beach chairs were readily available very cheaply for the day or by the hour and if the sun was a real problem, you could also rent colourful beach umbrellas. The beach umbrellas all advertising either beer or a local spirit 'Pitu', a very potent liquor made from sugar cane.

Left Fortaleza with the start of a good suntan and more amazingly, still with money in my pocket, for me the beach was a great way to pass time without blowing my bankroll. Attempted to speak to a few girls but the language barrier was too great and despite smiles, nothing materialised.

We spent the next couple of weeks sailing south down the Brazilian coast, calling at the same ports as we had done on my first trip until we arrived back in Rio de Janeiro, which was to be our final loading port before returning to the USA.

Rio de Janeiro

We arrived in Rio in the late afternoon and went to anchor in the scenic Guanabara Bay, which separates the City of Rio on one side from the twin city of Niteroi on the other. Our agent told us there was no berth available until tomorrow.

It was then that things started to go amiss. In Rio, harbour theft was a problem for vessels at anchor, so common that it was classed as piracy. Small boats came alongside in darkness, thieves boarded the ship, and stole anything they could find on deck. Mooring ropes, the ones we used to tie the ship up to the wharf were a favourite as they had a good, quick resale value.

The more aggressive pirates might then attempt to enter the ship's living quarters and go from cabin-to-cabin, relieving crew of their money and personal possessions.

All of us who were to take night watchman duties were called to the Chief Mate's office and told we had to be very vigilant in the coming night. Instead of the normal one watchman, we would now have two. For our four hours duty, we were to stay on deck and walk continually around the ship, keeping a close watch for any small boats approaching. If any concerns, we were to call the duty officer on the bridge, who usually slept in a reclining chair until woken.

I was on duty from midnight until 4 am and my partner was a senior Swedish seaman nick-named 'Malmo' as this was the city he hailed from back home. About one o'clock in the morning, a small boat approached and came alongside. It was full of whores who wanted to come on board. Our boarding gangway was raised so nobody could use it to get on the ship.

Malmo and I decided we would 'bend' the rules a little and let two girls come on board. Only two then nobody would know. He would get a 'quickie' while I kept the watch, his girl would then go back to the small boat, and another would come for me. He would then stand guard while I whizzed my lady off to my cabin. We figured that by three o'clock latest, the girls and the small boat would be gone.

As with all poorly conceived plans, things went so wrong right from the start. We thought the girls in the boat understood what we wanted, perhaps they did, but when we lowered our gangway for the first girl to come on board, they all rushed up, ran by us and disappeared through the only unlocked door into the accommodation. Two of the girls stayed with us, hampering us from chasing after the others, who were now knocking on every door, looking for a customer.

Amazingly in less than 5 minutes there was quiet, all half a dozen had found a willing partner. We waited for another 5 minutes, expecting the Chief Mate or one of the officers to appear, nothing happened. Well, we each had a girl, so first things first, we locked the entry door and went to our cabins.

Came out an hour later to find the small boat gone and eight hookers still somewhere on the ship. It was not that the girls boarding had gone unnoticed, rather that they had disappeared too quickly to be rounded up and sent off. At morning coffee break, Malmo and I were summoned to the Captain's cabin. The Chief Mate was already there, and I tell could from the expression on his face he was none too happy.

The older Captain had a weary 'oh not again' look on his face but otherwise did not seem to be unduly pissed off. It passed through my mind that one of the girls had dropped in on him, but we never did find out as they had hailed a passing boat and left while we were being scolded.

My accomplice Malmo copped all the flack and was even blamed for encouraging the younger person, me, to flagrantly disobey orders. He got a real blast in Swedish, which went right over my head, and it wasn't until the Captain switched to English that I learnt my fate. Both of us were told that we would be leaving the ship as soon as we docked back in New York. We had been fired! And this was what happened.

And I Decide to Become a Deck Officer

I now needed only a few more months of actual time on a ship before I would qualify as a full seaman or, as the rank was called, an able-bodied seaman.

I spent only a couple of days in New York before joining a Swedish ship from the same company and on the same service as my first ship. I would see Sydney, Australia again after an absence of over 3 years. The ship, the *Lake Erie* was to result in major changes, ending my happy-go-lucky existence and giving me a goal in life.

My duty hours were spent working with the Chief Mate and a young Swedish Officer cadet. Almost immediately, the Mate asked me if I had any thoughts of becoming a Ship's Deck Officer. Impulsively I said yes, although until then it had never occurred to me.

Every day the cadet, now joined by me, would spend from four in the afternoon until eight at night on the bridge of the ship with the Chief Mate. He coached us through the various subjects that made up the course for a 2nd Officer, using a company provided correspondence syllabus.

I was to spend nine months on this ship during which I saved as much of my wages as I could. I contacted a nautical college in the UK, forwarded the necessary documentation, which they verified, approved and I was duly booked in for the next 2nd Mates course start-up date.

During my stay on the ship, we had called in Sydney three times. Things had really changed. My best friend was in jail and most of the others had dispersed to God only knows where. I was able to make up with my family who were pleased that at last I was doing something constructive.

I left the ship in Sydney and booked a berth on an old Greek passenger liner for the trip to the UK. I took the cheapest possible ticket, which entitled me to a bed in a six-berth cabin on 'E' deck. There were no portholes or windows as E deck was way below the waterline.

My roommates were four other young Aussies and a 60-year-old retired bricklayer named Bill. The young guys had just completed their schooling and were hoping to find casual work in the UK, add some more to their savings, and then buy an old VW Combi van and tour Europe. According to them, young Aussies congregated in a lane behind Australia House in Central London where second hand vehicles such as the Combi they desired could be found.

The idea was to buy one, complete their European travels, return to London and sell the vehicle in the same place, recovering all or most of their initial investment. Sounded too good to be true but I later found out that many young people were successfully able to do this.

The bricklayer Bill was an old London Cockney, complete with the fascinating east end of London dialogue and accent. He had immigrated to Australia, spent his life working in and around Sydney and had, as he put it 'saved a few bob'.

When his wife passed away, he had decided to return to the UK to spend his final years in the city he had last seen as a young man. He liked a drink or two and had no complaints when we young guys would come staggering in late at night.

Each night on going to bed, he would take out his false teeth and put them in a glass of water beside his bed. In the morning he would take out the dentures, shake off the water, 'chug' the remaining water in a single swallow and then pop his teeth back in. With nothing more than a practical joke in mind, one night we poured the water out of his glass and replaced the teeth in neat gin.

Bill went through his morning routine and all but choked on the gulped mouthful of gin. We rushed to his bedside and pummelled his back, fearful for a few instants that we had killed the old bugger. His face went from red to purple before he slowly returned to normal. He scolded us but in no time was his normal cheery self again, but we had learnt a lesson.

Stopovers on the voyage were in Auckland where we took on more passengers and Papeete in Tahiti where the ship spent a full day and night. Went on a tour around the island by bus. Tahiti is scenically beautiful. I found out that it is considered a part of France proper, and we did see quite a few French soldiers in the bars.

The people are racially Polynesian, light brown skin and generally curly black hair. The majority are best described as solidly built, big shoulders, big boobs and big bums. The legendary exotically beautiful 'Wahines', the slender young women portrayed in all the tourist brochures are usually of mixed Polynesian and Chinese ancestry. There were quite a few of them and they were truly gorgeous.

The Chinese and some Vietnamese had been in French Polynesia for generations and to a large extent intermarried with the locals, and why not!

We went to a nightclub and tried to chat up some of the Wahines, but they were hookers chasing the big bucks and way out of our league. The club, if I remember correctly was called 'Lafayette' and it was the first time I had been in a place where the toilets were unisex, yes one toilet facility served both genders.

The same band that had greeted the ship when we arrived were in place as we left, playing the same Polynesian music. It was so easy to close the eyes and visualise the coconut palms swaying gently in the breeze as the last rays of the sun set in a perfect tropical paradise.

Au revoir, Papeete.

The Panama Canal transit was interesting as always and we had one further stop in Willemstadt, Curacao which is a Dutch possession off the coast of Venezuela. The ship took on fuel and the passengers were taken on a very 'commercial' tour where all stops were at shops eager to relieve us tourists of our money.

Left Willemstadt on the final leg of the passage across the South Atlantic to our destination Southampton in England.

Highlight of the final approach to the UK was a special dinner put on for all passengers on our last night at sea. After standard entrees and main courses, the dining room lights were dimmed and each of the various table stewards entered with a flaming ice cream dish.

It was spectacular right up to when our steward tripped and lost his footing, launching flaming ice cream into space. The passengers as one erupted in laughter, fortunately no one had been hurt, but our steward quickly disappeared to be replaced by another. The 'take two' ice cream dish was delicious.

Tying up in Southampton, we were greeted by heavily overcast skies with intermittent rain drizzle. Yes, we had arrived in England.

Life as a Student in London

I had put aside quite some cash but to last out the course, it was really going to be a 'study and starve' regime.

All but one of my fellow students had been cadet officers with their respective UK companies before attending the King Edward VII Nautical College. Coming from a lowly deck crew rating, which the college referred to as 'out of the foc'sle' was a disadvantage and socially some of my classmates, as ex-deck cadets, were at best distantly polite and aloof.

However, everybody makes friends, and I was fortunate to come up with two of the best. Talk about different background for these two. Faisal was a Kuwaiti; Dave came from a working-class family in the north of England and spoke with a heavy regional accent. They could not have been two more different persons in both physical appearance and character.

Dave had a fiancé who hailed from the same county as him, had just completed her nursing studies and worked in a hospital in the East End so was conveniently not far from our college, which was in the London borough of Poplar. She was a charming young woman who kept a tight rein on her future husband. She frequently would join us for a meal in local restaurants and was a million laughs.

It was at one of these evening meals when we went 'Chinese' that Dave freaked us out. We were ordering some desert dishes to follow the main courses when our waitress had obvious problems understanding what we wanted. Much to the amazement of all, Dave suddenly launched into what was apparently fluent Cantonese.

He had recognised from her accent that she was probably from Hong Kong but that did not explain his knowledge of her mother tongue. As a cadet, he had signed indentures with a non-descript British shipping company, which traded primarily in the Far East.

Immediately on joining his first ship, a grouchy old Captain told him he did not like cadets and that Dave would have to live, eat and work with the crew, who were all Hong Kong Chinese. To Dave's credit, he did not just walk off like most young English lads would have but stuck it out. Two ships and four years later he spoke, according to our waitress, excellent Cantonese.

As most of Dave's spare time was spent with his fiancé, the bulk of my social time was spent in the company of my Kuwaiti friend. Faisal was a direct contrast to Dave in that he came from a wealthy family in Kuwait.

His complete educational costs were paid for by the Kuwaiti Government through their London Embassy. These included rentals of a very up market apartment in Central London, return air tickets every college break, even if only for a few days, and incredibly also paid for the transport of his MGB sports car to and from Kuwait.

Just for good measure, a very generous monthly 'pocket money' allowance was thrown in. The only dark cloud on Faisal's horizon was that every month, the college had to forward a report on his academic progress. This used to annoy him intensely, not because it was a requirement, but because it went directly to an English student counsellor employed by the Embassy.

The man in question was quite strict on results and Faisal's style of study could at best be called relaxed rather than intensive. He was absolutely convinced that the monthly report should have gone to a fellow Kuwaiti in the Embassy, rather than one of their English employees.

I did see evidence of his family status in several instances. College rumour had him as a distant relative of the Kuwaiti Ruling Family. He never mentioned this, and I certainly never asked him, though I suspect the rumour was probably true.

The Embassy provided him with memberships of a couple of exclusive London Clubs frequented by wealthy Arabs. As his guest, I went several times to the Victoria Sporting Club in Kensington. It was, or maybe still is, an expensive West End Casino, which also staged big time boxing matches and had an excellent five-star restaurant.

I had many a free meal there, with no guilt feelings, as Faisal simply produced his membership card, added a 10% tip to the bill, and the Kuwaiti Govt. took care of the payment issue.

Met one of his brothers who 'worked' for one of the major oil companies that were heavily involved in the Kuwaiti Oil industry. Here we go again. His brother had an important title, a princely salary and an English 'assistant' to do his work. All 'Bro' had to do was turn up from time to time to sign prepared documents. Yes, there were such jobs, who would have thought!

One of Faisal's sisters visited London to catch up with him. She was attending a finishing school in Switzerland, open to all (with enough cash!) and especially catering for wealthy young women from the Arabian Gulf. She spoke perfect English and French and even with head scarf, in the looks department she was very attractive.

At all times, she was attended by a big middle-aged black man. I was puzzled and asked Faisal if he was family, as he was so black. My answer was certainly a surprise. He was her personal bodyguard since she was a baby. Wherever she went, he followed. And then the surprise came when I was told he was from Zanzibar and had been purchased by the father many years ago.

'Purchased', this would imply in the literal interpretation of the word, that this huge guy was, at least at one time, a slave! Maybe, maybe not but not my business to ask any more as his position in the family was certainly one of immense trust.

Faisal was a good Muslim and had a prayer room in his apartment. I had no doubt he kept the dietary laws but also liked to visit the local pubs and had a beer or two. Our choice of pub was 'The Rose' in Kensington and we would visit once a week generally on a Friday evening.

The pub was very well appointed, and like so many great British pubs, it had an excellent bar food menu. There was limited bar seating, many comfortable tables and chairs and on a weekend night would have seated well over one hundred thirsty customers. No live music, though the latest top 40 songs were routinely rolled out, just loud enough to enjoy while not interfering with ongoing conversations.

The place 'buzzed', had a great atmosphere and always had a good young/youngish crowd coming in often after finishing the weeks' work, grabbing a bite to eat and a few drinks before heading off to clubs, discos whatever to kick start their weekend activities.

One Friday night, seeing a couple of very presentable young women at an adjoining table, we decided to hit on them, and if not immediately rebuffed, offer them drinks. It was Faisal's turn to make the first move. He was a typical young Arab, good looking, well dressed, gift of the gab, slim and just 1.55m tall.

Off he strutted, the obvious ethnic look coupled with his lack of height was no hindrance and in a wink of the eye, we had company at our table. Lynne was a slightly built English woman with short curly brown hair and her companion, Helen, surprise, surprise, was a tall buxom Aussie woman with long auburn hair.

How things work out. I ended up with Lynne and Faisal with Helen. They made such a cute couple as he barely came up to her well-endowed boobs, though when we met she was wearing mini heels.

The evening was a big success, copious drinks ensured that there were no uncomfortable silences as we told each other all sorts of tales, some at least bordering on the truth.

As closing time approached, the girls, after a 'loo' pit stop, then asked us what plans we had for the weekend. Faisal jumped in and said we were planning to go to Brighton, stay Saturday night in a pub, then return to London on Sunday. Would they be interested? An immediate, "yes" and we agreed to meet them the following morning outside 'The Rose'.

Needless to say, Faisal's decision was a spur of the moment flash of brilliance, we had no previous intention to go anywhere as we had college assignments to work on, but sex or the distinct possibility of making out, instantly killed any study plans

They had wanted to meet at the rail station but when Faisal told them he had an MG sports car, trains were promptly forgotten. Again, perhaps a little to our surprise, the pair were actually waiting for us the next morning when Faisal pulled up in the MG and off to Brighton we went.

We continued to meet every Friday until one day Lynne was missing. Helen was very embarrassed to tell me Lynne's boyfriend had returned from work in Europe; whoops, did not see that coming, so sadly it was goodbye Lynne.

By this time, Helen had fallen big time for Faisal and he was concerned as she was starting to quiz him about possibilities of future marriage. He really felt the same about her, was nervous confronting her and asked me to explain to her how her life would be if they were to marry.

He gave me a detailed rundown of what huge changes, not only would, but would have to take place in her life. He realised she had absolutely no concept of what could be in store in Kuwait for a charming attractive young woman from a typical outgoing middleclass Aussie family.

I met Helen as usual on Friday evening, explaining that Faisal would be coming shortly and then told her what he had asked me to do. He would take over when he arrived as soon as I had broken the news, which indeed had brought on some tears.

Faisal's family were extremely wealthy and had a huge house in Kuwait City. His father lived his early years in the desert, emerging when the countries oil reserves changed forever the lives of the semi nomadic Bedouin Arabs. She would have to convert to Islam, wear the established religious apparel and at least for a few years, until the children came along, live in the family home.

His father had more than one wife. As the youngest wife, she would be ordered around by his father's other wives and by further wives of his brothers. She would have to learn Arabic. He would ensure that she got to go back to Australia with him to visit every year but that his future was bound up in Kuwait and they would have to return.

And if that was not enough for a western young woman to take in, he told me to tell her that because of his father's origins, the ground floor of the mansion was unsealed, just sand, no tiles, flooring of any kind, just sand, as that was how his father liked it.

On cue, he showed up and I took my leave. He thanked me later, telling me Helen wanted to talk things over with her family after the shocking news. This happened and apparently, they parted friends, but part they did, and I believe she returned to Australia shortly afterwards.

With the college study course now completed, the dreaded final exams were looming and 'party time' was over as we began studying in earnest. Back in high school, exams never bothered me. Then I simply didn't care, and my horrendous results reflected this attitude.

Now I had to be serious, my savings were now depleted, and I needed to pass, graduate and secure employment. Dave was in a similar position, only Faisal not overly concerned as apparently if he failed the exams first time around, he would simply repeat; life in London on his budget was not hard to take.

Miraculously, all three of us were lucky to somehow skim through the written exams and then pass the daunting orals examination conducted by a board of senior marine captains.

I was now a qualified 2nd Officer with a certificate to prove it. Now to find a job. I bought a British shipping newspaper, searched the various companies, and using the format taught us in college applied to three different firms. Within a week, I had replies from all three, thanking me and telling me they had no vacancies. By now, the cash flow situation was desperate, I placed an advert on the college notice board and my expensive Grundig radio was no more.

And then, completely by surprise, one of the three companies who had rejected my earlier application called and told me they now had a position for a 3rd Officer on one of their vessels. My response was immediate and a few days later, I received a second-class rail ticket to proceed to Liverpool for the obligatory interview.

I Join the *Bernard* as 3rd Mate

The *Bernard* was what was termed a passenger/cargo vessel owned by Booth Steamships, itself a subsidiary of the giant British Blue Star Shipping Empire. The term simply meant that in addition to normal cargo, it could carry up to twelve passengers in stateroom accommodation.

The ship was on a regular line between ports in North Europe to the Caribbean, North Brazil and then up the Amazon River to Manaus, the former rubber boom city in the heart of the jungle.

The company then had smaller ships, which went on past Manaus exiting Brazil to the upper Amazon ports of Leticia in Colombia and finally Iquitos in Peru.

I joined as the loading was all but complete. We sailed from Liverpool to Dublin and then Belfast for final top up cargo. The Captain was an old Liverpool Irishman with a ruddy complexion, indicating he surely enjoyed a whisky or two, a fact verified by one of the stewards who cleaned his cabin.

With me being a first trip Third Mate, he made frequent trips to the navigation bridge to make sure I was carefully following the set of orders he had hand written, a daily or rather nightly occurrence.

The crew were all from Liverpool and what a great bunch of characters they were. The Australian expression 'larrikins' as good a description as any. White, brown or Asian, everyone was a genuine 'Scouse' or Liverpool born and bred lad.

I guess I felt a certain kinship with them as my place of birth, Wrexham, although in Wales and not England, was only a short car drive away from Liverpool. One of them was on night watch with me to assist in keeping a look out for approaching ships. It was a very responsible job, especially in North European waters where there was so much shipping.

On my second night watch in the Irish Sea, my lookout came to the bridge door and called me, "Hey 3-O, gotta minute?" Not understanding him and thinking he had something to report, I went straight out. It turned out the '3-O' was his 'Scouse' abbreviation for 3rd Officer. He followed up with, "brought you a 'jambuttee sarny'."

Again, no idea what he was talking about until he handed me a sandwich wrapped in a napkin. Now I knew this was not how it was supposed to be, but nevertheless, I thanked him. And then he really ventured into no-go land when he said, "and something to wash it down with," handing me a can of beer. I told him I expected the old Captain to be up any minute, so please take the can down and please, please, no more beer when we were on watch.

A cheerful, "OK, 3/O," and off he went. 'Scouses' had the most wonderful sense of humour and after that when we would chat at odd moments on boring nights in the middle of the Atlantic, he would have me in stitches of laughter. To them, all people were equal and they had a tendency to disregard rather than disrespect authority, in a light-hearted inoffensive way.

We stopped at Las Palmas in the Canary Islands to take on fuel. I went ashore with the radio officer who wanted to buy a watch, or so I thought. He bought a dozen at throw away prices and told me I should do the same as for each watch, he could get a girl for a whole night in North Brazil.

The watches were distinguished by a green palm tree in the centre of the face and the outside bezel, I think that's what it was called, had a ring of imitation diamonds. They were cheap and looked cheap. I did not invest, perhaps I should have as it turned out he was not exaggerating.

The Mighty Amazon

Our first Brazilian Port was Belem, capital of the state of Para and situated on the mouth of a river of the same name. The Para River was one of several rivers which converged with the Amazon River proper to form the vast delta region of this great river before it flowed into the Atlantic Ocean.

The city of Belem had been around for almost 500 years as it was founded in 1616. The first Catholic Portuguese colonists named it 'Belem' after the city in which Jesus Christ was born, the name better known to the English-speaking world as Bethlehem.

The dock where we tied up was just a few hundred meters away from the bottom end of the main street, which despite the imposing name of Avenida Presidente Vargas was an area of bars, nightclubs and brothels, which were open for business 24/7. What else could be expected right outside the entrance gates to the port?

As you moved up the street and away from the port, the run-down decrepit slum atmosphere slowly changed. A walk of three kilometres and you were in the world of fancy shops, modern offices and hotels with 'lots of stars'.

Needless to say, not many of us made it past the bars and brothels so handy to the port. My friend, the radio officer was doing a roaring trade with his cheap watches. Those he did not exchange for sexual favours, he sold to the other girls.

There was an aquatic museum not far from the port and I paid a visit. The Amazon has a huge variety of freshwater fish, of all shapes and sizes and they were set out in several big tanks. I did not know there were such things as electric eels, but I saw them, and was told that the shock they delivered could kill a person.

We finished our unloading in Belem and headed off for our next port, Manaus, which was 1000 miles up the Amazon River. It was an incredible experience to be travelling in an ocean going freighter so far up a river. Nothing but jungle for the first day or so, but once clear of the delta region, we could see the land had been cleared on both sides of the river.

The Booth Steamship company had been running up the Amazon for decades and employed their own Brazilian Amazon River pilots and had their own carefully guarded charts of the river. These charts were of huge importance as the river was prone to changing navigable channels and water depths according to the time of year. The Amazon had a definite 'dry' season with moderate rainfall and an equally defined 'wet' season where cloudbursts of torrential rain occurred almost daily.

The rainy season extended from December through to May. During these months, it rained almost every day, generally around 2pm each afternoon, so consistent you could almost set your watch by it. The heavens would open, the rain so heavy that visibility would be reduced to a couple of hundred metres. However, it never lasted for more than an hour. When the rain would stop, as suddenly as it had begun, the air felt cool and fresh. It was the nicest time of the day; however, the oppressive heat and humidity soon returned.

We would frequently try to avoid floating 'islands of vegetation' drifting down the river. These were sometimes quite extensive and were detached sections of riverbank from 'somewhere' upstream that had broken away during the heavy wet season downpours and were now being swept downstream with the strong seasonal river current.

One day, we lost our steering and instead of changing course to round a bend in the river, we ploughed straight into the jungle. The front third of the ship was completely covered in, well, jungle. The pilot gave a call to all on deck to move into the accommodation while he attempted to free the ship.

He put the engine astern and effortlessly, we slipped back into the stream. He wanted everyone away from the vegetation as he said there was a small possibility that a snake might end up on deck.

In the wet season, the volume of water in the river increased enormously and in places, the river would become over two miles wide from bank to bank. It was then we relied so much on the skills of the river pilots who oversaw the navigation.

About halfway up the river, we passed by the City of Santarem. One of the pilots told us that after the American Civil War ended in 1865, a few veterans from the defeated Southern Confederate army settled in Santarem. He said there were still descendants of these in the city with their typically English names, though he laughed and said their old southern drawl belonged only in the past, and he doubted that most of those bearing these proud names could even speak English. However, the flag of Dixie still survived, engraved on some of the old tombstones in the city cemetery.

We stopped at Itacoaticara as our last port before Manaus to load bins of Brazil nuts, tonnes of them, and as they sold in 100 gram lots in Europe, they were no doubt worth a lot of money.

Manaus

And then to Manaus, a city founded on the early fortunes created by the wild rubber trees of the region.

The city, literally in the middle of the vast Amazon jungle fascinated me and instead of rushing headlong into the first bar or club, I decided to really have a look around. In just 40 years, from 1900 until the beginning of World War 2 in 1939, Manaus went from being economically nothing to a period of financial boom and then just as quickly back to bust again.

It wasn't until the 1970s that the Brazilian government encouraged investment in Manaus and the Amazon region and the city was now again emerging from its long slumber.

I visited a museum and read accounts of the enormous wealth accumulated by the so called 'rubber barons' all in the space of a few years as they endeavoured to supply the insatiable demand from the new car manufacturers in the USA and Europe who needed rubber for tyres.

A glittering opera house, costing millions of dollars, was prefabricated in Europe and shipped 1500 kilometres up the Amazon River, where it hosted some of the world's foremost singers and musicians of the time. A side note in the museum said that one of the first opera troupes to visit the city arrived from Italy and during their sojourn, over half ended up dying from yellow fever!

For the few at the top, it was a time of absurd extravagance. For the conscripted workers who had to seek out the isolated rubber trees in the dense inhospitable jungle life was hell. Malaria, Yellow Fever and the ever-present danger from wild animals ensured that many died alone and penniless.

The Opera House today, with its impressive dome, refurbished with its crystal chandeliers, ornate balconies and Victorian murals serves as a tourist 'must see' if only as reminder of the luxurious madness that instant wealth brought to those in power during the boom era.

The rubber boom died almost as quickly as it started. In the 1870s, a British scientific party had smuggled rubber seeds out of the Amazon to England and from there to the British Colonies in south-east Asia. Rubber plantations were established, thousands of trees planted in nice military lines with easy tapping access spelt the end of wild rubber in the Amazon.

There were numbers of indigenous Indians living in the jungles around Manaus. Some, especially in the more remote areas still chose to live in their traditional ways as hunters and gatherers, but 'civilisation' was slowly eroding this lifestyle.

They had been 'given' large reserves of land, supposedly their birth right, which were off-limits to all others. In practice, the isolation they sought was not working due to ever increasing illegal logging activities. Logging in many areas was completely illegal but flourishing due to corrupt state government officials and police.

The people of Manaus were a real bouquet of races from white to black while the vast majority were mixed race. As was so often the case with people from different racial backgrounds, many of them are very good looking. Those of indigenous Indian background were light brown, some with an almost Asian look about them.

Manaus was also a party city, with numerous bars and discotheques, and it was cheap. We made our favourite hangout the 'Veranda', a large club situated right on the edge of the river. It was basically an open-air bar. The roof projected well over the exterior balcony in case of rain, while the inside of the balcony was separated from the dance floors and bar by a fine wire mesh screen to keep out insects, in particular mosquitoes.

There was no air conditioning in a climate that was always hot and humid, but this absence was very efficiently overcome by several very large, slowly revolving ceiling fans. No matter how many people were on the dance floor, the fans did their bit, and it was never uncomfortable.

The female clientele were all hookers or would be hookers. 'Veranda' was a club the city's decent women never entered. It was here I met my first 'Cabocla'. A racial term indicating her father was of Portuguese descent and her mother Amazonian Indian.

Probably because of her dad she had completed high school, but what had gone wrong after school to where she now worked in this club was anybody's guess. Girls who had 'fallen from grace' usually became whores when their boyfriend made them pregnant, then disappeared never to be seen again.

The girls had to get money from somewhere with a baby to care for, and if they had even reasonable looks, they could earn far more selling their body than working in a variety of unskilled jobs.

Cabocla's were renowned for their good looks and this girl was no exception. She had never left Manaus and told me she had no desire to do so. She was saving to set up a beauty parlour and just hoped that one day she would realise her dream.

There was a saying in Manaus that anyone who sleeps with a 'Cabocla girl' will have a spell, or 'hex' as they called it, cast on them. This spell would guarantee the man would one day return to the Amazon and Manaus, lured back by the beautiful Cabocla women.

We stayed a whole week in Manaus with one incident standing out. I was the officer on night duty when our locally employed gangway watchman came running to me, babbling away hysterically in Portuguese. I could not get what he was saying but he pulled me to follow him quickly to the crew's mess room.

Three of our sailors had returned from the bars very drunk and had stolen his .45 calibre revolver out of his holster while he was dozing off. They were singing and one of them was waving the gun around. I realised that I had to do something before they accidentally fired a shot.

The guy with the gun pointed it at the floor and shouted, "Stand clear, 3/O. I'm going to make the watchman dance."

I shouted, "No, no, the bullet will ricochet and could kill someone, give me the gun." The watchman probably saved the day as he had disappeared out the door. One of the other guys took the gun and handed it to me. I said slowly and clearly, "guys, this never happened, do you understand, it never happened."

Returned the gun to the watchman and convinced him not to report the incident, telling him that if he said anything he would be in big trouble from his company. Fortunately, the matter died there. The last day in Manaus, we loaded a special tank on the ship filled with rosewood oil, another very valuable export product from the Amazon.

Departing Manaus, we headed downstream back to the delta region where we loaded timber products, both sawn lumber, plywood and a few valuable logs. The logs were hardwood, and with a specific gravity heavier than water that meant of course, they would not float.

To move them down the creeks and streams to the main river, they had light timber floats attached on either side. When we loaded them, the lighter floats would be returned to be used again.

It was in the river port of Breves that we encountered a certain Pieter Cornelius van Shirpenberg, one of the main timber exporters. His story was worth telling. He was Dutch and arrived in North Brazil just as World War II ended in Europe. Rumoured to be a Nazi collaborator who fled his country, perhaps true, or maybe his arrival in this remote part of Brazil was merely circumstantial.

Logging in this region had barely started and, as the story goes, he went to Government Officials in Rio de Janeiro which was then the national capital and managed to get a permit to operate a timber concession for a huge area of the Amazon delta rain forest.

He did not stop there. Again, he approached the government with the idea that he would like to take convicted prisoners from Rio's jails to use as his work force. He wanted some hardened criminals to act as overseers and guards. Again, no doubt money changed hands, but his request was granted.

He simply explained to the various officials that once at the logging site, it would be almost impossible for any of his 'workers' to escape as the nearest civilisation was 500 km away through dense jungle.

By the time we knew him, he was already very well established and was an old man. None of his prison workforce remained, they had either died or completed their jail terms and returned to South Brazil. He used to come on board our ship at lunch time always accompanied by his German Shepherd dog.

This was a British ship and lunch was always served in what they called the Main Dining Saloon with the deck officers sitting at a long table at one end and engineering officers at a similar table at the other end. In the centre was a large round table for the Captain, chief engineer and any passengers or shore guests. All the officers had to be dressed in full company uniform.

We had to be seated until the Captain entered when we would all stand up until he took his seat. It was an absolute hangover from the long-gone colonial days.

We had to admire Shirpenberg despite his probable murky past. He would stroll into the Saloon wearing thongs, a T-shirt, tatty shorts and with his dog on a leash, promptly sit down in a seat alongside the Captain. His entrance was so totally 'un-British'. It was almost as if to say, it's my cargo you're loading, I do what I want.

On one occasion, there was a discussion at his table about Piranha fish, which were found throughout the Amazon. Shirpenberg claimed they were only dangerous if there was blood in the water. Our Captain said he was not so sure of this.

His guest told him to come to the side of the ship after lunch when he and his dog would swim in the muddy water alongside our gangway. He then said he would come back on board, bringing a freshly slaughtered duck, stand alongside the Captain and throw the duck into the water he had just left.

By this time, just about every crew member was watching. He and his dog had a short swim, he came out and threw the blood-soaked duck into the water. It was instantly attacked by Piranhas. There were so many fish the carcass did not sink but just bobbed wildly up and down on the surface until only feathers remained. It took less than one minute. It was an impressive display by a man who certainly knew what he was doing.

He had his own seaplane to land on the river as there were no roads in or out of the village. I very nearly got to ride in it when I came down with fever. At first, it seemed to be malaria as the symptoms were similar. I had the high temperature, fever and was semi-conscious to where I was about to be air lifted to Belem when I began to feel a bit better.

The worst was not the fever but the intense migraine type headaches. Something had apparently bitten me, but it could not have been malaria as in a few days, I had completely recovered.

We topped up our loading for Europe with a repeat call in Belem. A call which had my good friend, the radio officer get a well-deserved black eye and several bruises. The watches he had exchanged for lust or sold for cash had 'died' and there were a bunch of girls out for his blood.

He had light blond hair and it was funny to see him going off the ship, wearing a dark beanie and sunglasses, and then taking a long detour to avoid the bars he normally frequented.

On our second trip, we loaded a British Trade Exposition comprising a huge collection of electrical appliances and tools. It included practically everything any proud homeowner could possibly use. Two large containers had been specially built to neatly pack away all the items.

Below and behind the navigation bridge was a promenade deck for our few passengers, and it was here that the exposition had to be set up each time we called in a new port. It was the crew's job, under us deck officers' supervision to assemble various stands and then display all the numerous items and multitude of brochures that accompanied them.

The British Embassy or Consulate invited large numbers of local businessmen, military and their wives in the hope they would like what they saw and place orders accordingly. Topflight local caterers supplied food, drinks as well as staff to serve the guests.

We hung up rows of coloured lights and strung up various ships' flags to provide the final decorative touch. Once set up, it certainly looked impressive, despite one of the seaman's comments that, "it looked like a backstreet bazaar in Bombay."

The guests rolled up and were escorted from the ship's gangway by cadet officers. Only the Captain, Chief Mate and Chief Engineer were invited to attend. They were all in their finest uniforms while the rest of us were told in no uncertain terms we were not to show up.

This performance was repeated on the second night of each port call. All the necessary preparation was in addition to our normal duties and kept us all working long hours. What hurt the most was that we were not only denied the booze that flowed freely, but that it seriously affected the hours we could spend enjoying a lively social life ashore.

Manaus was the last port for the exposition, and it was packed away for the trip back to the UK. By all accounts, it had been a success financially with good orders being placed.

Belem

We left Manaus and headed back down river to Belem where we had full cargo bookings for the trip back to UK/Europe. We arrived in Belem on the 16th of December. Loading was finally completed on the 23rd, just two days before Christmas.

The seamen were getting the ship ready to sail when the Chief Mate called me and told me the 2nd Officer, my friend the radio officer, the 2nd Engineer and the 4th Engineer were all not on board, and did I have any idea where they might be.

I knew exactly where they were, but told the Mate I thought I could probably find them. He told me to go at once, locate them and tell them to get back to the ship before he would have to tell the Captain they were missing.

I had been with them the evening before, in fact the 4th Engineer and I were hot on the heels of the same girl. The bar was in a cobblestone side alleyway a hundred or so meters off the main street and it took me only minutes to get there.

They were all there, well primed, just a few drinks away from being totally wasted. However, the radio officer was missing, they had all been upstairs for short times with their girls, but the horny radio officer had gone back for 'seconds'.

I said, "Hey you guys, we have to go back, the Mate is worried."

They told me, "Relax, the ship is not sailing for another 4 hours," and a drink was thrust in my hand. I like rum and coke and this bar served it in tall glasses filled with tiny round ice cubes. I had never seen ice cubes like this before and come to think of it, have never seen them since.

Well, one drink followed another, the radio officer came down, and then to the general comment, "we still have plenty of time," coupled with the arrival of some new and talented girls, I thought I'd better have a 'quickie' as well. I told myself it would be both my one and only Christmas present as well as a fitting farewell to Belem and Brazil. We went up to her room.

Time had gone by much quicker than we thought. The ship was ready to sail, and our absence noted. The Captain had called the local agent, who was an ex-company Captain and asked him to track us down and get us back to the vessel. The agent knew all the seaman's hangouts and did not take long to zero in on our hideaway.

I was still upstairs when he showed up, so unfortunately, I missed what followed. He was a youngish man in his thirties, with a decidedly arrogant manner. He burst in the bar door and immediately started threatening the 2nd Officer and 2nd Engineer with dismissal, fines and suspension unless they returned at once to the ship.

The only mistake he made was that they were drunk and surrounded by young whores. They stood up, one on each side, picked him up under the armpits and threw him through the bar door into the street. He bolted, who wouldn't after an undignified landing on cobblestones. The guys carried on as if nothing had happened. I came downstairs and heard the whole story.

In our fuzzy state, we knew we would be in big trouble; that was inevitable, so no point in going back to the ship now. We would face the music tomorrow. And legally the ship could not sail without us.

But we had got that wrong. Belem was a river port some miles from the sea. The Captain could shift the vessel downriver, with a port pilot to advise him, then drop anchor just before the river entered the sea. This he did, anchoring off a small city called Salinopolis.

Meanwhile, the bruised manager had sent a written note to the bar saying that a minibus would pick us up, sober, at 8am next morning to take us to Salinopolis. If we did not show up for the bus, he would send in the police and have us charged with desertion.

Happy Christmas, one and all. The party carried on unabated, we were all sexually satiated, and drunk as lords. With the young lady of our choice, we then crashed for the night. In the morning, we were all up and ready for the minibus but decidedly the worse for wear, nursing hangovers of varying intensity.

It was supposedly a three-hour drive to Salinopolis, but it took us over five hours. We had not gone more than a few kilometres, were still in Belem, when a mutual decision was made to stop for a 'livener'. Thought being that a really cold beer would bring us back into the land of the living.

Unfortunately, we did not stop with just the one beer but continued to stop the minibus at frequent intervals for just 'one more for the road' or a piss. By the time we reached Salinopolis, we were again feeling no pain. Not as drunk as yesterday, but high enough to not be the slightest bit concerned about our impending punishment.

A small boat was waiting to take us out to the *Bernard*. We all had a last bottle of beer in our hand as we drew near to the ship. The Captain was leaning over the bridge railing and his face was almost purple with rage. When brand new ships are launched, they are christened by some dignitary breaking a bottle of champagne on the bow of the vessel.

In a last defiant gesture, we decided to christen the good ship *Bernard* for the second time. Five, by now empty, Brahma Beer bottles shattered against the hull of the ship. The Chief Steward was at the gangway to meet us with instructions for all of us to go to our cabins until further notice. The ship at once, departed on the Atlantic crossing leg to our next port, Lisbon in Portugal.

The next morning, we were summoned by an angry Captain. The list of our offences, bad as they were, seemed to have multiplied. His dark mood no doubt magnified by the fact that this was his last voyage before retirement. After years of faithful service to the company, all he wanted was his last voyage to be uneventful and free of any incidents. Instead, he was facing no fewer than five of his officers, all guilty of numerous offences.

We were spared a long speech. Maritime Law required that he individually list our offences in the Official Ship's Logbook, after which he had to give each of us a copy of the entry he had made.

I still have my copy and looking at it, I feel a little sad. Not so much for what we had done, that was more youthful exuberance rather than wilful misconduct, but for the distress it had obviously caused the Captain on his last trip. He would remember his farewell trip, a grand finale to a long seagoing career for all the wrong reasons.

He concluded by saying each of us would have to front the Shipping Master in Liverpool when the ship docked and that we could face suspension of our licences. However there was still the Atlantic Ocean to cross and a port call in Lisbon before returning to Liverpool.

The Captain kept an unusually close watch on us offenders. He took to checking on me almost nightly, coming to the navigation bridge sometime during my 8pm to midnight watch. It was on one of these occasions that he really surprised me, so much so that I could hardly stop myself from bursting out laughing.

He was telling me that the behaviour of the young British officers was a disgrace to their profession and then he said, "Smith, you are the only one who has any excuse, you're an Australian and just don't know any better." I glanced at him, thinking he must be either joking or was just being very rude, but he was being sincere, he really believed this. The timing was not right for me to proclaim my Welsh ancestry, as in his own way he seemed to be excusing my behaviour.

The 2nd Officer relieved me at midnight as his duty hours were from then until 4am. Although only 25 years old, he already had a serious drinking problem, in fact was for sure a borderline alcoholic quickly heading for confirmed status as such. His favourite drink was a mix of cognac and crème de menthe which he called, "sol y sombre," Spanish for 'sun and shadow', which he would mix with lemonade. To say the least, it was a potent brew.

He was often very late relieving me to where I would have to repeatedly phone his cabin to get him on his feet. I was unaware that the Captain had noted this.

On the last night before arrival in Lisbon, he was especially late coming to the bridge. I thought I heard his footsteps, turned around to greet him and instead came face to face with the Captain. He said to me, "3rd Mate, where is the 2nd Officer?"

As if on cue, my relief came onto the bridge. He was a little unsteady and stood rigidly upright as the Captain asked, "Mr Brown, are you ready to take your watch?"

He replied, "Yes Sir," and promptly passed out, falling at the captains' feet.

The Captain told me to assist him back to his cabin, said he would take the 2nd Officer's watch and I was to go to sleep.

We docked later that morning, the 2nd Officer was dismissed from the ship and a replacement flown out from the UK. I called his home when we got back to Liverpool, but his mother said he had found another job in Hong Kong and had already left for there. He was a lot of fun; hope he was able to find some way of at least moderating his drinking.

The last few weeks had been quite eventful but there was still more to come.

Liverpool

Arriving in Liverpool, all the crew were required to sign off the ship before going on a leave break. Those who would be coming back for the next voyage would then sign on again when they re-joined. This was to be done the following morning after we had docked.

The signing procedures were carried out before the Liverpool Shipping Master, and before we did this, he had the Belem 'guilty 5' in, one by one, for the official 'dressing down'.

He told me I had burnt my bridges with Booth Line and what were my plans for the future. I had been talking to the seaman who was on the same duty hours as me and we had plans to visit a local club where according to him, the music and the girls were wild. When the Shipping Master asked me my plans, I wasn't thinking and told him I was going to a club with one of the crew.

The wrong thing to say, he looked at me with an amazed look on his face and told me it was time I started to take my career seriously and hanging around with some of these crew was not a good idea. This kind of surprised me, but the next morning I was to find out why he had seemed so hostile towards this crew.

It was afternoon by the time each crew member had signed off and we were all told we had to assemble in the main officer's saloon before departing from the ship. There were a couple of well-dressed guys waiting there and we assumed they were some big shots from Booth Line.

Captain and the Chief Mate came in and the door was shut. The two men then introduced themselves as detectives from Scotland Yard. They started by saying, "most of you will know why we are here, for those who don't, here is the reason." He then told us that the two special containers holding the British Exposition had been landed in the adjacent warehouse on the wharf during the night. They were then opened so that the various owners could collect their goods before the normal cargo discharge started the next morning.

To the amazement of all, the containers were empty. Every single item had been stolen, all that remained were numbers of empty boxes and cases together with the remnants of the advertising brochures. They assured the entire assembled crew that they would find out who was responsible, charges would be laid and for sure, some would end up in prison. We were told that if any of us had information, we should call or ring the local police.

They must have known there was little chance of this happening. We could not be held on board now we had signed off, and as there was no immediate proof that any person or persons had been involved, we were then free to leave the ship.

I never heard anything further and searched the newspapers for the next few days but there was no mention of the incident or of any arrests being made.

I Take a Sabbatical

Liverpool was a lot of fun just like my shipmate said it would be, but I was drinking too much and although the clubs were the best, I was getting tired of the constant partying. At various times during my day or night, the words of the Shipping Master would suddenly come back to me. What am I doing with my life?

In New York, I had been fired off my last ship as a seaman. I had spent difficult months studying for my Marine 2nd Mate's Licence. I then found employment with a good company on a line I really enjoyed. Now in Liverpool and after my first two trips as a newly qualified deck officer, I had been sacked.

My work record was starting to look decidedly shabby and the less said about my CV, the better. I would now find it difficult to get work on any British flag ship as new employers invariably contacted the previous company for a reference check and this would surely do me no favours.

It was time to go back to London and look for cheap lodgings in the Earl's Court area, home to so many visiting young Aussies living on meagre budgets. They could update me on any employment possibilities. If all else failed, and as a last resort, I would have to consider returning to Sydney.

Bought my second-class rail ticket and sadly departed Liverpool. It was a great city and the people I met were my kind of people. In the train, I sat in a compartment with three other young guys, and we started chatting. They were all Jewish, all from Liverpool and were going to London as part of a youth group preparing to go to Israel.

I told them I had been in Haifa and had celebrated my 21st birthday in that city. They asked me how I found the country and I told them I had really enjoyed my stay there. They then told me they were not only going to Israel but were emigrating there.

They would go first to a school to learn the Hebrew language and from there straight into the army. They told me they would meet up with the rest of the group in London and then go to Paris to meet a similar French group and from there to Israel. I had told them what I had been up to and the resultant consequences I now faced. Mentioned I wished I could come with them as it sounded exciting.

They said, "why not?" There were places still open with their group and if I wanted, they would ask if I could be included. I then told them I was not Jewish and as they all belonged to some worldwide Jewish Youth group, I would be a definite outsider.

The three of them then said that if I was serious, they would ask and leave my name with their London people. They gave me a London address and phone number and told me I must call the next day as the group were to leave in a few days.

Why not!

I called first thing the following morning and was told that if I could pay the fare that day, I could come with the group. I was then told if I went with them, I was not a part of the group and that once we reached Haifa, I would be on my own.

However, they did say that they could arrange for me to go to work on a collective farm, or kibbutz as they called it. They said that there was a kibbutz agency in the Haifa Port area, and they would pass my details to them if I so wished. I could then be met at the port and taken to the farm they had selected. Again, why not!

Paid my fare money which covered both train and boat costs and was given a written schedule for the trip, which was to depart in four days' time. As I would be travelling with the group, I was also entitled to a good discount.

Time flew by and at 8:30am four days later, met with the group at Victoria Station in Central London. Train, ferry across the English Channel to Calais, train again and we were in Paris.

Just two hours later, having met up with the French group, we got on another train destination Marseilles. I would say this for the organisers, they had really worked a tight schedule. As soon as we arrived in Marseilles, two buses picked us up and took us to the port.

Here we embarked on the *Iskenderun*, an old Turkish Passenger Liner. We had to share four berth cabins, way below the main deck. Later that night, we sailed. There were some forty people in the youth group, plus the one extra, me!

There were quite several other passengers who were mostly young people from France and the Scandinavian countries.

We also had a very second-rate English Rock Group on board booked for a series of concerts in Israel. The youth group members were quite excited and asked around to see if anybody had heard of them, and if so what hits, if any, this group had made.

Turned out they were seemingly unknown in the UK and Europe, with no chart hit successes of their own, and as one of the girls was quick to comment, they weren't even good looking. They had discounted fares with the proviso that they performed nightly during the crossing of the Mediterranean.

However on our first night at sea, all the nasty comments were soon forgotten as after a couple of drinks, they did provide some welcome music and as the alcohol flowed, dancing began. This all took place alongside the swimming pool with the obvious end results as young men will be young men.

Bodies, willingly or otherwise, ended up in the pool and when stewards tried to intervene, they too 'went for a dip'. From then on, ship security crew secured a net over the pool after dark.

We arrived in Haifa early one afternoon. Said farewell to the various youth group members as had made some good friends amongst them. A representative from the Kibbutz organisation was holding up a clipboard with my name as well as others.

It turned out the others were two Danish girls also from the *Iskenderun* who were allocated to the same kibbutz as me. Met the girls and we were told we would have a van ride of an hour to the kibbutz. Passports were stamped and off we went.

Life in an Israeli Kibbutz
Ramat Yochanan

We arrived at the kibbutz and were introduced to the Director of Volunteers. His name was Emmanuel, and he was a very friendly red-headed guy in his mid-forties. In common with many Israelis, he spoke several languages fluently.

Emmanuel welcomed us and gave us a quick description of the kibbutz as he took us around the various buildings. Centrepiece was a large dining room or in Hebrew 'Haderochal'. It was communal dining for everyone. It was huge and would seat at least 400 people. There appeared to be no seating arrangements, and all the members of the kibbutz took their meals there.

As new arrivals, we were each introduced to a family who would adopt us for the duration of our stay. At times, particularly on holiday celebrations we would be sure to eat with 'our' new family, at other times the volunteers generally chose to sit together where English or French would be the table language.

On the conclusion of our introductory walk, Emmanuel took us to get our issue of work clothes. Very similar for both men and women in that we each had long pants, shorts, shirts, work shoes or boots and a crazy little hat called a 'kova tembal', which apparently translated as silly hat! All the clothing was dark blue. All we had to supply was our own underwear and socks.

Equipped with our working wardrobe, we were then taken to our new living quarters. We volunteers were housed in what at one time were huts for the early settlers. There was a cluster of ten rectangular buildings each about 30 meters long by 10 meters deep.

Each building was divided into three rooms and each room generally contained three beds. In front was the entry door and one curtained window while the back wall had a further curtained window. The closest thing I have seen to these quarters are those that can be found in most old military barracks.

Not the most elegant description but they were very well maintained, clean and comfortable. Almost all the occupants, especially those who had stayed for some time introduced their own personal touches to the one third of the room they could call their own.

There were two toilet blocks behind the cluster, one for guys and one for gals, well equipped with cold water showers and enclosed toilets. Normally three guys, or three women shared each room. If a couple arrived together, they were given a room together, with just two beds, no double bed, which did cause some problems and a lot of laughs.

Two single beds could easily be pushed together, but all these beds had a pipe railing around the bed just a few centimetres higher than the mattress, which could seriously disrupt moments of passion. Most couples quickly put the mattresses on the floor, problem solved.

If a new relationship developed, all the eager couple had to do was to see Emmanuel and a two bedroom was theirs for the asking if available. This frequently happened, which was hardly surprising when all the volunteers were between 18-30 years old.

The volunteers came from all over the world. Such was the atmosphere in the kibbutz that in the six months I lived there, I saw no serious disagreements between any of the volunteers or between us and the kibbutz members. About half of the volunteers were Jewish but none were very religious. The kibbutz members themselves were generally not religious, however all the traditional Jewish holidays were celebrated and for a wedding, a Rabbi would show up.

Always there were between thirty and forty volunteers. I was the only Welsh/Australian, but we had several from the UK, at least ten from France, Danes, a Norwegian, a good number from the USA and 1 Canadian from Quebec. After I had been there for a couple of months, we received a group of twenty men and women from Hokkaido/Japan. It was a real little United Nations.

We worked six days a week. A volunteer's job list was posted every evening just outside the dining room so you could see what the next day had in store for you. There was a lot of variety, work wise. There were apple, orange, grapefruit and lemon orchards, huge chicken houses, a plastics factory, cotton plantations, olive fields, banana plantations, mechanical workshop, dairy cattle, sugar beef crops, kitchen duty, and I've no doubt forgotten some.

Our day started at 7am with breakfast in the dining room after which we headed off with our supervisors for our allotted task for the day. For breakfast, you could have what they called 'leban' a dairy product like yogurt, delicious and not sweet, boiled eggs, vegetable salad and freshly baked bread.

It was a self-serve meal, if you wanted ten boiled eggs you could take ten, not that anybody ever did. Out in the fields, we would have a snack break at 9:30 where we could have a sandwich or fruit with soft drinks, either orange or grapefruit natural unsweetened juice.

We would finish for the day at 1pm when we would head back to the dining room for lunch. The afternoon was ours. Evening meal was at 7:00pm.

My first work was picking oranges and grapefruit. I must have picked thousands, although picking is not the correct term. Using small scissor type tool, we cut the fruit off the stem, flush with the top, being careful not to damage the small 'star' between the stem and the fruit.

If the fruit is just pulled off, this 'star' is removed and apparently this greatly reduced the time the fruit would remain fresh. The fruit was put into huge bins which were taken to a sorting and packing yard. Most of our citrus was for export to European markets. Our bananas were also primarily for export.

I then spent time in the chicken pens and really did not like this work. There were six huge sheds and live chickens and fresh eggs made up a big part of the kibbutz earnings. I have no idea how many chickens there were, seemed like millions, but of course there weren't. Chickens, chickens and more chickens, from those freshly hatched baby yellow chicks to death row for those intended for the kibbutz kitchen.

The mature chickens spent their sad lives in long batteries of cages where they had minimal area to move around. There were conveyor belts running along in front of the cages, one for water and another for their food. They ate, slept and crapped in this tiny area, but most importantly, they laid eggs.

The number of eggs recorded daily on little pads on the front of the cage. Low production meant their days were numbered and Kentucky Fried Chicken or other commercial outlet would be their next stop.

My supervisor in the chickens was training me up for a permanent position there. He was a likeable guy and I was trying to figure out some way to get out of the job when fate intervened and I had an accident.

One morning, he told me my work for the day would be to sweep out the small silos used to store the crushed grain that, with undefined additives, was the conveyor belt supplied feed for the chickens.

Two of the silos were empty of feed but condensation inside them had resulted in thick grain dust becoming moist and adhering to the internal walls. My job was to sweep down the walls so the damp dust went to the bottom of the tank where it would then be removed via a vertically sliding gate through which the feed normally exited.

The silos were about 8 meters tall and the gate at the base around 600mm x 600mm. It was just large enough for me to squeeze through at a pinch. On top was an entry hatch with an internal ladder down to the bottom of the silo.

I climbed in and in an hour or less had finished the first and moved to the second silo. The dust was very slippery but having done the first cleaning, I was perhaps a little thoughtless or overconfident. The difference with this second silo was that the bottom exit gate had been carelessly completed.

The steel rods inserted during construction to strengthen the concrete silo walls had not been cropped when the gate was fabricated. Several rods protruded down from the top of the bottom gate opening. They made no difference to the discharge of the feed, but human exit was now out of the question.

The inevitable happened, I slipped on the dust and careered down the tank on my backside coming to a dead stop when one of the rods punched through the shinbone on my left leg. Initially I was in shock, but little pain and my yelling soon attracted attention.

The only way out of the silo was through the top. Now came real pain. With my supervisor now inside and assisting me, I had to move my injured leg until the rod popped out. I all but passed out with the pain. Now the stair rungs up to the top exit.

A couple of guys on top of the silo had lowered a rope, which the supervisor passed under my arms and back to the guys. I remember saying to the guys, "if this rope slips, I'll get fucking hung." They now heaved as my boss pushed my ass and slowly, we made it to the top and out.

I was assisted into the bucket of a front loader and lowered to the ground. An army jeep was waiting with a newly arrived American immigrant driving. He said, "I'm Willy and I'm going to take you to hospital in the nearby town of Afula." Off we went. Despite my pleas to slow down, Willy was driving like a maniac, and this attracted the attention of a police highway patrol car who flagged us down.

Willy, as a newly arrived immigrant spoke very, very little Hebrew and to the cops, his American English might as well have been Tibetan. When they saw why he had been speeding, they then went ahead and escorted our jeep to the hospital.

Spent two days in hospital while they took X-rays, removed some bone chips and then heavily bandaged, it was back to the kibbutz. Who came to pick me up, of course, Willy. He greeted me as a long-lost friend, as I reminded him, "Willy I've just come out of hospital, for heaven's sake drive carefully, what I really don't need now is a highway accident."

Back at the kibbutz, the volunteers had carved me a very handsome walking stick, and all of them had signed it. I was to use it for the next two weeks. I was not a person given to collecting souvenirs, but this stick was special and when it went missing months later, I was really upset.

There was a fellow volunteer who had broken her ankle. She was a lovely Danish woman named Jutte who was hobbling around on crutches. For the next two weeks, we spent all day, every day together so at least as invalid walking wounded, we had each other's company.

The real bonus resulting from my injury was that I was able to conn my way out of the chicken pens. Then for a brief time, I helped out in the kitchen and dining room, which was considered light duties, while my leg healed.

The job I liked most was working in the banana plantations and I had done just about everything associated with cultivating them. Initially, we would start off by cutting and planting the new suckers that shoot from the base of mature plants. These replanted would then become the next crop.

Cleaning the surplus dead leaves off each plant and keeping weed growth under control between the rows was a never-ending task. We would check the stems often until finally, when the fruit was still green, we would cut them off ready for marketing.

It was hard work and our boss and most of his kibbutz staff were army reserves from top combat units. The fields were often muddy so carrying a full stem of mature bananas was strenuous work. To them it was a form of exercise, and they would run down the rows with a heavy stem on one shoulder, dump it on the trailer and then run back for the next. We volunteers tried in vain to keep up with them, but nonetheless our efforts were appreciated. They were great people to work with.

There was a shop or store on the kibbutz. It was run by a lady who from time to time made sure that the shelves were always well stocked. However, for most of the time, she was not there and the shop, open for business, was unstaffed. It did not matter for all items were free.

If you wanted something, you just entered and took it. It was such a novelty to newcomers that they tended to take more than they needed but once they realised that they could drop in at any time, this tendency stopped. The shop had cigarettes and beer, so you were never without a drink or a smoke. The beer was 'Nesher', a very cheap low alcohol brand but it was beer, and it was free.

You had to be a determined smoker to avail yourself of the 'Degel' brand cigarettes. They were nonfilter, tobacco, loosely packed and were horrible, but for those addicted to tobacco, they sufficed. I'm sure many of the kibbutz people must have known that the main use for 'Degel' was to remove the tobacco from the paper, mix it with hashish then refill the paper tube.

It then became a far more popular cigarette and was enjoyed by many of the volunteers. The finished 'joints' were shared around behind the toilet block with a lookout posted in case any kibbutz member approached.

We really hit the jackpot one day. Two of our group had gone to Ben Gurion Airport near Tel Aviv to bid farewell to one of the departing volunteers. When they said their goodbyes, Jerry needed to have a pee before the bus trip back to the kibbutz. In the men's toilet, all the open area stand-up troughs were occupied but one of the lavatory closets was empty with the door open.

When Jerry entered, closed the door and started to piss, he noticed a bag stuffed behind the toilet bowl. Like he said later, "normally, I would not have touched it, but I was curious." He opened it and found it full of marijuana. He closed it tightly, exited the toilet and then gave it to his Dutch travelling companion Mieke saying, "pop this in your carry bag, please."

She said nothing and plonked it in her bag. They departed the airport, bussed back to the kibbutz, and it was only when they reached the volunteers huts, he asked for it back and showed it to her. She was furious, wacked him a couple of times, then burst out laughing saying, "Jerry, you Yankee bastard, I could have been arrested, jailed, certainly thrown off the kibbutz and maybe out of the country."

His reply was classic, "better you than me," got him more well-deserved clouts. I am sure Mieke will remember this to her dying day. Hashish was available everywhere, but marijuana was very rare on the streets. Some man had obviously panicked and left it in the 'loo'; bless him, it was a good-sized bag but did not last long!

Friday evening was when Jewish people had their traditional Sabbath meal. Observant religious people returning to their homes after worship would then eat as a family group, quite often inviting a guest, or guests they had brought back from the Synagogue.

The timing of the start of the Sabbath in modern Israel is determined to the exact minute. It was announced on TV, radio and by public address systems mounted on cars or vans going through the streets. Traditionally in olden times, it would begin when a glance at the sky would reveal at least three stars. It would end on the Saturday in the same manner. I didn't know how this worked on cloudy or rainy days.

The kibbutz while not being very religious did however turn on a special meal every Friday evening. The tables all were decked with white tablecloths, wine was provided, and the food was superior to the other days of the week.

After the Sabbath meal, it was also a big night for us volunteers. Every Friday evening, we would have an 'all welcome' volunteers party. By moving the beds up tight against the walls in one of the huts, we made enough free space for a surprising number of bodies.

Living on a farm which had literary hundreds of grapefruit and orange trees, we would prepare a huge plastic bowl of 'punch'. The kibbutz had an electric fruit juice extractor which was efficient, and we could squeeze the juice from 100 or more grapefruit in just a few minutes. There was a permanent soda water fountain at the entrance to the dining room so we would then add this to the freshly squeezed juice.

And then the unofficial addition was discretely added to the bowl. At first, we would buy a medium sized bottle of vodka from Kfar Ata, a near-by village and slip this into the punch. This would not alter the taste of the punch by much and was not discernible at all after the first cup.

It definitely added some zip to the drink, and it was readily noticeable that some of the quieter or shyer types quickly shed their inhibitions and were at least part way to becoming party animals.

The problem was the vodka, or rather the cost of buying it. There was an ever-present shortage of funds amongst the few volunteers whose discreet task it was to prepare the punch. And then a ready solution was found. One of the girls for some reason needed to purchase a bottle of 96% proof alcohol from a pharmacy in Haifa. When she got back to the kibbutz, she said she had been very surprised at how cheap it was. From then on, vodka was out and medicinal alcohol was in.

It took a couple of Friday nights before we got the mix correct. First, we put in too much of the 96% proof. People got high more quickly without realising why. There were no hangover headaches the following day, but an overpowering need to drink liquid. Soft drinks did not help, you reached for a second can shortly after drinking the first.

Water, and lots of it was the best cure. Once we had the alcohol-grapefruit juice percentages sorted out, we then introduced a small amount of sugar and the result was good enough to market, had it been legal.

We did have one major scare. A group of Tel-Aviv high school students came for a weekend visit to the kibbutz, and uninvited and unannounced arrived at our huts at party time. We welcomed them before we realised, they were helping themselves to the doctored punch.

We managed to scoop out most of the punch into jugs and remove them to another room before the kids were too noticeably affected. None the less, we were very relieved the next day when it seemed their alcohol intake had passed unnoticed by the kibbutz members.

And then the Japanese arrived. Twenty of them from the University of Sapporo on the northern island of Hokkaido. They were a breath of fresh air. They had been sent by the Japanese Government to study the kibbutz style of agricultural life. As we got to know them, we learnt that they had all volunteered not really to study kibbutz life but because it was an all-expenses paid trip to Israel.

All were in their early or mid-twenties, and all spoke good English. They mixed in very well with everybody and there was quite some competition among the kibbutz families for the privilege of 'adopting' them for their stay. They were to stay for four months.

Being Japanese, wherever they went they had their cameras, invariably very upmarket models and it was click, click, click throughout the day. A couple of the guys were advanced Karate and Judo exponents and they quickly set up classes for other volunteers and many of the young and not so young kibbutz members.

They loved our Friday night parties and when we told a couple of the guys the story of our punch, they thought it was hilarious and said they would not tell the Japanese girls. I was particularly friendly with one of the women. Her name was Kishko, or maybe that was her nickname, and during one party night, after copious quantities of punch, I said, "Kishko, you are very pretty, can I kiss you?"

She looked very serious and I thought whoops I'd gone too far, and then still very thoughtful and no less serious she said, "If I let you kiss me, we then have to make love." My reply as expected was OK, what do you think? She cracked a sweet smile and said a very definite, "No, Jake."

I told her if she decided to change her mind, just let me know. She laughed, the tension was broken and fortunately our friendship remained secure, so it was a celibate friendship. So, what!

Once or twice a month, the kibbutz would take us volunteers on trips to different parts of Israel. The country is small but with a history dating back some 3000 years, there were so many places to go to and so much to see. The trips were very well organised and totally free.

From somewhere, an army truck or trucks would turn up and we would load huge amounts of food and drink from the kibbutz kitchen. If we were to be away overnight, those who had sleeping bags would bring them, if not then kibbutz blankets, and off we would go. Overnight basic accommodation would be arranged in various youth hostels.

Our kibbutz supervisors were all steeped in the history of Israel from the time of Moses until yesterday and spoke several languages fluently. They gave us detailed accounts of the various places we passed through and told us to ask them any questions we might have about anything to do with Israel. They were bombarded with questions and were never stumped for answers. All of us learnt so much more about the country we were visiting.

In my time on the kibbutz, I saw most of the country, visiting the Galilee, the northern borders with Lebanon and Syria, a Bedouin encampment outside of Beersheva, a Druze village near Haifa, Nazareth where Jesus grew up, Bethlehem where he was born and so much more.

Bethlehem stuck in my mind due to a peculiar incident when we were taken to visit the Greek Orthodox Church, which allegedly stood over the site where the baby Jesus was born. The building as one would expect was magnificent and there were a number of bearded Greek Orthodox Monks in their black robes and typical hats, waiting to show us through their church.

In addition to us volunteers, we had some twenty young kibbutz teenage boys and girls with us, dressed as they always did in blue shirts and shorts, both the boys and the girls. As we got out of the truck, our supervisor came to me and said, "Jake, keep an eye on the kibbutz boys."

No reason given but I said, "OK, will do." When we entered the church, it became apparent that two of the monks were more than just interested in our young lads. One put his arm around one of the boys' shoulders and I had to move in, point my finger at him and say, "No." After this, they kept their distance. No move was made towards the young teenage girls, some of whom were decidedly attractive.

We went down into what they called the crypt and there was the manger supposedly over the very spot where the baby Christ was born. Bethlehem is quite close to Jerusalem. There is something very special about Jerusalem where so many of the buildings, both old and new, are built from a cream-coloured stone taken from quarries in the neighbouring hills.

It is a beautiful city which was sacred not only to the Jews but also to the Christians and Muslims. In Jerusalem, my visit to Yad Vashem was what would stay in my memory as long as I lived. This was the memorial to the six million Jews who were murdered by the Nazis in their notorious death camps in World War 2.

The main entry door was covered with intricate sculptures. The first few meters of the walls were constructed from very large rocks or boulders and on top of these, the remaining windowless walls of solid concrete.

Once inside the building, the walls were covered with photos of those unfortunates taken from Jewish villages throughout Eastern Europe. At first, confined in ghettos in the cities, then transported and murdered in the camps. A prominently displayed plaque simply says, 'A World Which Was and Is No More'.

From there into 'Martyrs and Heroes Remembrance Hall', a bare stone floor with the names of the numerous death camps superimposed on black backgrounds on the floor itself. An eternal flame illuminated the sombre scene. No one was speaking and when we came to walk out, we passed an elderly lady with tears running down her cheeks. I wondered what terrible memories she could have had of happenings so many years ago.

Kibbutz volunteers came and went frequently, none more interesting than Roland from the UK and his girlfriend, Marge. Marge was a young attractive English woman who had just graduated from university, very well spoken, neatly dressed and oh so British.

Roland was a gypsy who had spent his childhood and early teens living in old vans travelling the highways and byways of the UK. His family tired of being harassed by various local authorities had finally settled down in Kent and it was in a pub there that he had met Marge.

Once Roland came out of his shell, he proved to be a real comedian and had us in stitches with some of his gypsy tales. He was very proud to be one of the Romany people, to give them their correct name and said he could speak their language. He claimed he missed their traditional way of life which he said was gone forever in the UK but did say it was a hard life and that even in the good times, his people lived barely above the poverty line.

He had been to the annual gypsy festival in Sainte Marie De La Mer in France and intended to take Marge there in the future. They were the happiest couple which I suppose only goes to show that opposites do sometimes attract.

After nearly six months in the kibbutz, I was approached to see if I would be interested in becoming a member. It came just as I was getting ready to leave and head south through the desert to the city of Eilat on the Red Sea.

The kibbutz invite really took me by surprise and I did give it a lot of thought. The people were great, and after six months, I was really enjoying the communal lifestyle.

If accepted, I would first have to learn better Hebrew. To learn Hebrew, speak, read and write a completely new and different language, all newcomers or immigrants had to attend what could best be called a total immersion language course. The student's native language was supposedly pushed to one side and all dialogue between teachers and students had to be in Hebrew.

No problem on Ramat Yohanan as the kibbutz had a recognised Hebrew language school and it would have been free to a new member. Once through the initial course, it would be into the defence forces for the mandatory conscription service period, which for men was three years.

I would have had no problems with this. I finally decided not to accept their offer and my main reason for doing this was probably very immature at the time. I had been spending a lot of my free time with a newly arrived young immigrant woman, Ruth, who had just landed in Israel from India and was studying in the Hebrew Course in the Kibbutz, or 'Ulpan' as they called it.

Anyway, I was getting serious and then, 'out of the blue' and in the nicest possible way, she dumped me. Feeling a bit miserable, I had decided to go to Eilat with an American fellow volunteer.

Ruth was staying on to complete her course and I just wanted to leave. And I did. I spent just over six months of my life in Ramat Yohanan. Without a doubt, it was one of the happiest times in my life. I had made so many friends, both Israeli and travellers from, well you name it, and I sometimes look back and think how things would have panned out, if I had been accepted as a member of the kibbutz.

I guess all of us look back on major decisions we could have made at some point in time, wondering if we had done the right thing, it was hard not to do this. However, Eilat was beckoning.

Eilat, Israel's Red Sea Port in the Gulf of Akaba

Israel is a very small country and my buddy and I were going to travel from one end of the country to the other. Bus from the kibbutz to Haifa was the first step and took all of 45 minutes. A further bus from Haifa to Tel-Aviv took another hour.

Then the long stretch from Tel-Aviv to Eilat, again courtesy of Egged Bus Company, took just 6 hours. We had travelled practically the length of this ancient country in total daylight in less than a full day. Scenery was spectacular as we headed south from Tel-Aviv into the Negev Desert.

As we neared Beersheba, we passed several Bedouin camps or perhaps settlements. Understand, the Israeli Government was intent on putting an end to their nomadic way of life, which I suppose has a certain logic in a country as small as Israel. Just how the Bedouins would cope with this was uncertain as they had been desert wanderers since biblical days or even before.

The bus made its scheduled stop at the terminal in Beersheba for a ten-minute snack, drink and toilet stop. By this time the bus toilet, at the back of the bus was yuk! A good lesson learnt in that for any long-distance bus trip, book your seat as near to the front of the bus as possible as the toilet recess is invariably right at the back.

Bonus found in the terminal was an excellent well illustrated tourist brochure with the low down on Beersheba. And it was free. Historically, Beersheba dates to the days of the Jewish Patriarchs Abraham and Isaac around 2000BCE. They are credited with digging the first water wells.

The Romans with their mercenary legions were the first major power to lay claims to the region. There was sporadic Jewish presence over the many centuries that followed as the site or small township was occupied by various conquerors.

The Romans were succeeded by the Byzantines of Greek Christian background. When the Byzantine Empire collapsed in the 7th century AD and from then up until the 18th century very little happened, and the site remained little more than an oasis for the Bedouin tribes to water their sheep and camel flocks.

In the late 1800s, the Turks expanding their presence in Palestine built a garrison town for their soldiers in Beersheba and constructed a railway line connecting Beersheba with Arab cities in Northern Palestine and Damascus. They then began developing the town commercially.

The decision of the Turks to become allies of Germany in World War 1 was the first nail in the coffin of the widespread Ottoman Empire. The colourful legendry British soldier Lawrence of Arabia with his Bedouin tribesmen harassed Turkish soldiers, attacking supply trains and blowing up sections of the railway lines.

However, it was up to the British and Australians to defeat the main Turkish army when they captured Beersheba in 1915 in what was believed to be the last great cavalry battle in modern warfare. The British occupied Beersheba until they left their Palestinian Mandate in 1948 when the United Nations voted in the creation of the state of Israel.

So without so much as even leaving the city bus terminal, we had been able to get an insight into a city, town and former nomad site, which dated back into antiquity. Goodbye Beersheba and wait, has our luck changed?

Two new passengers had joined the bus, two very attractive women, and as luck would have it, had taken the seat in front of us. One looked Israeli and the other very Scandinavian.

It was not difficult to strike up a conversation with Israelis, providing there was no language barrier. These women were friendly and were going to Eilat to join their boyfriends who were doing their military service. Damn! So much for hitting on them; we had struck out again!

It turned out that both the women were Israeli's and were Sabras, meaning Israeli born. Natural blondes are not that common in Israel and this one was a real platinum blonde. Her friend was darker with the best suntan. It turned out that the blonde's family had emigrated from Finland, while her friend was of Yemenite descent.

Their English was very good and the remaining time to Eilat whizzed by, our chatting making a welcome change from eyeballing the endless desert scenery, interesting at first but what you saw in the first kilometre continued unchanged for the next fifty kms.

Eilat hove into site and the long bus ride was over. The city was sandwiched on a narrow isthmus of land with Egypt on one side and the Kingdom of Jordan on the other.

Other travellers we had met in the kibbutz had told us that there was a good free place to camp just off the town main beach and down towards the Jordanian Border. We had brought sleeping bags and cheap ground sheets with us and after asking around, were soon headed in the right direction.

From where the campers had settled, we could see the Jordanian sentry in his watchtower on the border and looking back towards Eilat, the plush 'many star' hotels lining the main beach. There were some twenty other fellow travellers already in 'residence' and they were friendly.

The camp was in an old wadi, or river bed. It very rarely rained in this desert area but could imagine this wadi might not be the safest of places if flash flooding was to occur following a torrential downpour. Everybody slept under the stars in sleeping bags on improvised groundsheets.

It was an incredible experience as the night was so still and once our talking had died away, total silence prevailed. The city lights of both Eilat in Israel and Aqaba in Jordan were only just visible in the distance. The night sky was so clear the stars seemed to sparkle in the dark heavens. It was awesome.

Our new acquaintances quickly filled us in on where to get some casual work that was often available. Apparently for the guys, the most common job was unloading trucks with some construction work open if you could show previous experience.

Eilat received most if not all their food and general supplies from the north of the country and trucks would make the long drive down during the cool hours of darkness, arriving in Eilat at daybreak, unload during the day then return the following night.

First thing in the morning, a bunch of us headed off and sure enough, there were trucks waiting to be offloaded. In conjunction with the truck drivers, a mean looking Israeli dude oversaw all the unloading operations. He would allocate our jobs and tell us how much we would be paid. He was the paymaster and could only imagine his percentage from each driver was a good one.

Physically he did nothing but then again, somebody had organised things rather than each driver having to separately negotiate a price. He was mean but fair, quick to jump on anybody slacking off. We all guessed he was some petty thug from Tel Aviv come to Eilat, for whatever reason.

They first job we scored was unloading a full cargo of crates of bottled orange and grapefruit juice. It was midsummer with the temperature peaking in the low 40s C. Of course, very hot but not totally unpleasant as it was a very dry heat, the humidity factor non-existent.

The truck driver set two cases of juice, one orange, one grapefruit alongside the truck cab and told us to help ourselves at any time during our work. The paymaster also told us to drink plenty as dehydration could quickly hit us with no prior notice and that could lead to heat stroke.

Normally two to three hours would see the trucks unloaded and we would be ready for breakfast. We would head off to 'Uncle Moustache's', a cafe run by a real character. His service was rough and ready, his food good, cheap and plenty of it. You simply fronted the counter and gave him your order.

One day, one of the girls told him she would make him a nice sample menu so he could have some printed. He replied, "No need, you come to me, I tell you what I got, you tell me what you want."

When ready, he would wipe your table with a 'cleanish' wet towel, your meal would be put in front of you and a knife and fork dropped casually alongside. Tables seated 6-8 persons. Tablecloths and napkins did not exist. I never heard any complaints, but then again, the food was good, and complaining might not have been a very good idea.

Earlier mentioned how great the night skies were. After a couple of nights, some of the others let on as to how much better they could be made. A local pharmacy sold bottles of cough medicine, which had the usual codeine content. Now if you skulled the whole bottle in a few minutes, the night sky really became magical. The pharmacist must have known what was going on, but after all business was business, and this was not an illegal drug.

However, we did have one Scottish guy who was a real addict. He was a bit crazy and wore a kilt, so keeping a low profile as far as the cops were concerned just wasn't about to happen. He had an Ethiopian girlfriend who worked in the Eilat hospital and supposedly she supplied him with morphine. This could not have gone on for long before she would have been nabbed by staff but as it happened, he got himself busted first.

High as a kite, one night he climbed onto the pointy roof of a restaurant on the beach and was sitting there still as a statue when somebody alerted the police.

They came, and the fire department followed. He was brought down, arrested and presumably deported as we never saw him again.

Eilat was a place where you did meet unusual people, none more so than a middle-aged French couple who arrived from Djibouti in East Africa together with a young female lion cub. How they got it through the Israeli Customs was anybody's guess as surely it could not have been legal. They used it to hustle money from tourists who posed with the cub.

After a couple of days, they then headed off north, no doubt paying one of the returning truck drivers to give them a lift. I had a great photo holding the cub, and sadly have lost it. It probably weighted 20-25kgs, but its paws were big, so it was going to grow and grow, just hope it ended up in Tel Aviv Zoo.

After lying through my teeth, I had landed a job as a short order cook in a small hamburger joint right on the beach. I would start at midday and finish at 9pm. The owner was an immigrant from England, and he was a miserable old sod. He had another proper restaurant up town and once he had shown me the ropes, he would disappear, returning only to close up, collect the day's takings, and pay me.

It was on one night when he came back that for some reason, he inspected the trash bin behind the shop and found a bag containing uncooked hamburger steaks. He was very upset and wanted to know how come? I told him sniff them, they are off, that's why I dumped them.

He did that and said they seemed fine to him and even if they were a bit 'past the expiry date', meaning off, I should still have used them as once cooked, the recipient would not know the difference. The verbal exchange got heated and he fired me. Had he known the truth, he would no doubt have called the police.

If we had had a busy day, and there were plenty of people on the beach, I would sell lots of hamburgers and hot dogs. Every so often, I would slip a hamburger steak into a plastic bag. On a good day, there would be quite a few steaks.

Just before my boss came to close up, I would drop the 'goodies' into the trash bin, retrieve them when he paid me and take the ill-gotten gains back to the wadi for a cook-up.

The Eilat police were now taking an interest in, to use their term, the vagrants camped in the wadi. They had made two visits in the past two weeks. We were puzzled as when they came, we assumed it had to be for illegal drugs, in this case hashish, and yet they never conducted a search of either persons or belongings.

It was an item in one of the national newspapers that shed a light on their behaviour. Young people from Tel-Aviv and Jerusalem had heard of these foreigners camped on the beach in Eilat and had decided to pay a visit. Most of them were young women, supposedly over the age of eighteen. Yep, they all looked to be eighteen but, well some would have been lucky to be seventeen. It was these young women the cops were looking for.

It was 'Uncle Moustache' who had translated the newspaper item, warning us that the cops were serious and that getting involved with underage teenage runaway girls would mean arrest and jail. He finished up in his typical fashion, "you guys, every day plenty older women on the beach who just come to Eilat for fuck, pick them up, they have nice hotel, you not have to sleep in the sand."

Back unloading trucks and with work over for the day, I was sitting on the beach when a man came up and asked me with a broad Irish accent, where he could find a pharmacy. Told him and we started chatting. He told me he was a radio officer working on an Israeli ship, presently in Haifa, and he had come to Eilat for a two-day visit as he had never been there before.

He looked at me in total disbelief when I told him I was a licensed 2nd Mate British Merchant Marine Deck Officer. He wanted to know what I was doing in Eilat. Told him, careful not to say too much now.

He then told me his company was actively looking for deck officers and was I interested in going back to work. Rattling my loose change in my pocket and with thoughts of another truck to unload tomorrow, I told him yes, not only interested but very interested.

He said that after he had been to the pharmacy, he would go back to his hotel and call his company in Haifa. He would then come back to the beach and let me know the result. Off he toddled. I thought, well that sure was a surprise, nice talking to him though don't suppose I'll ever see him again.

Wrong! Two hours later here comes my newfound Paddy friend and bringing good news with him. He told me he was going back to Haifa tomorrow and if I still wanted to go for an interview with his company, when could I be in Haifa? I now had no reason to remain any longer in Eilat and told Bill that was his name that I could leave by bus tomorrow.

He was flying, but that I could be in Haifa the day after. He asked if I had the fare money, told him yes. I then went back to his hotel with him. He phoned his boss again, told him my name and passed the phone to me. I was told they would expect to see me, and to show up at the office as soon as I arrived in Haifa. Bill gave me their address and phone number.

He then made my day when he said let's go and have a few beers, I'm paying. You have bad days and occasionally, a good day rolls around, well this had been a very good day.

Said goodbye to all my friends, had really enjoyed the company of most of them, but as with travellers, a goodbye was usually just that, the inevitable 'catch up with you again sometime' not likely to happen.

Au Revoir, Eilat
Hopefully, A Job Beckons

The bus journeys back to Haifa were uneventful and arrived in the Haifa Bus Terminal mid-afternoon. Found my way to the office address and was pleasantly surprised when a guy at the front desk said, "Hi, been expecting you, take a seat."

I was then taken into the office of Captain Sharon who was the Operations Manager. The interview that I had been dreading went off OK. I was later to find out that my Irish friend Bill had been with the company a long time and was very well thought of-thanks again, Bill.

Introductions continued when I met one of the owners of the company. I was impressed by the informal way these senior executives behaved, the questions they asked were right on the mark, but their approach so totally different from the stuffy ways of their British counterparts.

The shipping company was called Mediterranean Seaways who owned half a dozen cargo vessels trading between Israel and various ports in the Mediterranean and North Europe.

The company had been established by two brothers, Sami and Juli Hershcovitz who I believe had come to Israel from Rumania. Juli ran the Haifa Office while Sami was London based. They were excellent people to work for and Mediterranean Seaways was a company very much on the move upwards as they bought more vessels and spread their operations further afield.

Later, the brothers were to do as many Israelis do and changed their European family name to the Hebrew name Ofer. As their shipping business evolved into a shipping empire, the company diversified into several specialised divisions, some not marine orientated, and the name Mediterranean Seaways was retired.

I was delighted to be back on a regular salary and was assigned as second officer on their vessel *Iddan*. Joined the ship directly after my interview was concluded and met the new crew who were a mixture of European, Turkish, and Israelis and with a Dutch Radio Operator.

The ship was on a semi-permanent run from Haifa, Ashdod and Gaza to the Croatian port of Rijeka. We carried oranges out and cars and general cargo items for our return to Israel. I had never been to Rijeka before and George, the Dutch radio officer assured me the nightlife was great.

On my first duty free night, set out with George and several other crew to the Plaviadran night club. There were plenty of women, well dressed and attractive. George had told me they were not hookers. The way he threw his money around, he was quickly the centre of attention and many of the women obviously knew him from previous visits.

If you had the intention of spending the night with one of them, there were the obligatory expenses. Croatian women liked to drink, and I was soon to realise that they were not the demure lady type who would sit on one drink for ages, it was hard to keep pace with them. They were not in the least backward, if a woman liked you, she would ask you straight out if she could stay with you.

This was what hookers did and these women were not hookers, they were single women simply wanting a night out with someone they found attractive and sex to follow at the end of the night. George had told me all this and he had said, pick one you fancy quickly, and the others will not bother you.

Fortunately, Rijeka and the Plaviadran were not overly expensive. Firstly, the drinks, then a meal, taxi to a hotel and the room charge all did add up. Again, George told me do not attempt to offer the lady any money as she would be very offended and would think you believe she was a prostitute.

It was a very happy ship to work on, we always would have at least one night in Rijeka and the same in Haifa or Ashdod.

Gaza

On one trip, we were sent to Gaza to load oranges. The loading took place with our ship at anchor offshore and barges laden with oranges were towed out and tied up alongside.

Now, Gaza is an all-Arab city and when we went there, the Israeli army were in control. The Arab labourers would come out to the ship escorted by the Israeli soldiers. The soldiers would then station themselves at pre-determined spots around the ship while the loading took place.

I was on duty when each of the following incidents occurred. A young Israeli soldier came to me and said he had lost his assault rifle and please don't tell my sergeant. He had had to make an emergency trip to one of the ship's toilets for a 'number 2'. Did his business, departed the toilet leaving his rifle propped up inside and now he couldn't find the toilet.

None of the Arab workers were allowed to go inside the ship's accommodation but nonetheless, a soldier couldn't be parted from his weapon in what could be called enemy territory.

Fortunately, I took him straight to the toilet in question and he and his rifle were reunited. He was shit scared I would tell his sergeant and I had to reassure him that I would not, at the same time scolding him for losing a weapon, which had it got into the wrong hands, could have ended up shooting me.

The second incident involved the very same sergeant who had the soldier shaking in his boots. I was chatting to this sergeant near one of the ships lifeboats asking him questions about the particular model Uzi he was carrying. He very casually just passed it to me. He said, have you ever fired one of these before, and I had to tell him, no I had not.

Now some 200 meters off was a Greek cargo ship that had completed loading and the crew were tying big cargo nets over the pallets of oranges on deck ready for the vessel to sail.

The sergeant said point the gun to the sea and fire off a burst. Wow, this was exciting! What he had not bothered to tell me was that when firing these Uzi's, they will kick upwards, and also only fire very short bursts.

Sure enough, the gun kicked up and I heard the ping of bullets hitting the side of the Greek ship. I said, man I think some bullets might have hit that ship; just hope I haven't killed a sailor. Could see no indication from the ship that they were aware they had been shot at. Meanwhile, the sergeant thought the whole incident was hilarious, he just could not stop laughing.

I knew he should never have let me fire his weapon, but he was a veteran soldier and was quite sure he could have explained the missing number of rounds. In all, it was quite a day.

The Missing Submarine

A change from our routine as a cargo ship.

The Israeli Navy had purchased a submarine from the British Royal navy. With an Israeli naval crew, it duly sailed from Portsmouth in the UK, bound for Israel. Could assume that for most of the voyage, the naval authorities in Haifa were keeping track of their new vessel.

However, just a couple of days out of Haifa, all communications ceased. For some reason, the submarine called *Dakar*, translated meaning swordfish, had disappeared. Immediate air searches revealed no debris or oil traces on the sea surface. The authorities decided to implement a thorough sea search of the area they thought the sub might have foundered.

As an Israeli flag ship, we were called in to assist in the search. A couple of naval officers and two ratings came on board, we refuelled and sailed. We were shown the type of grid search that our navy people would supervise. We would steam on a set course for so many miles and then alter course 90 degrees, repeating this process until we had completed a square.

We would then do the same again this time on a smaller square. Several other vessels were participating in similar search patterns. After three days, the area had been combed and the search was called off. Some debris had been found, although we found nothing.

The story that did the rounds was that the *Dakar* had been sunk by a Russian submarine. It was most likely that Israel did find the reason for the sub's disappearance but suppressed the news. Perhaps years into the future, the whole story might come out.

After so many trips away from Israel, the number depending on the length of the voyages, we would be entitled to a short leave. Once again, I had fallen madly in love with a girl. She was born and still lived in Jaffa, the ancient former totally Arab city just south of Tel Aviv. Naturally I was always eager for a few days off. More about this beautiful young woman later.

My leave over, I joined another ship on what would be a new run for the company. We were to load in Israel, proceed to Adana in Turkey, and go from there to Marseilles in France then return to Israel. I was really looking forward to this trip as I had never been to Turkey. I was destined to spend longer than planned there.

When the Israeli ships were preparing to leave port, the junior deck officer, in this case me, always worked alongside the seamen securing the ship's cargo loading gear. While doing this, I received a long scratch from a wire down almost the entire calf of my right leg. It was a very shallow scratch, did not openly bleed at all but left a long bloodline. It caused no pain, and I continued working, the ship sailed, and I carried out my normal sea watch duties.

The next morning, my calf had swollen up to where the skin was stretched tight, but again no pain at all. I showed the Captain, as mounds of paperwork must be prepared for even the slightest shipboard injury or incident. He could not believe I was feeling no pain and said he would gently push the area around the scratch to see if this would cause me discomfort.

When he pressed on the skin, the resulting indent stayed after he removed his fingers and had to be gently massaged for a few minutes before returning to normal. And still no pain. We were due to dock later that evening and he contacted the agent, advising that I had to have medical attention as soon as we had tied up.

It happened as planned and in next to no time, I was being checked out by one of the doctors in the Adana hospital. The medical verdict was blood poisoning, and I was to be admitted immediately to hospital. The ship was to sail the next day, minus me. Some of my belongings were brought to the hospital and I was told that if I recovered in time, I would be sent on to Marseilles to re-join the ship or flown back to Israel.

The doctor who was treating me was a character and spoke reasonably good English. He was very keen to improve his command of the language and would frequently stop by my bed and chat for ages. I said to him one time, "Doc, don't you have any other patients to attend to?"

He casually replied, "No, they all died"! I trust he was joking.

There were lots of young good-looking nurses with one most unusual feature in that none of them wore shoes. I don't suppose it really mattered, the hospital was as clean as hospitals in the western world were, I just never imagined nurses working in the wards bare-footed.

Many of them had auburn hair and I asked my doctor friend if such hair colour was normal in Turkey. He told me that they were not Turkish but were Kurds from some remote part of the country and that the auburn colour of their hair was because they put henna in it. He then had to explain what henna was.

We were watching a couple of nurses cleaning the floor and I commented on how attractive these women were. He seemed really surprised that I seriously thought some of them to be beautiful. He didn't seem to think so.

He then 'jerked the mat out from under my feet' when he said which girl do you like. I will arrange it so you can marry her. I said, "Are you serious, I don't think any of them speak English and if I was to pick one, she might not like me at all."

Again, I was not sure whether he was joking or not when he said, "she will like you for sure, you are a rich European, she is a poor woman from a remote Kurdish village, working here for very small wages, don't worry, she will like you. If you want, I will arrange everything, you must convert to Islam and then you can marry."

A few days prior, I had kissed my girlfriend goodbye in Tel Aviv, and now this. I told the doctor, "Let me think about this." But to this day, I can still see those Kurdish nurses, and some of them were very attractive.

My treatment was progressing, and the doctor said that using crutches I should get some exercise, walking around the hospital grounds or go into Adana city itself. If I got lost, I was to call him on a mobile he lent me. I was bored and welcomed the prospect of a walk so took him up on his suggestion.

Even moving at a snail's pace with my crutches, I covered quite some ground and yes, got totally lost. I bailed up passer-bys but could not find anyone who spoke English. So, time to call the good doctor. Stopped a young guy and passed the phone to him and he told the Doc where I was. A few minutes later, he showed up and said he would drive me around Adana and show me the city.

Cities were cities and really Adana was nothing special until he took me to a street where, according to him, the best prostitutes worked. He said that their beauty was such that they were in great demand. I was thinking that if I'm going to perform on crutches, this was going to be a bit tricky.

And then we saw them. I began to understand why the good doctor did not find the slim, small breasted Kurdish women attractive. These women, the elite of their profession in Adana, were attractive in that they were good looking, but they were all big women. Big boobs, big bums and gigantic thighs. Perhaps Turkish men prefer bulky ladies, I could see that the doctor certainly did.

Our shipping agent called by, telling me that if the hospital would agree to discharge me the next day, he would then book me an air ticket to Marseille as the ship would be there. Hospital gave their OK providing I used crutches, which I still relied on, until I reached the ship.

Their reasoning was that staff in the airports would then better assist me and take care of my luggage. Although seemingly almost healed, the hospital did not want me putting undue stress on the leg until I was safely back on board the ship.

Flights were with Turkish Airlines from Adana to Istanbul, a change of plane and onto Marseille. I had a six hour wait in Istanbul. I don't know what caused it, maybe the breakfast on the flight from Adana, but I came down with diarrhoea. When this happened, you 'gotta' go to the nearest toilet, and you 'gotta' go quickly. Arrived at the 'loo', ass cheeks clenched, and fortunately found it was empty, no occupants, and no janitor.

There were four 'number 2' booths and all vacant and all 'squatters'; no western style toilets here, just the hole in the floor and a handrail to hold onto. No toilet rolls, just a wash down hose for the clean-up when the job was done.

The above was no big deal, unless you happened to be on crutches. The cubicle was small, the crutches big, and how to position over the target with a gammy leg and in a super big hurry.

Huge sigh of relief when the job was done, I was quietly praying that there would be no further visits, but at least I knew how to handle the situation if it arose.

A further prayer when I boarded the flight to France as aircraft toilets were very small. All went well, my prayers must have been answered and it was such a relief to get back on the ship.

Back in Tel Aviv, I was telling my girlfriend of the ordeal and said I wish you could have been there to help me. Her so feminine reply, "me, help you, Jake come on, no way," such was true love!

And so, to the girl I should, 'maybe' have married.

Orli

It was one of those nights when I did not feel like going to a bar or club and decided to go ten pin bowling. My ship was docked in Kishon Port, adjacent to Haifa so just a short bus ride into town.

The bowling alley was busy, but I was able to get a lane and started to play. I hadn't played for ages and even at my best, I was not a good bowler. However, was enjoying the game when a strikingly attractive young woman sat down in the seats behind my lane. I thought she must have been waiting for someone so gave her a quick smile and continued playing.

Fifteen or twenty minutes later, she was still alone so I decided to ask her if she would like to join me. She said she did not feel like bowling, but she would like to chat with me when I had finished playing. The last few frames were played at record speed. And that was how I met Orli. A meeting that started an on, off love affair that lasted for over two years.

We left the bowling alley and went to a small nearby snack bar, had a hamburger and coke and talked for over two hours. I asked her where she was staying, and she said she was visiting an aunty in Haifa but lived in Tel Aviv. She asked me what time I had to go back to Kishon, and I told her I had to be back to start work at 7am next morning.

We were really getting along well and jokingly, I said we should find a small hotel room for the night. Israeli girls were very forthright but even so I nearly fell off my chair when she said, OK that would be nice.

I said what about her aunty, she said she would ring and tell her she had decided to return to Tel Aviv. And that's what we did. I was a real sucker for young women and fall head over heels in love at the drop of a hat.

Met Orli the following evening for another wonderful romantic dream night. Told her the ship was sailing the next day and how could I contact her when we returned. She told me to give her the company phone number and she would call them to see where the ship was and when it would be back and that she would wait at the gates of the port at 6pm on our arrival day. I told her she could get a pass from security to come directly to the ship, but she did not want to do that.

We called at two regular ports on the Israeli Mediterranean Coast, Ashdod near to Tel Aviv and Haifa/Kishon, some 70 miles from Ashdod.

"Uncle Bar-Lev"

It was when we were in Ashdod that she said we should take the bus ride to Tel Aviv as she had a friend there who would let us stay in a spare room in his apartment. So why not.

Her friend turned out to be an old lawyer named Bar Lev and his even older wife, Hanna. He had retired from active practice although from time to time, he would represent, free of charge, clients who had no funds whatsoever. He loved his work and before retirement had been very successful.

Orli had met him through a former American boyfriend who was a distant relative. The American faced with pending Israeli military service had returned to the USA.

He welcomed Orli and then me with open arms. He was from an old Hassidic family in Russia, his father being a renowned Rabbi. Bar-Lev had fallen out of favour with the father when as a youth, he had become involved in a socialist Zionist youth group very much against his father's wishes.

He had then left Russia just prior to the start of WW2, with his wife-to-be and travelled to what was then Palestine. His family that he left behind in Russia all perished in the Holocaust.

He had a large apartment in Hayarkon Street with two spare bedrooms and said Orli and I could stay there whenever we wanted. Now every time I had leave for a few days we would move in, his only request was that we could take him and Hanna out for coffee or a meal, certainly a good deal as his apartment was in the heart of Tel Aviv.

When Orli was not around, the old man and I would take a short walk to Dizengoff Street and drink coffee in Cafe Kassid, a popular place with a distinctly bohemian, artistic crowd. Bar-Lev was at home with these people, knew all of them, and I met and heard some extraordinary true stories about Israel and its people.

One morning over breakfast in the apartment, Bar-Lev surprised me by asking what I knew about his 'daughter' Orli. I said, "Well, not much other that I know she lives here in Tel Aviv."

He then said, "If I tell you her story, I want you to promise me you will not let her know I told you." He then told me I would be in for a shock. I called Bar Lev 'uncle' so I told him, OK uncle spill the beans, whatever you tell me will remain totally confidential.

He started by telling me that Orli was not her name, though that was the name she went by. Orli was a Jewish girl's name, meaning 'light from within'. Her real name was Salima, she was not Jewish, but was an Israeli Arab woman. Her father was a Bedouin and her mother an Arab woman from a small village. She was not 21 but was 27 years old.

She did not live in Tel Aviv as such but in Jaffa. At the time of independence, Jaffa was an all-Arab city some eight kilometres from the heart of Tel Aviv. Most of the Arabs fled to neighbouring Arab countries when Jewish forces captured Jaffa in 1948.

At that time, Orli's father was in prison, arrested by the British occupation police for supplying arms to the Jewish Underground forces. Her mother was very young, had no children and hid in their home until the fighting was over. She was one of the few Muslim Arabs who remained in Jaffa.

Her father was released by the new Israeli Government but turned out to be a habitual thief, who was to spend much of his time in the now Israeli prisons. On release, he would return to his wife, make her pregnant and then end up behind bars for another extended period.

Her mother had several children before Orli came along, most of them boys, all of whom left Israel for Jordan. Her elderly mother was really struggling to feed herself and the two remaining daughters when Orli first came under the attention of the police in Jaffa. Her crime, as a young teenager, was stealing food for the family.

She had exceptionally good looks with a figure to match, spoke Hebrew fluently as well as Arabic, English and French. She posed as a 'Sabra' the name given to kids born in Israel, explaining that her parents were from Morocco as were so many Israeli immigrants.

She was a very intelligent woman, who solved the family problem of poverty by becoming a high-priced prostitute who frequented bars in the most expensive hotels.

She targeted well-dressed men in their late forties or fifties, always tourists or businessmen, and was very well rewarded for her favours. Apart from buying the clothing, which was a job-related necessity, all her earnings went to her Mum and younger sister. Of course, they knew what was going on.

Between 'assignments', she wanted to lead a normal life as a young woman on the lookout for a lover, partner or husband. She was a Muslim and no longer being a virgin, made marriage to any Arab a problem, but she was very insistent that, come what may, she would not marry a local Arab.

She would, however, expect her husband to be a Muslim or convert to the faith before marriage. One time when we were in bed relaxing after love making, she told me stories of how some Arab women who were no longer virgins on their wedding night managed to conceal the fact.

She said the wedding ceremonies were very formal and could go on for two or three days at the end of which the bride and groom would go to a prepared room to consummate their marriage. When they had made love, the bed sheet with the virginal blood would be taken out by the groom and publicly displayed to the assembled guests.

However, there were always ways to circumvent any problem be what it may. A bride who was not a virgin would arrange for a girl relative, cousin or sister to smuggle a container holding fresh chicken blood into the room at some point during the early celebrations. At the appropriate moment, the bed sheet would be dowsed with the blood and the bride's honour would be unquestioned.

We had become very close, almost inseparable whenever my ship returned. It was Orli herself who one day confirmed all that Bar-Lev had previously told me. It came about in most unusual circumstances.

My ship had loaded a full cargo of ex-NATO military equipment in Belgium. Included were a number of tanks, all of which had been completely disassembled. We had tank turrets in one of our cargo holds, engines in another, crawler treads in another and so on. The story I heard was that NATO were not permitted to sell complete tanks but could legally do so if they were in pieces.

If this was true, it would have been playing into the Israeli hands as all these tanks would be modified, perhaps much modified, before going into service, and they would arrive in Israel already for this to begin.

As well we had taken on thousands of artillery shell casings, innumerable crates of heavy machine gun live cartridges and unmarked large wooden crates whose contents were supposedly known only to the ship's Captain.

At this time, when Israeli ships containing military cargo arrived in Ashdod Port, it was always on a Friday morning. Non-Israeli flag vessels would be sent to anchor outside the port. The ships would be unloaded by military personnel and not by regular stevedores.

And so back to my girlfriend. Orli was waiting outside the port gates when one of the security officers asked her what she wanted. Remember she looked totally Israeli, a descendant from one of the Jewish communities in North Africa.

She told him she was waiting for her boyfriend who was the 2nd Officer on the ship *Bat Golan* which, due to its cargo, was the only ship in the port.

The security officer in charge was himself a newly arrived immigrant from India and while his spoken Hebrew was good, his ability to read the language was not so good.

He said, you don't have to wait here, you can go to the ship. She had always avoided doing this, but here was the Head of Security giving her the go ahead. As required, she left her ID with him and entered the port and came onto the ship.

An hour later we were in bed, fortunately not in the act, when there were thunderous knocks on my cabin door. Opened to find the Captain and two-armed MP's. We were told to get properly dressed and come with them to the Security Office. One of the head security officers assistants had routinely picked up Orli's ID card and seen that she was an Israeli Arab, and she had been given the OK to visit a ship carrying military cargo. As expected, there was a general panic in security.

Before we arrived at the office, security had already run their checks and her police record was known. She had faced cops before, was not unduly fazed, and openly told them I was her boyfriend and that she had told me she was from a Moroccan immigrant family. She was saving my ass, God bless her. Luckily, we both got severe warnings on what could have been considered a major security breach.

I asked her one day if she would like to come with me to the Red Sea, city of Eilat for a few days as she had never been there. She said, "Jake, I can't, don't you know how I get my money." I replied I had an idea. She was crying and then confirmed what Bar-Lev had told me. What to do?

My job did not pay mega bucks, but I said I could give her some money each month. She then told me she could make as much in one night as I did in a full month. She could not come to Eilat as a wealthy client from Italy was arriving for a few days.

It was strange that after this revelation, logically we should have drifted apart or broken up, but just the opposite happened, and we became closer than ever now there were no secrets. What eventually killed our romance was when the ship I was working on started making very long voyages from Israel to several ports in the Far East and Australia.

We had a sad farewell and I must admit I shed a tear or two, but I assured her I would be back in Tel Aviv before six months were up. However, it was eight months later, not six that we finally arrived back in Eilat. I had been writing her letters, care of Bar-Lev and she had always answered but the extended absence was starting to take its toll.

To make matters worse, I had received a letter from her which brought me bad news. It was Bar-Lev who, at her request had helped her write the doom and gloom letter. She told me she had met a wealthy German client, thirty years her senior, who had visited Israel on several occasions.

He had made her several promises which so far, he had always kept, and wanted to take her to Germany and marry her. If she approved, he would then arrange for her mother and sister to also move to Germany if they so wished.

What could I say? I wrote her a long letter, thanking her for telling me the news, told her I was heartbroken, but then wished her every possible success in her venture, telling her this guy could offer her everything that I could not, and that she should take it. I was depressed for weeks after, and then another letter arrived from Bar-Lev.

She told him that she would not contact me further unless the German proposal failed. And then came the bombshell. She told me her Mum would like me to consider marrying her younger sister who was just sixteen. By this time, I had met both the mother and her sister, so knew them.

Her sister, although a Muslim, had been educated in a Catholic school in Jaffa and spoke English with the huskiest accent, as well of course, fluent Hebrew and Arabic. An Arab baker from Nazareth had approached the family through a 'broker', offering her a marriage proposal together with a big cash dowry offer. She had never seen him, which was not all that unusual, but he was thirty-five and she was not over enthusiastic.

I had to reply to Bar-Lev, telling him to thank the mother, no doubt through Orli, but I was virtually bankrupt, and it was Orli I was in love with and not her sister.

I hope all went well for her in Germany. Months later, she sent me a postcard from a city called Wiesbaden, really just a hello, how are you greeting, the only address was the city name.

I have never heard from her since, though I would never forget her, and I sometimes wondered what might have been had circumstances been somewhat different. It was the first time I had really fallen in love.

Another of Bar-Lev's close friends was a Professor Steiner, and did he have stories to tell. Born in Russia and as a very young man, he had served in the White Russian forces, which opposed the Communists or Bolsheviks in the revolution, which saw the end of the Russian Czars.

The White Russian forces were defeated, and the remnants had to flee the country. Like many Russian Jews, Steiner headed for China where eventually he taught music at the Shanghai Music Conservatorium. When the communists came to power, he left China and headed for Israel.

He spoke very good English, although with a heavy Russian accent, and I would listen for hours when he would relate his past experiences to Bar-Lev and myself.

He had arrived in Tel Aviv with all his family's money in gold bullion, but by the time I met him this had disappeared, and he was eking out an existence teaching piano to young Israelis. He loved a drink and although a very old man, had problems with young female students. He liked to touch them, and this had got him into trouble on more than one occasion and was how he had first met the lawyer Bar-Lev.

He claimed that he could predict the future of some people simply by intently studying their faces. Recalling the previous experience, I had with a fortune teller in the USA, I asked him if he could foretell what lay ahead for me. He had a curly beard and when he stared intently into your eyes, it was scary. There was a kind of mystic aura about him at these moments and I remember thinking at the time, my God, he is a re-incarnation of the mad monk Rasputin.

Of course, he wasn't but the thought did flash through my mind. After perhaps ten minutes of intense concentration, the only comment he made was that I would come to serious harm through acquaintance with a black lady, he would not say a young or old woman.

So far, touch wood, this has not happened. I find some black women very attractive and the most beautiful woman I have ever seen, and I'm jumping way ahead here, was a woman working as a prostitute in the Sunshine Club in Mombasa, Kenya.

Her Mum was a Somali and her long gone father, a Danish seaman. Of course, nowadays most top modelling agencies have black models, often from Somalia/ Eritrea where their high cheekbones and easily straightened hair make them very beautiful in an exotic way.

Logs and Plywood from Africa

My next ship was a stately old lady of the sea. She had been built in Norway just before World War II and in her day, must have been one of the most modern vessels afloat. By the time I joined, her best years were long gone.

She, yes ships are 'she's', had been bought by my owners supposedly when she was headed for the scrap yard. Paying just over the scrap metal value, she would have been a cheap buy. It turned out a smart deal, but Jewish businessmen were renowned for money making deals.

I joined her in a shipyard in Malta where she was having steel plating replaced in the bottom of the ship beneath the engine room. Malta had been chosen as supposedly surveyors who issued the ship with a sea worthy certificates were known to be more lenient there than in neighbouring countries.

Leaving Malta for West Africa, our first stop was an anchorage off a township named Tabou in Cote D'Ivoire, perhaps better known as the Ivory Coast. Here, we took on some 40 African crew who would live on board for the next few weeks and under a French superintendent, would load our cargo of logs.

Don't know what their wages would have been, but they worked twelve hours every day. Two of their team were cooks who prepared their customary meals. I tried their food which was basically fish, sweet potatoes and mysterious other ingredients, which made up a spicy sauce. The food had a strong smell but tasted fine.

They joked with me, telling me this food was a real sex stimulant and that if I would go back to Tabou with them, they would introduce me to nice girls. They spoke French after a fashion as it was very much their second language, and with my minimal bar room French, our conversations were hilarious, assisted by facial and hand movements.

Logs were floated down the rivers in long rafts guided by tiny local tugs. Each individual log had two steel eye pins, hammered into the wood, one at each end. Steel cables ran through the eye pins linking the logs together. There could be up to 100 logs in a raft, which were then secured along each side of the ship and the loading would take place.

Each log had an owner's or company marking cut into the wood. I asked if this was to avoid theft as these tropical hardwoods were valuable but was told this was not the case. Apparently, the rafts sometimes broke up with the logs drifting out of the river into the sea and ending up on nearby beaches.

Their owners could then identify and retrieve them according to the markings. The work was dangerous and the workers not safety conscious in the slightest so that our job as deck officers, in addition to tallying or counting the logs loaded, was to always watch them and stop loading if an unsafe situation arose or looked likely to develop.

Every worker had been issued with work boots, hand gloves, safety hard hats and safety glasses. The problem was that apart from the hard hats, they did not like to use the rest, especially the boots, which were packed away, shiny and new, to take back to their village when the job was completed.

After Tabou, we headed to Abidjan, the capital city of the Ivory Coast. For years, it was known as the Paris of West Africa and the city centre with its wide tree lined boulevards, modern shops and restaurants could almost have been in France itself.

Unfortunately, the Ivory Coast, like so many African countries had found the road following independence from their past colonial masters to be a very rocky one.

There were no doubt many reasons for this. Colonial powers bled the countries dry. Most key positions in governments and private companies were held by citizens of the ruling power and even when it was apparent that independence was inevitable, they did little to prepare the nationals to take over the job of running the country.

Tribal enmity which had been controlled in the colonial era surfaced and until now was a key factor in the seemingly endless violence in so many African countries. As always those who suffer the most were the women, the children and the elderly.

The lovely Ivory Coast had seen far too much violence and senseless killing in recent years. Our time in Abidjan, outside of the routine work, was one of contrasts. Going into the city, we could eat at first class French restaurants and when it was party time, we would head off into the nearby suburb of Treichville, which was alive with bars, loud music and girls.

Here, the prices were reasonable and there was no such thing as closing time. As long as there were customers, the bars stayed open and one could see the 'hostesses' reappearing, sometimes more than once, after their 'short time' social alliances.

Pussy was cheap, and the girls varied from jet black, true African women with frizzy hair to mixed race women of all shades of brown. The better, meaning more expensive bars, had the younger attractive women and many of them were really beautiful. Typically slim with legs guys only dream about, boobs that did not need bra assistance, and decked out in the most mini of mini dresses or tiny shorts, they were sensational.

With their looks, had they been born in Europe or North America, they could have been anything. But not to forget the European women, they too had come all the way to Abidjan for a holiday that certainly included the services of a generally much younger African stud. There were plenty of these ladies too, mostly German and French and not at all bashful.

They knew what they wanted, were going to get it, and were having a ball as the guys moved in on them. Sure it was all about money, and obviously the ladies, just as with us, did not mind spending hard earned banknotes to support the age old sex industry.

An interesting and surprisingly good thing apparent in all bars was that when a customer was ready for a liaison, he or she could pick up a condom (from a vast selection on offer) at the bar for a token payment.

Could only say that for any bachelor, playboy or playgirl, if it was a holiday in a place where you had fine foods, excellent hotels, top beaches and a vibrant nightlife put Abidjan, the capital city of the Ivory Coast in your little diary, chances were, you would not be disappointed.

The loading of the logs had been completed in Tabou and in Abidjan, after which we headed to Port Gentil in Gabon to top up our ship with bundles of plywood. A farewell to our African stevedores, no injuries, not even a scratch, and we headed back to Israel.

One thing I remember about our crew was the radio operator, who hailed from Belgium. He was a friendly enough guy but was weird in that whenever he touched anything, he would rush off and wash his hands. It must be a sickness, washing your hands countless times each day. I asked him why he did not wear gloves and had to quickly apologise as he got very embarrassed.

The ship was called the *Ela*. I believe the ship may have been named after one of the owners' daughters. He was a Captain in his own right, and he also had a degree in Marine Law so was a highly qualified man.

His name was Ike Ahronovitch and I had the privilege of meeting him for a brief chat in the Haifa Office. He was a quiet, dark haired little man, no taller or heavier than most racehorse jockeys.

He was a part of the history of the founding of the Jewish state in that he was the Captain of probably the most famous of the so-called immigrant blockade runner ships that attempted to bring Holocaust survivors from the Nazi death camps in Europe to what was then called Palestine.

At the time, Britain controlled Palestine and was under enormous political pressure from the Arab population to restrict the immigration of further Jews to the country. These poor souls were amongst the lucky few who had survived the horrors of World War II.

Jewish underground forces in Palestine were able to purchase old ships around the world and convert them to carry large numbers of passengers. The ships were old, small and overcrowded for the run through the Mediterranean Sea to the shores of Palestine.

The British navy, based out of Malta, set up a blockade of the Palestinian Coast, determined to prevent any of these ships succeeding in their mission. Ike was appointed the Captain of the ship *Exodus*, an appropriate name relating to the departure from Egypt of the Hebrews under Moses so many centuries ago.

With a staggering 4,500 persons on board, death camp survivors, the *Exodus* secretly departed from France in 1947. Approaching Palestine, it was confronted by, boarded and then seized by a British warship.

During the boarding operation, three of the passengers were killed. Many years after the British Captain said his crew, knowing the background of the passengers, regretted the incident but it was purely a political decision from Whitehall and as members of his Majesty's navy, they had no choice but to follow orders.

The British then sent the ship back to Europe where the remaining passengers ended up in Germany, an act which generated media sympathy for them around the world. This was the man who was now one of my bosses.

The *Ela* was to complete a number of further voyages in the African log trade but age was finally catching up with the ship to where necessary running repairs would be too costly and the ship, once again headed for the ship breakers, this time without a reprieve.

Encounter with a Warship

We had loaded a full cargo in the Israeli Port of Eilat in the Red Sea Gulf of Akaba. The cargo was a transhipment from another vessel and had originated in Japan.

At the time, there was turmoil in Rhodesia, soon to become Zimbabwe. The basically white government was resisting African nationalists from assuming power. To help the nationalist cause, the UN and Britain were determined to prevent essential supplies from entering the landlocked country.

Our cargo was destined for discharge in the Port of Beira /Mozambique and from there via a rail link, it would go to Rhodesia. In point of fact, we were assisting in breaking the blockade on Rhodesia.

Nearing Beira, I was on duty in the early morning hours, closely monitoring the radar and watching a vessel approaching our stern at a much faster speed than we were making. I called the vessel on radio to advise that as they were overtaking us, would they alter their course to keep clear as they were going to pass far too close.

The immediate reply was, "This is the British County Class Destroyer 'Kent', and we require you to provide your destination and cargo."

I replied, "We are in international waters and you are coming too close for our safety, I am going to call my Captain."

The Captain was an Israeli navy veteran and quickly came to the navigation bridge. By this time, the warship was only 100-150 meters off our port side and repeated their demands over the radio and also their public address system.

I asked the Captain what we should do. His reply, "nothing, just ignore them, they are acting illegally, I'm going back to my cabin, call me if they should try to come alongside and prepare to board us, but I can assure they won't do this," and off he went.

The PA message was repeated several times and I kept radio silence. They maintained their position, which was certainly worrying but made no effort to come closer. My duty was up and I handed over to my relief, a Chief Mate also ex Israeli Navy. The warship kept station until daylight and then pulled away and disappeared over the horizon.

A New Career Change

We arrived and tied up in Ashdod early one morning and as normal, the ship's agent came on board to officially clear the vessel back into Israel. He was a good friend of mine, a drinking buddy, and he called me to one side and pointed to a ship at another wharf.

He said it was an American tugboat, which had come to Ashdod to participate in a new oil drilling operation that was to start up off the coast, and that they were looking for a Chief Mate. Was I interested? I told him my licence was only as a Second Mate not a Chief Mate.

His reply, "don't worry, your licence is for ocean going ships, this is just a small tugboat, if you want, I'll take you on board and you can speak to the American Captain."

This happened and I met Captain Polk from Louisiana. He questioned me and showed me around his newly built ship and asked me if I would be interested in joining. The crew were all Americans but were going off in the next days to be replaced by Israelis, the only Americans to stay on would be the Captain and Chief Engineer.

I thought, why not give it a go. I was due leave from my ship and my replacement had already arrived, so I called the Haifa Office told them the story and their reply was great, "go ahead, you have a month's leave and if you are not happy on the tugboat, come back to us."

The tugboat was called the *Cay W*. Went back and told Captain Polk I was free to join. The boat was contracted to an oil drilling company. He called their personnel department on the phone and passed the mobile to me. The Personnel Manager introduced himself as Jim Weiss, and said, "welcome to Storm Drilling and can you make it into Tel Aviv today to sort out contract paperwork?"

Wow, unbelievable, it seemed like I had been hired, sight unseen and without the usual interview!

Jim was the friendliest guy. He said straight out, his background was as a college football player in Texas, after which he completed a course in personnel management and came to work with Storm Drilling. He said he understood the oil drilling side of things but knew nothing about boats, so he really could not ask me anything but apparently Captain Polk had been satisfied.

He then took the wind right out of my sails when he said, "Now Jake, what sort of salary do you want?"

Yes, I was in a completely different world, commercial shipping companies never ask such a question, they just tell you how little they will pay you. I was tongue tied and after a pause, he said, "Would $1500 a month be ok?"

OK! Would it be OK! It was three times what I had been earning, I managed to mumble, "that would be fine, Jim."

He then said Captain Polk had told him I had experience operating and maintaining some of the navigational equipment and he would include an extra monthly bonus if I would take care of this equipment. Would I agree to this? Was this for real or was I dreaming? It was real alright and the paperwork was duly drawn up.

This was big bucks to someone whose rental on an apartment in downtown Tel Aviv was $20 a month. Reported for work the next day. The American crew were leaving in a couple of days and Captain Polk told me my first job would be to interview Israelis who would take their place.

I was then told by Storm Drilling that we would work two weeks on and then have a week of time off, all on pay which was apparently a requirement requested by the Israeli union. As such a priority would be to hire another Chief Mate who could relieve me during my time off.

Quickly got the crew sorted out and they were a good bunch, some Israeli born, some immigrants and one a tourist from Finland who was an experienced engineer. And now time to start work. We were to work with a drillship called the *Typhoon*, which had just arrived after being towed from the Louisiana. The towing tug had already departed back to the USA.

The *Typhoon* would be anchored over the selected drilling site, and it would be our job to run out and set the anchors for them. Captain Polk and the Chief Engineer Mr Mac had done this work before.

It was all new to us and they now repeated over and over the procedures we would have to follow in doing the work. The job itself was not difficult, but due to the work involving big anchors, very heavy wires and powerful winches, safety was the key factor.

It would be my job to supervise the activity on the big back deck of the tug, while the Captain would manoeuvre the ship and the engineer would drive the giant winch. While giving the crew instructions, I had to always watch them to make sure they were not in a place where they could be injured if we had a wire break or jump unexpectedly. Such injuries would not be cuts and bruises, more likely broken bones or worse.

As this was to be the initial anchor job for both the rig and the boat, the oil company decided that for this time, work would only take place in daylight hours and they stressed that safety was of prime importance, not speed. The training went well, the job ran smoothly and in two days the *Typhoon* was ready to start drilling, or to use the oil field terminology 'Spud-In'.

We were slowly getting used to words and expressions peculiar to the oil field. Popular T-shirt designs called us 'Oilfield Trash' and a lot of our new fellow workers took great pride in being just that. Typically, hardworking, hard drinking, hard swearing types, many on their second or even third marriage, they were a breed apart. At least half had spent time behind bars for any number of reasons.

These were my new colleagues. The first drilling location was very close to the port being just twenty minutes from the wharf to the oilrig. It was the first time any drilling had been done off the Israeli Coast and this first exploratory well was to be drilled to over fifteen thousand feet. The drilling team encountered various problems and progress was very slow.

Meantime, we had been joined by a smaller vessel, the *Anna M* whose job was to transfer personnel to and from the rig. She would sometimes make three or four trips a day. Our ship, the *Cay W* supplied the rig with all the drilling requirements, the various types of pipes used, chemicals, fuel, water, special drilling tools, food for their complement of some eighty crew and the list went on and on.

It sounded like a heavy work schedule, but Storm Drilling planned very efficiently, and we would usually do just one or two trips a week, tying up alongside the rig, sometimes overnight and then returning to our base in Ashdod Port.

The port had given the drilling company and us a permanent berth, which was generally not used by commercial shipping and for the two weeks of our duty hitch, or 'swing' as it was called, we would spend most nights tied up to the wharf.

It was not far into Ashdod city and there were worker buses from the port entrance into town at regular intervals. We had to always carry a radio with us when we left the port, in case the rig needed a 'hotshot' item that could not wait until the following day. This only happened a couple of times.

With no effort, our crew had developed into a good team, and we would generally go into Ashdod in a group, leaving just a couple of guys on board to monitor the ship's power supply generators. The chief engineer, Mr Mac never went ashore and at least one of us deck people had to stay on board as well. The Captain had brought his wife and her terrier dog to Israel and the company provided him with an apartment in the town.

Ashdod was a very friendly place; many, if not most of the people were immigrants from Morocco, Tunisia and Algeria. This being the case while all spoke Hebrew many, especially the older ones, would speak French amongst themselves.

I became friendly with one such family and had a standing invite every Friday evening to join them in their home for the Sabbath evening meal. If we were alongside the wharf on a Friday, I never missed the chance and quite often the elder brother who worked in the port would come by my ship and pick me up.

What to do in Ashdod?

We would start off in a cafe cum bar in the centre of the city, enjoy a coffee, a couple of beers, maybe a snack and then if it was dance night, move on to the Ashdod Seaman's Club. There would always be a number of women there the downside being that most of them either came with a boyfriend, or with another girlfriend. You could speak to the single girls but watched by all their peers, there was no way you would ever get beyond a chat.

When the dance ended, there was still one place to go if your hormones were demanding action. An enterprising 'pimp' had set up a tent in the sand dunes between the town and the port, He served cold beer, cognac and coke and had two or three reasonably good-looking hookers standing by. Where to go for a short time, why, into the dunes out of site of the tent.

Not all did, those of us that had girlfriends remained true to them, although it was questionable whether it was a case of being faithful or more likely not wanting to get sand in the cheeks of our ass.

A good friend of mine was in the last stages of completing his national service in the navy and he was based in Ashdod. Then it was the practice for the navy to cruise around inside the port during the night in inflatable rubber boats and throw percussion grenades beneath the ships tied up alongside the wharves.

The purpose was to bring any possible terrorist divers to the surface with their eardrums shattered. My friend was called Nino and when he learnt I was working on this tug, which most nights was tied up at the wharf, we had no peace. He would wait until 2-3 a.m. before attacking.

We laughed it off, quietly cursing Nino, but it did have a serious effect on our chief engineer. I explained at length to him that this was a customary practice in the port, but he remained convinced we really were about to get attacked by Arab terrorists.

The navy base was only a couple of hundred metres from the ship, so I called there and asked Nino to try and give the *Cay W* a miss on his late-night patrols. I told him our old chief engineer was rapidly heading for a nervous breakdown. What made it worse was that our berth in the port was in relatively shallow water with just a couple of metres of water beneath the flat bottom of our ship. These facts resulted in the grenade explosion noise being magnified until it was really deafening, and it literally shook the ship.

We were all concerned for Mr Mac and then about 7 o'clock one evening 'came the straw that broke the camel's back'. To test the navy's security, an army unit entered the port without being seen. They placed dummy explosive charges on some of the port cranes and buildings and then as they withdrew, they launched a surprise attack on our ship. They should never have done this as our tug was flying the American flag, however they did.

Mr Mac and one of the ratings were sitting in the mess room, watching TV when the door burst open and heavily armed troops, faces camouflaged, rushed in. Their leader said in Hebrew and then in English, "do not move, do not be afraid, we are Israeli soldiers, and this is a security exercise." They then left as quickly as they had intruded.

For Mr Mac this was too much, and he lost the plot completely. He did not move from his chair, just sat there saying over and over, "The Ay-rabs are here, we are all going to die." The rating had called the Captain and myself and we arrived back on board within minutes of one another.

Mac was still raving, I went to the Port Infirmary and returned with a paramedic. The Captain called the agent and told him what had happened. The agent called the Port and an ambulance arrived alongside the ship shortly afterwards. Mr Mac left, holding onto the Captain's arm, still saying we would all die as the Arabs had taken over. We had explained to him many times that the soldiers were Israeli's, but he simply could not comprehend what we were saying.

It should never have happened, but these things do. No doubt exercises such as this were simply part and parcel of life in a country that had been theoretically at war surrounded by implacable enemies since the state was created so many years ago.

The next day, we packed Mr Mac's possessions and sent them to the hospital where he was being treated. A week later, Captain Polk and his wife were asked to escort Mac back to the USA as mentally, he was not fit to travel alone.

A new Captain and new chief engineer, fresh from Texas arrived on board. Some months later, we heard that Mr Mac was back at work and had recovered but still told all who would listen how the Arabs attacked his ship and that he was lucky to be alive.

Our new Captain Harold was a giant of a man, all 435 lbs of him (194 kgs). He was an ex-US Navy veteran who had found his way onto the oilfield boats. The chief engineer, Fred hailed from Brownsville, south Texas on the Mexican border. In character, they were total contrasts to Captain Polk and Mr Mac.

At the same time, one of our young Israeli seamen was called up for national service and his replacement was an amazing English Jewish guy who had recently arrived in Israel.

Introducing 'Curly King'

Curly was our new replacement seaman. He had never worked on a ship in his life, so how come he was hired as a seaman. In his words, his story went something like this.

He was a London 'Cockney' and proud of it. He was 43 years old, looking somewhat older, which as his story unfolded, may well have been the case. His parents had arrived in the UK as refugees from Russia just prior to World War II and had settled in the east end of London, which at that time was a Jewish locality.

He had scraped through the schooling system before abandoning further education to begin a life of petty crime. He was soon to 'graduate' into the big time when he was accepted and became a member of the notorious London east end-based Kray Brothers gang.

I recall him telling us one day how he was listening to the BBC describing a big payroll robbery, when he and other gang members were counting and dividing the proceeds.

The Kray brothers had one other 'mob' contesting their 'turf' and in all probability, it was a member of this gang who shot Curly one night in a dark Soho Street, dragged his body into a shop entrance and left him to die.

A passing police constable on his routine patrol heard noises, investigated, found Curly and summoned an ambulance. Off to hospital, an emergency operation and Curly pulled through, ironically a London 'Bobby' had saved his life.

Fully recovered, he resumed his gangland activities. At this time, a chain of London betting shops was being targeted by organised crime, possibly on their failure to pay 'protection money'.

Assigned to this case was a well-known Scotland Yard detective who was obsessed in trying to bring the Kray gang members to justice. He and his sidekicks stopped a car Curly was driving and searched both him and the car. In the trunk, they found several detonators. Curly was promptly arrested as being involved in the betting shop 'bombings'.

He was sentenced to seven years in prison and began serving his sentence. All along, he had proclaimed his innocence, insisting the detonators had been planted in the car by the cops. Not surprisingly with his police record, scant attention was focussed on his pleas.

He had served more than half of his sentence when a dramatic change of events saw him released. The Scotland Yard detective who had arrested him was found to be mentally deranged and the case against Curly was annulled. So, Curly guilty of many unsolved crimes was now back on the streets again but with a bonus.

He received a cash payment to cover the years of his wrongful arrest and to top it off, a letter from the English Prime Minister at the time, pardoning him and declaring him innocent of the charges laid against him. He was very proud of this letter and used to show it around.

His stories were endless, and funny as could be, but that's what Cockney wit was about, and served as a good cover for his darker side. Being Jewish and with his London future somewhat bleak, the Kray brothers were in prison, Curly decided to take up the state of Israel's offer of the 'Law of Return'.

This law entitled any Jewish person from any country in the world the right to return to Israel, the Jewish homeland, provided they could prove their Jewish identity. Persons with criminal records were supposedly barred, but Curly managed to dodge under the radar screen and entered the country as a new immigrant. New immigrants were permitted to bring in certain items tax free among which was a car.

Curley solved the car problem by buying an old bomb in London then trading it in on a brand-new MGC sports car. He was able to pay the minimal deposit on the vehicle, the remainder to pay off on time payment. He then drove to Dover, boarded a cross channel ferry and watched the fabled white cliffs of Dover fade into obscurity as the ship closed in on France. A drive through France to Italy onto Greece and another ferry to Israel and Curly landed in Haifa, greeting his new home. So goodbye forever to Mother England.

He still had most of the payoff he had received on his prison release but somehow, and he would never say how, he had increased this amount substantially. And how did he get a position on our ship?

He met one of the oilrig hands in a Tel Aviv discotheque and over drinks, the guy gave him the drilling companies address and told him to put his name down for a roustabouts (rig labourers) job on the *Typhoon*.

Curly rolled up, fronted the same Jim Weiss and asked to put his name on the roustabouts list. Jim said, "OK but right now we are full, but we need an experienced seaman for one of our tugboats."

Without batting an eyelid, Curly said he was available as while he had never worked on a rig before, he was a seaman in his younger years. Jim hired him.

When Curly arrived on board, the Captain sent him to me as I would be supervising his work and in fact, giving him his daily jobs. He said straight out, "Jake, I told a few 'porky pies' (lies) to land this job and I've never worked at sea before, but I'll do you a good job so give me a break."

I said, "Have you told the Captain this?"

And he said, "Well, no."

I said, "OK Curly, this is a secret between you and me, I will show you what needs to be done, and as long as you get along with everybody and do your work, there will be no problems."

However, I told him, "if you fuck up big time, I will see the Captain and have you fired, this is not a threat, and I just want to make things clear at the start."

We shook hands on what was to develop into a good friendship.

My Apartment in Tel Aviv
"Home Is What You Make It"

For my week off after every two of work, I would go back to Tel Aviv. Some months previously, I had taken a place at No 8 Hayarden Street, just a stone's throw away from the beachfront in central Tel Aviv. It was small, just one room, perched on the roof of a three-story building. The building was old, constructed out of granite blocks and from the outside, looked a bit run down.

I had the entire roof for myself and diagonally opposite my room, some twenty meters distant, was an equally basic but functional toilet cum shower. The cosmetic appearance of the roof top was enhanced by loads of old junk furniture.

The floor below my 'palace' was a chess club frequented by old religious Jews from Europe in one corner of which was a small coffee-sandwich bar, which fed the oldies and supplied, for a token amount, my breakfast and morning coffee.

The bottom or ground floor was the chess club office tended by an ancient Rumanian Jew. Every month, I would go and see him to pay my rent, 70 Israeli Shekels equivalent to twenty USD. I would enter the club through the big main door then veer left and up an old circular staircase, past the entrance to the chess club, then climb a further spiral staircase to the roof top.

I really loved this place, but I was young and basically it was a dump, but youth see everything in a very different light from older people and I looked at it as 'home' even though it was just the one small room.

Inside and out, my 'apartment' was painted bright orange with paint 'borrowed' from the tugboat. Nowadays, this type of paint is now banned due to a very high lead content, but so far, touch wood, it had not affected my health. The dazzling outside orange brightness was however very short-lived as the chess club manager quickly made me repaint the exterior brown.

Working some 35 km from Tel Aviv, I really needed transport as my International Driver's licence still had a few months validity. Looking no further than my own street, I found a rather beat up Fiat 500, better known as a Fiat Bambini with a 'for sale' note on it.

The owner, an Israeli student just back from study in Europe, spoke perfect English and the price was negotiated. In next to no time, we cleared up the paperwork and I was the proud owner.

It was light grey and had a lot of surface rust. My workmates in Ashdod later cleaned the rust and painted the spots with a maroon undercoat with the intention of painting it bright 'Ferrari' red. We never got around to applying the quality finish paint job so with the spots, the poor little Fiat looked like it had an infectious rash.

It lived and was parked in the street directly in front of the main door to the chess club. The licence plates were from Germany of a type indicating it had been bought in a duty-free zone.

Walking home one afternoon, I found an old lady spitting on my car. She angrily spoke to me in Yiddish, which I totally did not understand, not even a single word. She did not speak English and my super basic Hebrew was also no help. A passer-by came to our rescue.

The old dear was a Holocaust survivor and was very upset with the Germanic car number plate. It was explained that the previous owner was an Israeli student who had studied in Germany, had brought the car back to Israel, and then sold it to me.

Somewhat pacified the lady moved on, but I could not help but imagine what she had gone through in the past, it bothered me for days. In between fooling around in Tel Aviv, I was seriously dating a girl from Jerusalem.

The age-old beautiful city of Jerusalem was surrounded by hills and climbing these rises would see the little Fiat slow down to 20-25km as the clutch was about shot. Nonetheless it was a fun car, and quite often carried four people, no doubt a major factor contributing to the lack of speed.

My girlfriend loved it as it meant I could come to Jerusalem and pick her up from her home. Going to Jerusalem was always a slow trip as much of it was climbing the hills leading to the city but coming back, we had a lot of downhill and were almost able to keep pace with the other cars.

In my week off work, I would come to Jerusalem on Wednesday to pick her up then go back the following Monday. She worked as a hairdresser and her boss was OK with her being gone, off pay, for a few days every couple of weeks. She was the eldest daughter of a wonderful family who had been amongst the mass exodus of the Jewish people from Yemen when Israel became a country in 1948.

The Jewish community had been in Yemen for centuries, long before the Prophet Muhammad began preaching and spreading the words of Islam. For years, the ancient Jewish faith and the new Islamic religion coexisted peacefully but gradually laws and customs came into place whereby the Jews became second class citizens in the country.

One example being that they were not allowed to ride camels, as this would mean their head could be above that of a passing Muslim. The Jewish women dressed exactly the same as their Islamic counterparts in that they wore the full black burka, their body covered from head to foot with just the opening around the eyes.

The Jewish men were readily distinguished as they all had the long side curls down either side of their head reaching to their jaws. The community, isolated for centuries, retained their Hebrew language and were deeply religious, although of course, their daily language was Arabic.

They were famous craftsmen creating all kinds of silver jewellery and finely decorated curved daggers. Daggers important in that traditionally the head of every Arab family would wear a dagger around his midriff.

My girlfriend was called Hadassah and had opted out of doing national service, which was permissible for young women as she came from a religious family. Both her sisters went against the family's wishes and did do their military service, although this was not a big issue.

At work, the drilling operations continued smoothly and as far as we knew without any notable 'finds' of ether oil or gas. We continued to shift the rig around without any accidents and had a great crew in that everybody was happy, and we had no changes in personnel. It was much the same story on the rig.

Curly meanwhile had found a nice apartment in Tel Aviv, and with his sports car, money, dyed auburn hair and, despite his age, was a well-known identity in Tel Aviv's premier discotheque. He loved to flaunt his apparent wealth and had little difficulty in picking up the more gullible young women. He invited me and another crew member to check out his new apartment.

We arrived and entered what was certainly an upmarket apartment. Curly was sitting at the dining room table with a pile of banknotes in front of him. In a nearby chair was a glamorous young disco type girl, apparently his latest conquest. We said hello and Curly showed her out.

When he came back, he said the money is just for show, these chicks are taken by it every time, and then I put it back in the safe. In the bank, it would earn me a little interest, here it gets me women. To each his own I guess, I kind of felt sorry for him, but then again, I could be pretty sure none of his disco conquests would have been innocent virgins.

It came the time to apply for my car driver's licence as my French International one was about to expire. Yes, I was a competent driver, no problems there since teenage years, but still missing was a piece of paper that legally said I could do so.

My first driver's licence was obtained in the Bois de Boulogne just outside Paris when I managed to get a French International Driver's licence without producing any national licence, not being French, and only able to speak a few words of the French language.

Heard about the 'deal', 'scam', call it what you will, from a backpacker and sure enough for a small extra 'consideration', it was quick and easy to walk away with a genuine French International Driver's licence.

Now I needed an Israeli License and a friend from Ashdod was able to help me out. We went to the motor vehicle registry and queued up behind a huge Russian immigrant, apparently one of those from Georgia, who were famous for being very quick tempered.

The MVR clerk was a timid little guy, and he did not understand one word of Russian or Georgian Russian. He tried to explain that he would go back into the office and find someone who could attend to this 'gentleman'. He started to explain again very slowly in Hebrew what his intentions were when, 'bam', the Georgian punches him in the chest. Down goes the little clerk and then scurries for his life back into the office.

My friend and I had already taken a few steps back in case this lunatic decided we were next. The Georgian continued standing in front of and leaning on the now vacant counter as if he had done nothing wrong.

In less than 5 minutes, the cops arrived with one who could speak to the guy and to our surprise and relief, he walked out peacefully. The little clerk was back. He was shook up. I did an eyesight test and unseen, my friend completed a road rule questionnaire for me in Hebrew. I got a required photo and shortly thereafter I had my first genuine driving licence. While I collect it, my friend was babbling away in French as he knew the clerk couldn't understand, of course neither could I.

I was now a legally licensed driver. Our new Captain was the best and so proud of being from Texas. When we would go out to the rig, he would play 'The Yellow Rose of Texas' at full volume on the ship's PA system. As many of the rig senior drilling crew were also Texans, this was well received, and Harold S. was somewhat of a hero.

This huge man told us he was married and had a couple of children with a tiny Japanese woman he had met and married when he was seconded by the US Navy to Sasebo in Japan. However, he was soon to lose weight and a lot of weight at that.

The company had allowed the USA Captain and Chief Engineer to share a VW beetle car on permanent rental. One night driving back to the boat, and only 100 meters from the ship, Harold ran into a railroad flat car. For some reason, the port had left a string of these cars, without an attendant engine, laying unlit in the port. The railroad tracks crossed the internal port road system in several places.

The big guy was hopelessly trapped in the vehicle, he was just too big to get out as the car was quite badly damaged. Roving Port Security quickly spotted the car, were able to speak with him and he told them he thought his leg was broken. The port fire engine arrived, and they stood by until the Ashdod Police came and were able to cut the car around him so he could be lifted out.

We were watching him and his last words before the ambulance took him away were, "Man, I was in so much pain until they gave me that injection, oh boy it was good stuff, I'll have to hit them up for another."

We were suddenly a Captain short, and I was asked if I thought I could fill in until a new body arrived from the US. Told them sure, Captain Polk and Captain Harold had been teaching me how to drive the boat. For ten days, I was Captain until a new guy showed up.

My crew teased me relentlessly especially when we would be in Ashdod, calling me Captain in a loud voice. Then when the new man came in, they told everybody we knew that I'd been demoted because I was such a bad Captain.

Captain Harold had a broken hip and before the doctors would do whatever they had to do to fix him, they told him he had to lose weight and they put him on a rigid diet. He used to beg us to bring him cold beer into the hospital, which of course we did.

When he recovered sufficiently to walk, the company decided to fly him back to the US until their medical staff would declare him fit to go back to work. There was no compensation at all from the port and only the feeblest excuse-ridden apology. So, it was goodbye to Harold S. an excellent Captain.

Meanwhile, the two American Chief Engineers had met local girls, fallen in love and proposed to them. Both women accepted but there was a major problem. Neither of our engineers Fred or Ramon were Jewish and in Israel, it was not possible for the marriage to take place.

However, they did what so many similar couples had to do and that was to make the short flight to Cyprus, tie the vows and return to Israel. By this time, we knew most of the crew on the oilrig and had started to socialise with them. Where we did at least start an evening's drinking, at 'Bernie's'?

Bar Life in Tel Aviv Bernie's

All free time on leave from the boat was spent on Gordon Beach in Tel Aviv, either that or in Jerusalem. At nights, if my girlfriend was not in town, I would generally start the night out in Bernie's Bar in Dizengoff Street. The bar owners Bernie and her husband Bob were a middle-aged immigrant couple from Chicago. Personality wise, they were two total opposites.

Bob, behind his normally expressionless face, was the silent type, if you got a "Hi" from him that was about it and meant that you were a regular customer.

I always associated Bernie with the French word 'formidable'. She was loud mouthed, funny with a high-pitched annoying laugh, and an opinion on anything and everything. Together, she and Bob made a good team, and the bar was generally crowded.

They had put a sign on the door, 'Welcome but please speak English'.

For bar staff, they hired visiting young women tourists from wherever, the only requirement was that they were good looking and outgoing. Excellent music at just the right noise level made animated conversation easy, the place was always jumping and a lot of fun.

Hookers on the prowl were not encouraged but there was so much competition from Israeli girls looking for a good time and out to score with English speaking guys, that the pro's would have found it hard going. It was a home away from home for oil workers and there was always someone you knew propping up the bar.

Started drinking mid-afternoon one day with a bunch of hands from the rig, and by the time it got dark, we were far from sober. One of the guys was a little Irishman called George. He wore thick-rimmed, tortoise shell glasses and what remained of his hair was really red as in orange red.

Everybody had regular girlfriends except George. For weeks, he had been trying to score or even get a girl to sit and chat with him, with no luck just rejection after rejection. Now well inebriated, he decide to end it all, life was just not worth living.

Dizengoff Street immediately in front of the bar was lined with restaurants, bars and coffee shops, a busy thoroughfare with almost bumper to bumper traffic, especially in mid evening. George announced he was going to go out into the middle of the street, lie down and wait to die. This was greeted with uproarious laughter, none of us believing him.

He got up, lurched out the door and with car horns blaring and irate Israelis bellowing, he first sat down, and then laid down right across the white line in the middle of the road. However, it was just not George's day! All the traffic slowed right down and continued to abuse him as they carefully moved around him.

Watching through the glass panelled door, we were initially shell shocked, then realising that sooner or later, the silly bastard was going to be run over, we rushed out, blocked the traffic by weight of numbers, rescued him and returned him to his bar stool.

George just kept saying, "I don't understand, they just kept avoiding me." Bernie consoled him with a drink on the house and before long, he had forgotten the incident.

On another occasion, one of the most senior rig managers was arrested after leaving Bernie's at closing time early one morning. His crime, caught stealing two full bottles of milk from the front steps of an apartment building. Again, he was very drunk and his excuse to the Tel Aviv constabulary that he just felt like a drink of milk was not accepted. The owner of the milk was well and truly paid for his inconvenience and the errant manager spent the night in the holding cell for drunks, not being released until daylight.

My best workmate was a Finn and if it was to be a night on the town, we would generally start out together, invariably parting company as the night wore on, especially if we had picked up girls.

My friend Risto had met two women from the Finnish Embassy; hot, he assured me, and arranged for us to go out for a drink. Now I'm 1,72m and Risto 1,96 so I thought I'd better check on my date in case she was also a Finnish giant. He assured me she was not, and I was soon to find out that Finns also tell lies!

They were both tall and were strikingly good-looking blondes. Risto's excuse was that he really fancied his date, but she insisted her friend came along as well, and OK she was a 'bit' tall. Had it got around to good night kisses, I would have had my nose right between her two delightful boobs.

Where could we take these women for a drink or two? Well, of course, to Bernie's, where else. Before we met them, Risto and I had a few starters, but that was no excuse for what followed when they drank us, almost literally under the table. Give them their due, they paid drink for drink and were a lot of fun, even to the point where they had to put us into a taxi and drop us off at our respective addresses. Risto continued to see his date but mine no longer insisted on making it a foursome. So, I never knew what it was to fuck a Finn!

There were a lot of bars and clubs within a short walk from my room so there was always a place for a nightcap or two if the night was quiet. I picked up a young lady cop one night, out of uniform I might add, and when we reached home, she wanted to play the old Simon & Garfunkel song 'Bridge Over Troubled Water', which was on one of my CD's.

Put it on repeat and played it over and over while we made love. Why mention this? A few days later, when we were on our way back to Ashdod and work, Risto told me he had picked up this woman whose favourite song was, guess what?

We had a good laugh. Neither of us saw her again though we looked for her. Fancy a lady cop for a girlfriend, then again in Israel this would be considered quite normal where so many beautiful young women are in uniform.

A final tale from Bernie's. Left the bar with Risto and another equally tall Finn. We were drunk and were having an argument on where we would go next. They were speaking in Finnish, and I asked them to speak in English. Barely breaking stride, they picked me, one on each side, turned me upside down and deposited me face down in a garbage bin.

Garbage bins in Dizengoff Street were conical in shape, secured to one-meter-high pole set in the sidewalk. This to stop dogs scattering the contents. My Finnish friends continued walking still arguing loudly, meanwhile my shoulders were wedged in the top of the bin, face in the litter and my legs waving in the air above the bin. Fortunately, a couple of soldiers extracted me, there was no way I could have freed myself.

The next day, I asked Risto what they thought they were up to, and he didn't believe me. When I finally convinced him, he was full of apologies and said he had no recollection of even leaving Bernie's or of what happened in the street. It turned out that the two of them had gone on to an upmarket disco in the classy Dan Hotel, only to be refused entry.

The stories that came out of Bernie's were legendary, but on the positive side, romances did start up, ending on at least two occasions in marriage.

My Humble Apartment

At night, the short Hayarden street was taken over by Yemenite hashish drug pushers and street prostitutes, with frequent raids by the city vice squad. The address really had 'class'!

The street was cobblestoned, and the pushers would hide their wares in hollowed out areas beneath the stones. It was hashish, the similar cannabis family drug to marijuana and was the recreational drug of choice in Tel Aviv as marijuana was difficult to find and because of this, very expensive. The hash, or so the popular story went, was supposedly smuggled across the Israeli border from Lebanon in the stomachs of Bedouin camels.

Apparently, the poor beasts were somehow induced to swallow plastic bags and then when safely in Israel, they were similarly enticed to pass them out the back door. True or otherwise, a lot of the dealers' sales were to gullible visiting tourists and such tale would no doubt have spiced up the backpackers' stories when they returned to their own countries.

Hash was sold by what the dealers called a 'finger', which was a small rectangular block about the size of an average girl's thumb. It was so cheap. The blocks or mini cakes were very hard and the way most prepared it for use was to hold a burning match under one end after which you could then crumble it in your fingers and then add it to tobacco previously removed from a standard cigarette.

The mix would then be carefully repacked into the empty cigarette paper tube. One could become accustomed to Hash and perhaps feel the need for a joint occasionally, but I don't believe it was in any sense addictive in that you just had to have it. In fact, the more you smoked, the longer it took to get a buzz on, never mind feeling stoned.

Drugs at work on the boat were taboo, which was good as after two weeks work then getting back to Tel Aviv for a night out, it just took one good joint to kick start the evening.

One thing I noticed was that some of the rig guys were binge drinkers in that they would scoff down liquor, particularly Jack Daniels or the like just to get smashed in as short a time as possible, after which they would become very aggressive.

It was hard to explain what possessed them to do this as women would then generally avoid them apart from the real hard case whores who would proceed to rip them off big time.

And yet, and I have seen this several times, when these same guys would smoke just one joint before starting to drink, they would be so laid-back, be talkative, funny, be everybody's friend, and the last thing on their stoned mind was to start a fight.

What was in this hashish?

Returning Home After a Night on the Town

The working girls around that downtown area were mostly Moroccan or Rumanian, were rough, and most of them, perhaps if unfairly compared with cars, could be said to have quite some mileage. They did their business on the stairs above the chess club, which was the last flight leading up to my domain on the roof.

Most of the clients were Arabs. When the act had been completed, the girls would clean their vaginas or elsewhere using cotton wool. They would then just throw the soiled wool on the stairs. If the girls had a good evening with plenty of customers, there would be wads of cotton wool everywhere.

Sometimes on my getting back in the wee hours after a night out, I would have to discreetly edge past a couple busy humping away. The girls' didn't care and the customer too busy to pay attention, even when one time I inadvertently trod on his little radio.

Early morning, an elderly lady would clean the stairs from top to bottom. She was Russian born and I would sometimes see her as I went down to the chess club for my coffee and cheese sandwich. As far as I know, she never complained about the cotton wool, perhaps it reminded her of snow in the old country.

All Good Times Must Come to an End

The drilling company had let us know that the present well they were drilling was to be the last for the time being in Israel and that the rig and the boats would be leaving. It could all be over in just a few weeks and apparently, there were several options for the next destination.

There were those of us who had to break the news to our girlfriends while a few of the others were happy to sail off into the sunset without so much as a goodbye. And then the news arrived.

We were going from the sunny Mediterranean to the Canadian Arctic. There was no great urgency as it was now late March and the location we were going to would be icebound at least until June.

In the meantime, a decision was made to dry dock the oil rig and the boats in Toulon, France before crossing the North Atlantic Ocean to St Johns in Newfoundland. There final preparations would be made for the trip north to the Canadian Province of Labrador.

Sad farewells all around, and Bernie's threw a going away party with eats at the bar and free drinks for one miserable hour. Still, I guess it was a nice gesture although for sure the cash register would miss the free spending 'oil field trash'.

Hadassah came to Tel Aviv for a last goodbye and in typical Israeli fashion, she just bluntly said, "Are you coming back?" I told her yes and it would be in six months as that was the new agreement we had been asked to sign if we wanted to go on the trip.

The company had guaranteed that I would be repatriated to Israel on completion of six long months. She gave me a lovely big facial portrait photo for me to keep in my cabin.

Our Israeli crew were not coming on the trip and my friend Curly decided life was too good in Tel Aviv, and "what about my car?" Convinced him not to come with us.

A new Captain arrived for the sea voyage during which we would also be towing the oilrig. He was from Panama City in Florida, was 1.55m tall which no doubt gave him his nickname 'PeeWee'. When it was confirmed that we were Arctic bound, his comment was, "gosh darn, the only ice I've ever seen was in the bottom of a glass."

I was going to be the navigator along with my counterpart on the rig and like Captain Peewee, I had no Arctic experience but I did have the benefit of an excellent course on ice navigation while studying in London. The rig actually had an engine but an old very low powered model, and so by connecting our towline, we would add the extra horsepower, hopefully to give us more speed.

The trip from Ashdod to Toulon was blessed by fine weather until we entered the Gulf of Lyon on the last few miles of our run into Toulon. This area was prone to a very strong offshore wind, locally called the 'Mistral'. From calm flat waters, in no time a big head sea could build up, which was exactly what happened.

I was on duty when a big wave crashed over our bow and took out one of the navigation bridge windows. I had my head buried in the radar at the time and did not even see the wave hit us. The bridge took in a lot of water which flowed down into the next accommodation deck.

I called the Captain and by the time he rushed up, I was already speaking to the rig. I had reduced power to enough to hold our boat and the rig into the seas and then happily handed over to Captain Peewee. Miraculously, only our second radar that had copped the full force of the wave was out of action.

The force of the wave's impact was such, the tiny pieces of glass were embedded in the tough vinyl wall cladding at the back of the bridge. Had I been directly in line, it might well have killed me. Peewee told me to take all available crew and see if we could find plywood to cover the gaping hole that just prior had been a window. We were able to do this.

The entire incident had occurred with just 60 miles to steam to port and when we were already thinking we were home safe. We spent a long night, I don't think anybody really got any sleep, but by daybreak the wind had died, the sea had moderated, and the rig Captain asked us to take in our towline. This done, we made the final few miles to the pilot station where pilots were waiting for both the rig and us. Straight into port and the dry-docking people were ready for us.

By mid-afternoon, we were sitting high and dry in a dry dock, which was plenty big enough to take both the *Typhoon* and the *Cay W*. The plan was to remain in dry dock for seven days, but the rig manager and their support team from USA decided they would carry out some additional work on the drillship and the program was extended to two weeks.

All that was done to our ship was to water blast the hull, removing a lot of marine barnacle growth, replace what were known as anodes, metal zinc rectangular plates that were welded onto the underwater hull of the ship to control corrosion and then finally apply various coats of paint.

The painting could only be done when the rig was also ready for this job, as once the special paint was applied, the vessels had to go back into the sea water within a certain time.

Living on a ship in dry dock was no fun. To go to the toilet or have a shower, it was necessary to climb up long gangway onto the dock itself where such amenities were provided. However, we got a break when we were all shifted to a really nice hotel right in the middle of Toulon where we were to stay for two days and nights.

This was no act of generosity on the part of our owners but a necessity. The oilrig had become infested with cockroaches and we had noticed a few on our boat as well.

They are nothing new to ships and at one time or another, most vessels had the little buggers, and they bred rapidly. They came onto ships when boxes of food provisions were loaded and there were a lot of boxes when an oilrig had a crew of 80-100 persons at any given time.

The most effective way of eliminating them was to chemically fumigate the entire ship. This meant that all accesses into the ship had to be properly shut off, and crew taken off for the time the job took to complete. No complaints from the combined crews who were split up amongst three different hotels.

We had already had a good look around the city, been to a couple of night clubs, found the prices high and the girls not particularly friendly, so decided use the days to sight see the famous French Riviera. Our manager arranged for a minibus to be available if we could supply enough names to fill the bus. It worked out that in the end that so many guys wanted to go that he had to end up hiring three such buses.

The first day, we took a bus trip to Juan Les Pins, and the second of our two-day holiday from work, we did the same again, this time to Cannes and Nice. For a century or more this coastal strip had been home, or more likely one of the homes, of the very rich. We just kept passing luxurious villas with immaculate gardens. These bus trips came with a multilingual driver who kept up a running commentary, particularly focussing on the eccentricities of some of the famous who had, or still did reside along the coast.

The fabled beaches were to say the least disappointing. In many places, pebbles rather than the golden sand we associated with beaches, no surf at all, and the entire beach area filled with tightly packed deck chairs interspersed with beach umbrellas. According to the driver, the deck chairs were rented by the hour with a discount if you took one for the whole day.

The beaches were however clean and with their deckchairs and umbrellas colourful, so the obligatory photos were duly taken. In both Juan Les Pins and the next day in Nice, the drivers would stop at the better-known restaurants and cafes.

Before de-bussing, they would give us an idea of how much it would cost for a drink, prohibitive, or a meal, absurdly high, and then tell us where to go nearby for cheaper but just as good deals. This was a surprise as normally drivers get a commission for 'clients' introduced to shops, restaurants and so on.

I imagine if our drivers had had a mixed load of tourists, they would not have mentioned the cheaper alternative. And then again none of us could be mistaken for 'high rollers' with money to burn. Back to work on our cockroach free ships, and not a sign to be seen of one. I guess the 'fumigators' must have removed the myriads of tiny corpses.

The dry dock completed, the painting was done and couple of days later, the dock was refilled with sea water. Small tugs pulled us out and we were ready for the North Atlantic crossing. Well, not quite ready. We were instructed to drop anchor just outside Toulon Harbour for a day while the *Typhoon,* which had some engine work carried out in the dry dock, was given what they called sea trials to make sure all was as should be. Trials were successful and we were called in to once again connect our towline and head off on the long haul to Canada.

By now, the navigator on the *Typhoon* and myself were good friends and were looking forward to the sea passage. As a result of the incident on our way into Toulon when we had a window taken out by a rogue wave, our management had fabricated portable aluminium covers to fit over all of our forward bridge windows.

Each cover had a small circular glass porthole inserted for our essential look out duties. These covers must have cost a pile of francs. We installed them for the first two days at sea and then took them off as the weather was so good. Weather wise the North Atlantic had a bad reputation, and we were a small ship towing a large underpowered oilrig across the whole expanse from east to west.

Sailor's superstitions were such that if you sailed from port and had not paid the whores, then you would have nothing but bad weather. Well, if there was any truth in the old saying, then our crews must have been paying the 'ladies of the night' better than ever before.

The notorious North Atlantic was a virtual mill pond for the entire crossing. As a result, we made a slightly better speed than anticipated, arriving off St John's, Newfoundland two days earlier than planned.

Saint John's Newfoundland

We tied up right astern of the *Typhoon* with a most unexpected welcome to the city, and indeed to Canada. Waiting on the wharf in large numbers were officers of the Royal Canadian Mounted Police. As soon as our respective gangways were in place, they swarmed on board and began an intensive search.

The Mounties had erected a long barricade down the wharf some 50 metres away from the tied up vessels. Behind the barricade were large numbers of the townspeople as well as the media with their TV cameras.

On board, we had no idea what was behind all this until our Captain was told that Interpol had notified the Canadian Authorities that there were supposedly unspecified illegal drugs on board either or both vessels.

According to Interpol, the French Police in Toulon had arrested drug dealers who admitted supplying commercial quantities of drugs to some American crew members.

They searched the *Cay W* for over three hours and found nothing, however on the *Typhoon*, the search went on well into the night and was intensive. We could see some of the Mounties climbing way up the drill ships, drilling derrick some 70 metres above the deck.

All they found was a hashish pipe in the radio operators' cabin, which showed traces of cannabis resin. Steve, the operator was arrested. Our Captain Peewee had told me to place a sign on the gangway. 'No visitors permitted to enter the ship' and our agent had said we should say nothing to any of the waiting reporters, and that he would deal with them.

It was no doubt big news for the quiet city of St John's and the media were out to make the most of it. As soon as the police left and removed the barricades, the locals came to the sides of the ships, eager to talk with any crew member. They were all convinced that indeed there were drugs on board, and they were eager to buy.

Next day, we featured on both the local and national TV *wake up good morning* shows and made the headlines complete with photos in the daily newspaper. Radio operator Steve faced the court and as the owner of the now famous pipe was found guilty of using a drug even though none had been found.

He had already been fired by our ultra-conservative oil field management and was not given a jail sentence in St John's but was deported back to his home town of Philadelphia.

Steve did not take life or authority very seriously best shown as when the verdict was announced, he said, "well, now with this hanging over my head, I'll never make President of the USA, my childhood dreams have been shattered."

Our American crew members now had to be replaced by local Newfoundlanders or 'Newfies' as they liked to be known. In a city where unemployment was high, we had no problems in lining up a good crew.

Newfoundland classed as one of Canada's Maritime Provinces was different from mainland Canada. The people spoke with an accent more Irish than mainstream Canadian English and they had no time for the French Canadians from the neighbouring Quebec Province.

I was told that until 1948 Newfoundland was a British Colony. Economically, Britain was in poor shape after the five long years of World War II and was reluctant to retain a colony, which to be impolite, did not generate enough return on investment.

So, Newfoundland was offered to the Canadian Government who expressed little interest. The Newfoundland Government then approached the USA to see if Uncle Sam was in the market for another state to add to the many. Apparently, the USA also getting over the war, was none too excited.

If the above story is true, and the person who told me was quite convinced it was, then Canada ended up accepting Newfoundland as well as Labrador, which was part of the package. I could say that on our exploratory drives around the beautiful city of St John's, it was not uncommon to see the British Union Jack flying alongside the Canadian Flag on poles in front of some of the up market homes.

Economically, the province depended on fishing, primarily cod fishing from the near offshore Grand Banks and lumber, timber exported as both natural wood or processed into paper pulp. As mentioned, unemployment was a problem particularly in the long winters when a lot of outdoor work came to a halt.

We were to be chartered by the oil giant Conoco and their local office told us we could expect at least a couple of weeks in St John's as the sea at the intended drilling location was still solid pack ice.

In the meantime, after work hours we were free to enjoy the city night life. There was a big dance hall open most nights of the week and it was a great place to go. No hookers, just local young men and women out to enjoy a few drinks and chance their luck on making out.

What really made it good was that the local people were very friendly and did not resent newcomers trying to pick up their women. No worry if you were a bit shy, the women would just as soon ask a guy to dance as wait to be asked. If you said you were a lousy dancer, they replied, "Come on, I'll show you," end of story.

The dance would end just before midnight and we, with company if we were in luck, would head for 'Paddy's Inn', a local cafe cum restaurant. The weather was still cold, like just above zero Celsius and Paddy's served the best possible light meal to wrap up a night of drinking and dancing.

It was simple, it was cheap, and it was fabulous. Hot freshly cooked potato chips bathed in the richest gravy. The secret was the gravy, it was so good, and the chips or fries were cut on the premises and did not come all the same size as from a supermarket packet.

If you wanted more gravy for your remaining chips, it was simply a case of fronting the counter and another ladle full was free of charge. If you had 'scored' and a night of lust lay ahead, the women either had their own place or you went to a hotel. The luckiest wound up with a woman who not only had her own room but also had a car, which meant a ride back to the port come daylight.

After two weeks, Conoco told us we were to sail and go to the small port of Cartwright in Labrador and wait for the rig to follow once the sea pack ice still reported on location had broken up. We would use the port of Cartwright to take workers to and from the rig. Those going on leave break had company chartered flights from Cartwright down to St John's from where they would have routine flights back to the USA. The American rig crews worked 28 days on the rig followed by 28 days of time off.

For all other operations of rig supply, our base port would be St John's, a three-day voyage from the drilling site. We sailed and headed north towards Labrador. Navigation had to be precise and excellent lookouts had to be always kept. We were passing through an iceberg area and quite frequently we would sight them.

These icebergs had broken free from the permanent ice off and around Greenland and would then drift south. They were huge and could weigh several thousand tonnes. Although only about 10% protruded above the sea surface, they were readily visible and did not present any real problems.

It was when small chunks of ice broke off the bigger bergs that we had to be very careful. These were called 'growlers' and again might weigh hundreds of tonnes. Collision with one of these could be disastrous. As they were smaller, very little ice might be visible above water. The constant action of waves against these 'growlers' resulted in the part above water becoming rounded.

During daylight, a well-kept lookout could pick up these smaller 'growlers' but at night, we relied on our radars to supplement the lookout's task. Radar worked on the principle of transmitting signals, which bounced back off a target and returned to the vessel where the time taken determined the distance of the object from the ship.

Radar signals were best off vertical or angular targets and worst off the low rounded targets symbolic of 'growlers' where the signals were deflected and fewer returned to the ships receiving antenna. We used two lookouts at night, alternating hour about and provided them with night vision binoculars.

All went well for the first two days, although the weather had turned bitterly cold. We were pushing into a slight sea, which resulted in constant spray coming over the ship. The moment the spray hit the cold metal superstructure, it turned to ice. With more spray, large deposits of ice quickly formed.

Ice build-up had been expected and in St John's, we had been supplied with big wooden mallets and wooden shovels. It was now the crew's job to break the ice off using the mallets and then shovel it over the side. All of them had at one time been fishermen and this was something they were used to and good at. We began to encounter pieces of pack ice.

It was on Peewee's next night watch that the phone rang in my cabin waking me from a deep sleep.

"Jake, come to the bridge, we're stuck in ice."

Peewee was nervous, excited and not reacting well in a stressful situation. I normally did the radio work for him, and he told me to call the US Coast Guard for advice and possible assistance. It was difficult to try and tell your superior what you thought was best, but for the moment he had really lost the plot.

I said, "Captain, just a suggestion, we are stuck in pack ice, not moving at all, do you think we should stop our main engines now in case ice comes into contact with our propellers and damages them?"

His immediate reply. "Yes. Yes, I will call the engine room now while you call the coast guard."

Again, I interrupted him and said, "PeeWee, we are in Canada. I think we should call their authorities rather than the US Coastguard."

His response, "call both quickly now."

He called the engine room and they had shut down the main engines. I started by calling the Canadian Coast Guard and almost immediately, my call was answered by the Captain of a Canadian ship. His accent so totally gave him away as a Newfie.

I gave him our position and he told me his vessel the steamship *Cabot Strait* was also stuck firmly in pack ice some forty miles ahead of us. He asked if all was OK on board. I passed the phone to Peewee, which was not a good move as he was more freaked out than I had thought.

He at once told the *Cabot Strait* that he had never been in ice before, was worried, had no idea what to do, which was why he had his deck officer calling the two Coastguards. He then passed the phone back to me, gee thanks Peewee. Our chief engineer had come to the bridge and was trying to calm the Captain down.

The Captain of the *Cabot Strait* told me that as long as our vessel had suffered no damage, there was no need to panic. He explained that a wind shift had driven the pack ice in towards the shore, making progress through it impossible for anything other than a specially built ice breaker.

He assured us the wind would change in the next day or two, the ice would break up and we could proceed on our way. The only reason to call for assistance from the Canadian Coast Guard would be if our ship was in danger of sinking in which case, they could attempt rescue of all crew using a helicopter.

Peewee was calming down. If ever there was a time for Valium, this was it! The *Cabot Strait* told us they would listen for us on a frequency they gave us, and we should give them a call if we had any problems. In the meantime, they said just sit back and wait for the weather to turn.

Their vessel was a Canadian Government ship which, once the long winter was over, ran supplies to the isolated little settlements along the Labrador coast and up into Hudson Bay to the Port of Churchill. Churchill, exporting iron ore, was the only commercial port in the vast region. This was their first voyage of the coming spring/summer season, and they were not surprised to get ice bound.

When daylight came, we were able to step down from the ship onto the ice, which we guessed was 1.5 to 2 metres thick. Walking around the ship securely stuck in ice, miles from the nearest land was certainly a new and exciting experience. Areas of the surrounding ice were stained a brownish red colour. We mentioned this to the *Cabot Strait* who provided the answer.

Environmentalists and fellow Greenies, you are not going to like what we were told. Every year when the young seals were born, the indigenous Inuit communities had the right to hunt these baby seals for their pelts. The hunters travelled out on the ice on their skidoos, (powered sleds), and the little seals were clubbed to death. Hence, sadly, the stains we could see on the ice were seal blood.

As predicted after two days, the wind did change and the ice broke up. Where it had been one solid sheet, we were now surrounded by broken slabs of pack ice as far as the eye could see. We had a tad less than 100 nautical miles still to go to reach our destination of Cartwright so how best to continue?

We came up with the practice of edging up to one of the larger ice flows until our bow was in contact and then slowly increasing engine power. Normally, the ship was steered automatically but now we had to revert to manual steering. We found that by pushing the ice flow ahead of us on our desired course, we would clear a path through the broken floes. We could sometimes steam for up to half an hour until we had to back off, choose another large floe and repeat the process.

We did this for a whole day and as darkness descended, we could see more and more clear water between the flows as the wind continued to drive the ice back offshore. By nightfall, we had some 50 miles to go, and the ice was no longer a big concern.

Peewee decided to run at slow speed during darkness so that by day light, we could reassess the situation and hopefully make it into Cartwright before nightfall. All went as we had hoped and were able to tie up at the township's little wharf just after lunch.

The Isolated Township of Cartwright, Labrador

The town was small with something under 1000 inhabitants. Seemed like most of them were on the tiny wharf when we tied up. With no room to spare, we took up the entire length of the little wooden wharf.

First to board was a sergeant from the RCMP. I wondered how concerned he might be as he must have heard of our 'welcome' from his fellow officers when we arrived in St John's a few weeks earlier.

The sergeant was not only the protector of law and order but pretty much was responsible for everything that took place in the town. The health, education and welfare of all were just some of the areas for which he was responsible.

He came on board in his resplendent red RCMP uniform, which was impressive and after introducing himself to the Captain, told him to summon all the crew to the navigation bridge so he could address them.

He gave us a friendly welcome to his domain and then spelt out the does and don'ts we were to follow at such time as we were in port. The big number one on the 'don'ts' was that under no circumstances were we to supply alcohol to the locals.

He told us that some of the younger women might enjoy sexual experiences with a newcomer, and this was not going to happen. He told us it was such a small place that everything that happened sooner or later reached his ears and if we did not comply with his instructions, our company would be told to take us out immediately. Welcome to Cartwright.

As it turned out, he was a great guy and nobody got into strife, under some duress I might add, as a couple of the younger women, part Cree Indians were stunners. At the end of the little wharf was the place where all business in town took place. This was the Hudson Bay Trading Company Store. They stocked food, clothing, electrical appliances, fishing and hunting equipment, in short everything from a women's bra to a skidoo.

The Hudson Bay Company was a part of Northern Canada's history. Set up by the British in the 1670 originally to buy furs from the trappers, it had survived bigger and better until the present day. In Cartwright, the only source of income came from two main sources. The annual salmon run, and the harvest of young seals.

The salmon run was so important to the community that when it started, school was closed for the six weeks or so that the fish were caught. Families set up camp along nearby rivers and all participated until the run was over. Apart from the fish kept for their home consumption, the remainder was all sold to the Hudson Bay Company. In a normal season, many tonnes of fish would be caught.

Hudson Bay had a fixed price per kilo for the season. Each family had an account with them and was credited for the amount received from the fish the family unit caught during the six week 'run'. They would use this slowly diminishing credit to pay for food and household necessities for the remainder of the year, hoping to last out until the next salmon season.

They told me that bears could be a nuisance during the fishing season as they too wanted their share and did not mind intruding on an area claimed by a family. They were protected and could only be killed if they attacked humans. The families used noisy, but harmless explosive charges to scare off persistent offenders.

The children loved the salmon run, firstly because no school and then because they enjoyed helping in the fishing itself, another annual event was the baby seal hunt. It could be very profitable but was already under pressure to be stopped. It was also risky.

Cartwright had lost four skidoos in the previous season. They had left their sleds grouped together while they went out on the ice to stalk the young seals on foot when suddenly the ice fractured, dumping their valuable skidoos into the icy sea.

A third source which was declining was the trapping of fur animals, most importantly mink. In earlier decades, this had been a big and at times lucrative business, but in Cartwright there were only a few old men who still ran their trap lines during the winter

The Canadian Government was trying to induce people from these small mixed settlements to move south to join up with bigger communities. Mixed settlements meaning places where the inhabitants were of European, Indian or mixed of both races, and did not include settlements that were 100% Inuit or Eskimo. From the Governments point of view, hamlets such as Cartwright were economically not feasible, but in a democratic society you cannot just resettle people against their wishes.

We had an example of what the government was on about one day when we were at the wharf and one of the township women suffered severe life-threatening problems while giving birth in the tiny local medical centre. A Royal Canadian Air Force helicopter with two crew and a doctor flew in and took her and her husband down to St John's.

From a humanitarian viewpoint, it was so efficient but of course the costs prohibitive. While they were bringing the lady from the clinic, myself and two of our crew chatted with the pilot and he showed us his helicopter, which was equipped like a mini hospital.

He told us that they made such flights all the time to small communities and today's flight was 'a piece of cake'. He then went on to tell us it could be a very different set of circumstances in winter with bad weather, snow or blizzard conditions. The helicopter landed on the wharf between us and the Hudson Bay Store.

I asked him if they still would fly in such winter weather, and he said if it was a patient in a life-or-death situation, they would certainly do all possible to make the rescue flight.

Of course, the major problem in Cartwright and like communities was the almost non-existent employment opportunities. Hudson Bay employed a handful of staff, there was a doctor and two nurses in the clinic, two schoolteachers and our friend, the RCMP sergeant. That was about the sum of those who had permanent jobs.

The children liked to come to visit our boat and Peewee loved kids so despite company regulations, he always invited them on board and made sure each got at least an ice cream or soft drink. I asked them, would they like to move south to a bigger town or city and the emphatic replies were, "no way."

I said, surely the cold winter months with the long nights and short daylight hours must be boring and was surprised to hear that these were their favourite months.

Why? They all had pet huskies or husky/wolf mixes and wintertime was the time they had the big dog sled races. This and the local natural ice hockey rink kept both the boys and girls out of mischief, all happening in temperatures often below zero.

I am a dog lover, perhaps surprising as I had never owned a dog. A little local girl told me that one of her dogs had just had puppies and would I like one. I checked with Peewee, telling him I was going to get a puppy, and would he have any objections. He said fine go ahead but make a little kennel for it on deck as he did not want the puppy inside the accommodation.

Next day, she proudly bought this little puppy on board and said I could have him. He was snow white and she said his mother was a husky and his father a passing wolf. I queried this asking her how come a wolf had come into Cartwright and she told me the story, at the same time assuring me that wolves did not come into the township.

Some years previously, when a government ship had called into Cartwright, possibly the *Cabot Strait*, they had a few tourist passengers on board. The tourists had gone on a walk around town when one of their small children wandered off, was attacked by a husky, and died of its injuries.

From that time on, huskies were only allowed in Cartwright during the fall and winter months. In summer, they had to be shifted to some of the numerous little islands in sight of the settlement. The owners would go there every couple of days to feed them and make sure their long tie up leads were not tangled. Apparently, while her dog was 'vacationing' away from town, a horny wolf passed by, and her batch of puppies was conceived.

I thanked her and asked her how much money she was asking. She said, "Nothing Jake, it's a present for you." I told her to run home and ask her Mum if I could give her ten dollars. She took off and was soon back telling that was OK, so the deal was sealed.

My new acquisition was given the name Kali and was to be totally spoilt by all the crew none more so than by Captain Peewee. The puppy had thick body hair, but his belly was almost hairless. He didn't bark like normal dogs more like howled and quickly adopted the front deck of the boat, where we had placed his new kennel, as his territory.

As far as I knew, he never once went in his kennel, which was a work of art built by one of the Newfy seamen. We had been in Cartwright for over a week and a Conoco helicopter flew over the drilling site and confirmed that it was still iced over. The helicopter then came into Cartwright and Conoco asked Captain

Peewee if he could spare a couple of guys to go with the helicopter for two days while radio base stations were set up on prominent points in the area.

We all wanted to go and I shamelessly pulled rank and became one of the two lucky ones. The stations were to provide key reporting points for the rig crew change helicopters as the flight from Cartwright was all over open water. The pilot would have to report as he passed stations designated as A, B and C on his way to and from the *Typhoon*.

The man in charge of setting up the stations was a French man who had wintered with an Inuit family the previous year. We asked him what it was like to spend month in an igloo, and he burst out laughing. Igloos, he told us, were a thing of the distant past, and most Inuit would not know how to build one these days.

We asked him if it was customary for Inuit men to offer their wives to visitors and again, he said this may have been the case a long time ago, but no longer. However, there was a twinkle in his eye! After spending the winter with the family, he was given a going away present in the form of a polar bear skin.

These are big bears and of course, they have magnificent big snow-white skins. The polar bear is heavily protected, and the only people allowed to kill them are the Inuit. It may still be the same but at that time, each family had a permit to kill one polar bear each year. They could if they wished, then would sell this permit to wealthy sportsmen hunters, generally from the USA.

The term sportsmen hunters was an ugly description as these guys, armed with a high powered rifle and their precious bought permit would then charter a light aircraft, locate their victim and acquire their trophy. The only upside was the high dollar premium the Inuit family could expect from parting with their permit.

Another true tale about the polar bears. They were a real menace around the port of Churchill in Hudson Bay where they routinely came and scavenged in the rubbish dumps around town. Being protected, there was little that could be done about this. The worst enemy of these big bears was the slow global warming, which was melting away their traditional ice hunting grounds.

The base stations were set up like clockwork, the Frenchman was very organised, and the two days allocated for the job were more than enough. We did get the chance to look down on the Labrador scenery. Lots of small rivers entering the sea and many freshwater lakes, still frozen over. Cartwright bordered on the zone where trees gradually disappeared, and the vast tundra began.

The forest trees were all pine trees not much bigger than the Christmas trees people in Europe and the USA decorate their home living rooms with every December. I asked why the trees were so small and was told that below the initial topsoil, the ground was permanently frozen, stunting further growth.

After two weeks in Cartwright, we were told the location was now ice free and the *Typhoon* had sailed from St John's. We were told to proceed to location at once. It was a twelve-hour run. Once there, we were to provide details of any remaining sea ice in the area, the presence of any ice bergs and to get some idea of the present prevailing ocean currents.

The location was clear of ice though there were three large icebergs within a ten mile radius. Conoco had employed a team of experts from the UK who were to track any icebergs, which might cause a danger to the rig once it was on location. The rig arrived and with it, a second tug similar to the *Cay W*.

We worked together and in 48 hours had set the rig's eight anchors. Once the anchors were run out, the rig put a load test on them to check they would not slip if we got any severe weather. All eight anchors did not hold under the test load and the insurance surveyor said we would have to double up anchors.

That was insert a second anchor on the same anchor wire as the initial anchor. This generally would satisfy test requirements. The rig only had eight spare anchors. This took a further three days to double up on the anchors but was successful. All anchors now were holding, and the rig prepared to start drilling.

Very simply to start drilling, they use a large drill bit for the initial hole opening. Once they had reached the desired depth with the large drill bit, they pulled it out of the hole and run-in steel pipe which was then cemented into place. This stopped the hole from caving in.

As the well got deeper, the hole size got progressively smaller, and each new section drilled had further smaller diameter steel pipe cemented in, and so on. The problem the rig was having was that each time they pulled out of the large initial hole to install the steel pipe, the hole would collapse. We were sent to St John's to fit a special survey tool, which would hopefully determine why the hole kept doing this.

The tool and an operator were waiting and after only an hour in St John's, we were on our way back to the rig. The tool worked and revealed that the exact location picked for the well was centred over a 300-meter-deep depression in the sea floor. Over millions of years icebergs had been moving across this area and the depression had filled up with debris in the form of large boulders, deposited by these icebergs. The result was that each time drilling would pull out of the hole to run the steel pipe, the boulders would fall back into place.

Solution was for the rig to move some 200 meters to clear this depression and at last, they were able to make a start. There seemed to be a continual run of problems with the drilling. Springtime had become summer, and summer was rapidly becoming fall with the advent of winter soon to follow.

There was always at least one iceberg within a ten-mile radius of the rig and the iceberg specialist team on the rig were kept busy plotting their paths. The problem with icebergs was that they do not move in a direct line. Their path was very much determined by their underwater shape and 90% of the iceberg was under the water.

We tried an interesting experiment where we ran a large diameter rope from our stern around the iceberg to the stern of the second tugboat. There was no way we could tow anything as massive as an iceberg and that was not the intention, all we were trying to do was to turn it a few degrees so it would then set off on a new path away from the rig. We kept breaking the rope and our experiment failed.

Meanwhile, our trips to St John's continued and we usually would stay in port for two or three days. By this time, we knew lots of people and our social life was becoming a little overpowering. I had been seeing Kristy, a 22-year-old nurse and we got along fine but she was starting to get very serious wanting to know if I would have time to visit her folks in Cornerbrook, which was a town quite some way from St John's. I was writing to my girl in Jerusalem and had not mentioned her to Kristy, perhaps I should have but it was a bit late now.

And then there was the incident with my rapidly growing puppy, 'Kali'. We were at the wharf in St John's when the Conoco drilling manager, instead of coming up the ship's gangway, decided to just jump onto the foredeck of the boat from the wharf.

This was Kali's turf, and he did not like it one little bit. He seized the guy behind his right ankle and clamped his teeth. The dog would not let go despite the man hitting him repeatedly on the head with his fist. Incidentally, you could hit a husky's head all day with your fist and all that would happen was you'd get a sore fist.

One of the Newfy seamen grabbed the dog and coaxed him free. The Conoco guy was hurt and furious. He stormed into the mess room and told me my 'wolf' had attacked him, that the dog had to go today, and I would be hearing more about this.

Captain Peewee saved the day. He and the Conoco man were both from Florida and maybe this helped, but then Peewee diplomatically told the man that he had not followed safety regulations by jumping on board instead of using the gangway and in any incident report, this would have to be stated.

However, the dog did have to go, and I was able to give him to one of our seamen. This man had a Newfoundland dog that was very old, and he used this dog to pull a sled through the woods to collect old pine branches and pinecones for firewood during the long winter months. He said pinecones were the best as they generated the most heat.

He planned to hitch Kali up alongside the old dog and he would learn what to do. Huskies were quite big dogs but the longhaired, always black, Newfoundland breed were a good bit bigger. We were all sad to see Kali go, but at least he had gone to a good home.

The drilling was a long way from completion, but the weather was getting colder by the day and ice was starting to form on deck. Conoco were already talking about stopping drilling for the season and to continue next year. On a crew change trip into Cartwright, there was already some snow on the ground.

Conoco did not make the decision to stop drilling, the decision was made for them by the Captain on the *Typhoon,* who in part panicked prematurely. We had not one but three icebergs moving towards the rig but with the closest still some 10 miles away, the *Typhoon* Captain ordered drilling to stop and welders to get ready to cut the rig anchor wires, freeing the drillship.

Yes, the icebergs were tracking in such a way that one or more might have ended up on a collision course with the rig, but they were a minimum of 10 miles distant and moving at a speed of just over two miles per hour.

Both boats immediately asked for permission to start retrieving the anchors but this was denied by the *Typhoon* Captain who was just waiting to cut the wires as soon as the drilling crew told him they were ready for him to do so. This he did, leaving thousands of meters of big diameter wire and sixteen anchors on the seabed.

The *Typhoon* steamed off location headed for St John's. We, together with the other boat, were left to recover the mess on the seabed. We worked solidly for a whole week and had recovered all but four anchors and two wires, by which time our deck was full and ice on deck was becoming a big safety issue.

Conoco gave us the OK to head for St John's. A further surprise was still in store as Conoco, under pressure from the Newfoundland Government, wanted us to return to location and complete the clearing of the seabed. The other assisting boat was off-hired, and we were the 'lone ranger' to go back to the site.

Orders were orders and off we went. In just the week away from location, winter had really set in. We did manage to retrieve two of the four remaining anchors and one wire, but the work deck had become a skating rink and myself and the deck crew had a couple of narrow escapes before Captain Peewee called a halt to the operation and told Conoco we were returning to St John's.

Hope to See You Again, St John's

A few days only in St John's with time for a final last-minute fling with our girlfriends and we were off. As seafarers and oilfield trash invariably did, we promised to return soon, some of us no doubt meant it, from others, it was no more than empty words.

My farewell was one of tears with Kristy. There must be something wrong with my character as while we got along fine, I did not realise that she had really fallen for me. It was usually me who got dumped but now the shoe was on the other foot.

We steamed independently out through the narrow entrance to St John's harbour, once clear, again connected our tow wire to the *Typhoon* and began our trip down the east coast of Canada, then the USA, all the way to Florida where we rounded the Florida Keys and headed up into the Gulf of Mexico.

We were to drop the rig off in Gulfport, Mississippi and then continue onto Freeport in Texas, which was where our company had their head office. The trip went with incident, a day alongside the wharf in Gulfport as both vessels were cleared back into the USA and then onto Freeport.

A day out of Freeport, I got a phone call from the owner of the company asking if I would stay on for a couple of weeks as he was short of crew and needed a deck officer for another vessel working in nearby Galveston Port. Told him OK, the extra bucks would certainly not go amiss.

Tied up in Freeport, a car to Galveston and a new ship the *San Jacinto*. Three days later, another call from the owner, telling me I had to get off and would be sent back to my initial point of hire, which was Tel Aviv. The owner was apologetic and said he had omitted to tell the local US Immigration that I was not a US citizen.

He knew them personally in Freeport, which probably saved him from a fine and he requested, and was granted permission for me to stay three days in

Freeport to relax and look around. This I did and from that time, Texas and the Texans have always been 'number one' for me.

The owner's name was Eddie and he sent his crews for their scheduled crew changes to different ports along the Gulf of Mexico Coast. He said I could ride shotgun with the driver of the crew minibus, which they termed a 'carry-all' and in this way, I was able to get a quick look at Alabama, Louisiana, and of course, Texas as we delivered and picked up various crews.

Back in Freeport, I was handed my air ticket to New York with a connection to Tel Aviv.

Israel Again

I had asked Eddie if I could have a ticket to Paris in lieu of Tel Aviv but he said, "Sorry Jake, we are responsible and obliged to send you back to where we hired you, and that was Tel Aviv. If we were to send you to Paris or elsewhere and for some reason, you got into trouble there, then we would still be liable for your ultimate return to Tel Aviv."

Told him that was fine. I was going in any case back to Israel to meet up with my girlfriend and just thought a short break in Paris would be a nice stopover on the way. Jokingly I said, "Eddie, you could always get me a ticket New York/Paris/Tel Aviv."

His reply, "nice try Jake, it ain't gonna happen."

Thanked him and the office staff and got ready for the trip to Houston Airport and from there onto New York. At the last-minute, Eddie said he might have further work for me in Malta as he was tendering for a contract there, but this would be three months off. I had been booked with the Israeli National Carrier EL AL for the flight back to Tel Aviv.

At the check-in, I said to the woman, "Please tell me all those people are not going on this flight."

She said, "Why do you ask?"

I told her, "Sorry but I really don't want a long flight surrounded by this lot."

I was not usually too bothered but the entire flight, seemingly minus my seat, had been booked by a congregation of ultra-orthodox Hassidism from a New York Synagogue. For those unfamiliar with Hassidic Jews, they were best described as a separate Jewish community within the Jewish Tribe or family.

They did not mix with those not of their kind and could be a real problem in buses, trains or planes. They prayed loudly, sang and danced around and would not stay in their seats once the seatbelt sign was turned off. The women wore long dresses, head scarves and had lots of kids.

The men dressed in black, sporting traditional side curls, long beards, broad brimmed black hats and with prayer shawls around their tummies were clothed as their ancestors would have been in Eastern Europe some two hundred plus years ago.

They paid absolutely no attention to the limits of cabin carry-on baggage and the overheads would be jam packed. This was OK but every few minutes, they would find the need to open the overhead and retrieve something. Hasidic men would refuse to sit alongside a non-Hasidic woman and would insist that other passengers change places to conform to their wishes.

On arrival in Israel, they took forever to exit the aircraft again with time out for prayers. It was not that I did not respect them for their obvious religious devotion, but just as they were with me, I preferred to have nothing to do with them.

For cabin staff, they must be the proverbial nightmare. These were to be my fellow passengers The check-in young woman burst out laughing and said, "I am an Israeli, and I also would not like to sit in a plane full of these people."

She then said, "according to your papers, you still have one full day before you have to leave the USA. We have another flight tomorrow, which would be better for you, would you like me to put you on that flight?"

"Yes. Please!"

She then told me of a hotel very close to the airport, which was not expensive and provided free pick-up and drops for passengers. Chatted for another couple of minutes when one of the elderly Hassid's came to the counter, so thanked her and headed off to the hotel.

Next morning, a good flight followed and hello again to Tel Aviv. Phoned Hadassah from the airport and told her I would stay at a friend's place in Tel Aviv. She told me to call her when I had arrived there. Did so and she said she would be coming down that evening and I should not go out until she arrived.

We enjoyed a very happy reunion. I told her I had been saving carefully, a bit of a 'white' lie, as I wanted to get enough money so we could go on a holiday to the UK. For some reason, England was the one country away from Israel that she really wanted to visit. I told her my boss had said that in a couple of months I might have another job in Malta.

She told me her sister had gone to live in a kibbutz with her boyfriend, and to avoid spending my savings, and now that my apartment in Tel Aviv had gone, why did I not go back to a kibbutz while waiting for my next work assignment.

Sounded good to me and Hadassah phoned her sister in Kibbutz Beit Alfa who was able to confirm I could go there and work as a volunteer. Hadassah was happy as she could then visit me there.

I Lose My Passport

An English friend on the kibbutz suggested we go into Haifa after work one day, look around and then have a few beers at a club I'd been telling him about and then catch the last bus back to the kibbutz. It turned out we did not need the bus into Haifa as a kibbutz truck was going in and we hitched a ride with them.

Walking around Haifa was tiring as it was built on the steep sides of Mount Carmel and after a while, our enthusiasm as tourists had rapidly declined and we decided to stop at a pleasant little bar halfway up Mt Carmel and enjoy a few cold beers.

As is so often the case, a few beers led to a few more until the sun went down and we were already half pissed. Not a problem as the club I had been telling him about only opened at seven o'clock in the evening. It was down near the port and walking downhill was no problem, it was cooler, and in a short time we found the club which had already opened although we were among the first customers.

This club had always been very popular with the 20 something's age group and before long, it started to fill up. We were now drinking Bacardi and coke, which was not the best idea following the number of beers we had drunk. By ten o'clock, we were drunk but were still relatively coherent and knew it was time to head for the bus station if we were to make the last bus. Somehow, we managed this and found seats at the back of the bus.

That was the last I remember of the bus ride. I woke up, cold, confused, and wondering where the hell I was. During the ride, I had either moved intentionally or otherwise to the long back seat of the bus, laid down and passed out. I had then fallen off the seat and rolled back underneath it.

It was not until my friend had got off the bus and looked around for me that he realised I must still be on the bus, which by then was disappearing into the night. As there was nothing he could do about it, he walked back into the kibbutz and crashed out.

Meanwhile, the bus had reached the terminal in Beit Shean. A quick glance by the driver would have shown an empty bus as his only remaining passenger was concealed under the back seat. Sometime later, waking up in total darkness, where was I? Slowly, it all came back to me, and I badly needed a piss.

I remembered seeing a bus driver open a door by pressing a small button on the base of the door, but on the outside of the door. Could there be a similar button on the inside? Thankfully, there was and the door opened. Relief as I whipped out 'willy' and drained my bladder.

It was 4:30am in Beit Shean, which was very close to the Syrian Border, not a good time to be wandering around as for sure there would be security prowling and the last thing I needed now was to get shot at. Played it safe, got back in the bus and waited for daylight. Dawn broke and with it, life returned to the bus terminal. Shortly after caught a bus, which dropped me at the entrance to Beit Alfa.

Just in time to change into my work clothes and grab a breakfast. Took out my wallet to see how much, or how little remained after our night out then went to grab my passport from my back pocket. Whoops, oh no, back pocket empty. Went to the dining room met my friend, just in case for some strange reason he had my passport. Nope!

My job for the day was in the apple orchard and I told my supervisor that I thought I might have lost my passport in the Haifa bus. She told me to go to the kibbutz secretary and let him know. This I did and he said to check again as if it was lost, I would have to report it at once to the police in Beit Shean. Did that and was now sure it was missing.

He then said he would drive me into Beit Shean. Filled out the relevant paperwork at the police station and was given a copy of their report. They told me to contact my embassy and let them know what had happened. Why so much concern over a lost passport. Well, there were certainly good reasons.

Israel had always had a security problem with Palestinian terrorists and one thing these people really looked for was 'new' identity. They had experts who could change out a passport photo and personal details on what was an original passport issued by a national government and 'Voila' another identity had been created.

My lost passport was an Australian passport and as such in high demand by terrorist operatives as it was valid for entry into practically all the world's countries. I called the Embassy and told them I would come to Tel Aviv the next day to do whatever was required to obtain a new passport.

Reporting to the Embassy, I got a very cold reception, when in a roundabout way the officer suggested that I might have sold my passport as the 'going rate' for an Australian passport was $400 American dollars. I heatedly denied this. The paperwork completed, the Embassy gave me a date when I could return to pick up the new document.

I asked them if they could give me a letter saying my new passport was being prepared. They said there was no need for this and why did I want one. I told them frequently buses would be stopped, and border police would enter and randomly check all person's identities.

Now I had no identity and as such could be arrested. The Embassy Officer's reply to this was, "if that happens, one of our staff will come and visit you in jail." Thanks, my friend! Happy to say that I made it back to the kibbutz without being required to show any identity.

The roadblocks set up by the police were many, were simple and highly effective. Two heavy metal plates with closely spaced 10 cm high thick protruding spikes were placed across the road. Each plate extended well over half the width of the road.

The plates were placed far enough apart so that a bus or truck could only weave between them at very slow speed. Had a vehicle tried to crash the roadblock, the tyres would have been totally shredded in seconds.

A few weeks later, I got a call from my boss in Freeport to tell me the Malta job had not eventuated, but they would keep me 'on their books' for any future work. They had 38 ships but almost all worked in home waters and as a foreigner, I was ineligible.

Work prospects were decidedly not too rosy when unexpectedly, I got a letter from the chief engineer on the *Cay W*, telling me a school friend of his was the manager for another oilfield boat company and had been put in charge of their newly established London office. If I was looking for work, I should give him a call using my friend Fred as a reference.

Called London, the manager was out of the office, but his secretary confirmed they were looking for people and could I come to London. I had been calling my old company Mediterranean Seaways to see if they had any openings, they didn't, but was also put back on their lists.

Called them again asking if there was any way I could work my passage back to Europe. It was a cheeky move, but they came to the party and a few days later, I sailed out of Haifa on the *Bat Snapir* headed for Marseille. OK, no wages but a big saving for me in eliminating an air ticket expense.

It was now train time. Marseille to Paris, Paris to London and time to knock on the door of Zapata Marine, the company my friend's buddy was now the manager. The company was in the west end of London in a prestigious Curzon Street address.

I was shown in and introduced to Charles the manager. He was seated in an expensive swivel chair with his feet resting on a highly polished table. Not a single file or paper on the desk, only his laptop.

He said, "Hi, Jakob Smith, what can I do for you?"

I said, "One of your friends gave me your name and I phoned your secretary from Israel. She said to call in if I made it to London. Well, here I am and I'm looking for a job."

He said, "Which of my friends was this?"

And I told him, "Fred Brown."

He replied, "That bum calls himself a friend of mine."

He must have seen a worried look on my face as he quickly continued, "Where is Fred these days and by the way, he is an old friend of mine." Phew, there must have been an almost audible sigh of relief on my part, I'd been thinking that in less than two minutes in his office and I'm out on my ass.

The ice broken, we then went on chatting. He was particularly interested in our Arctic work. The secretary brought in coffee, we bullshitted some more when he said, "it's lunchtime, have you been in the Playboy Club before, it's just down the street."

As with all healthy young men, I had read Playboy magazine, got all hot and bothered ogling the gorgeous pictures and wishing my girlfriend of the moment had boobs just like the centrefold model. But been inside a Playboy Club, no I surely had not.

My respect for Charles rocketed when two of the Playboy Bunnies greeted him by name as we went in and were shown to a table. Menu was extensive but with a heavy bias towards American fare and I could see why Charles was obviously a regular customer. We had excellent hamburgers, French fries, as our American friends call chips, all washed down with Coca-Cola.

Meal over, it was back to the office. I'd been with Charles for two hours and so far, no word about a possible job, but that was about to change.

He said, "I'm gonna send you to Nigeria, we have a bunch of boats there. They need people and our Port Manager there is a guy called Bob and he will assign you to a boat."

While we had been talking and then taking lunch, the secretary had prepared a contract for me and all I had to do was sign it, all this when Charles had not even told me I had a job. I needed a work visa to enter Nigeria, and this was to take a minimum of two days. In the meantime, I was booked into a very nice hotel just around the corner from the office.

As I left for the hotel, Charles said, "While you are waiting for your visa and if you feel like lunch again, call into the office at midday as I eat at Playboy every day." No need to be asked twice and I enjoyed two more lunches before heading off to darkest Africa.

Charles gave me a couple of gifts for staff in Nigeria, told me to make sure I bought a bottle of Glen Livet Whisky for the local manager and instructions to buy the latest daily newspapers; English, German, Polish and French for the mixed nationalities of the officers on the boats.

My flights were to be to Paris with British Airways and then with Alia Royal Jordanian Airlines to Lagos/Nigeria. From Lagos, I would fly to Warri with an internal airline. Three different flights.

A Pickpocket Strikes

My flight out of London went to Charles De Gaulle Airport in Paris. I had a four-hour layover there, which suited me as I still had to buy the various newspapers Charles had mentioned.

Found my way to the airport news agency shop and spent some time selecting quite a bundle of different newspapers. So, the guys would have more reading, I had picked the largest of the papers and must have had over five kilos in all. It didn't matter as I was flying business class and the extra carry on was no problem.

Decided to take a coffee on my way to the boarding lounge and went for my wallet to see how many francs I still had. Well, that was easy, I had no francs and no wallet. Minor panic, big body search including my bundle of newspapers, and no wallet found.

Retraced my steps to the news agency, and they confirmed I had not left my wallet on their counter. They directed me to the airport police. They said straight out any money, credit cards, driver's licence or such, which you may have had in your wallet are gone, you will never get them back. The pickpockets that work here, both men and women were experts and often worked as a team, one distracting you or bumping you while the other removed your wallet.

Of course, I was pissed off but still with some admiration for whoever had stolen my wallet. I always kept the wallet in the front right-hand pocket of my jeans, which while not skin-tight, the jeans were close fitting rather than baggy. And someone had managed to get their hand into this pocket, remove the wallet while I was totally unaware of anything untoward.

The police went on to tell me that once a wallet or handbag was stolen, the crooks would immediately remove anything of value and then dispose of the article in a post box or trash bin generally in the airport. I completed the required police paperwork and went on my way. Crime had in this case paid off as there was over $USA 800 in the wallet.

However it was not the end of the story. Some four months later, I received a form from the French Police 'Lost and Found' deposit centre in the airport area advising that they had my wallet, empty apart from my name and phone number, and that I could call and collect it, producing the said form.

My wallet was a 'cheapy' but my curiosity was aroused and I thought if I went back through Paris at the end of my hitch, I'd check out this 'Lost and Found' deposit. I did go back via Paris Charles De Gaulle and I did go to the 'Lost and Found' address.

I gave the form to one of the desk clerks and watched him go into a small open room where there must have been hundreds of wallets. A couple of minutes later, he emerged with my wallet. The final touch was when the clerk then told me precisely in which post office box it had been dumped.

I couldn't help thinking I wished the airport police were as efficient in catching these pickpockets as the lost and found department was in documenting and storing the pilfered items. Arrived in Lagos, a short transfer to a STOL-Short Take Off and Landing aircraft-and proceeded onto Warri, a major port in the Nigerian Offshore Oil industry.

Laden with gifts, I found out that London had forgotten to advise the local manager of my flight schedule, it was just by chance that a company driver was at the airport with a departing crew member. Met Bob the English manager, who was happy to receive his whisky and told me the ship I would join would not arrive until tomorrow and in the meantime, I would stay in the Mid-West Inn.

This hotel was owned and run by Lebanese, was good and had an excellent restaurant. For the first time in my life, I ate frog's legs, and they were good. First thing in the morning, I was picked up and taken to an older vessel, the *Olympic Service*, where I met Captain Harry and chief engineer Hans, the remainder of the crew were Nigerians.

I changed into my work clothes and told Harry I would look around the ship. He said, "There's no hurry, we will load today and sail this evening." I asked him what we were loading, and he told me pipe, but a shore gang would look after this and that I should get ready to go to the Warri Club with him and the engineer for a few beers before coming back to the ship for lunch.

We left the ship at 10:15 for our few beers and arriving at the Warri Club saw that crews off other boats were already there. Star Beer was a Nigerian brew, and it was a good drop. I tried to pay for a round but was told to put my money away as soon I would have plenty of the local Naira currency.

I couldn't help but notice that the other guys were pulling out wads of money from their pockets. The morning pre-lunch session ended at midday, and we all headed back to our ships. Lunch was served, roast beef and Yorkshire pudding and then it was time for a siesta.

If the ship did not sail that afternoon, it would then be back to the Warri Club for the evening session. So far, I had not done any work whatsoever and from what I had experienced on my first day, it looked as though every day spent in port alongside the wharf would follow the same pattern. I enjoyed a beer or two but not every day, morning, noon and night.

I was also to find out that roast beef and Yorkshire pudding was the only English meal our cook was any good at, and that it was the fixed lunch day-in, day-out. Warri was a river port some five hours steaming from the sea. We sailed late afternoon, and I stayed on the bridge with the Captain.

The ship was steered by a local River Pilot, and really no navigation skills were required on our part as his knowledge of the narrow winding river was intimate. Our only concern was when we would have to pass an inbound ship, but the officers all knew each other and would chat away on the radio non-stop.

After two hours steaming, the Captain dropped anchor in the river off a small landing at a place called Bintulu and said we would be staying there for a few hours so I might as well turn in and he would call me if needed. When he did call me, we were just leaving the river into the open sea. This was at Escravos, a name which in the Portuguese language was the word for slaves.

I wondered how many unfortunate captives last sight of their native land was here as the slave traders forced them onto ships bound for the Americas. Harry had set the autopilot on course for the rig we were serving, and it was some 24 hours steaming away. He handed over the sea watch to me but before he left the bridge, I had to tell him that I had found a pile of Nigerian Naira money on the little table beside my bed.

He said, "That's your share Jake, last night we pumped off a little surplus diesel fuel to a local buyer. It will happen all the time. Right now, you can see we are running on just one of our two main engines, and we are only going at half speed. However, as we have to account for our fuel usage to the oil company chartering the ship, we record maximum fuel consumption as though running at full speed using both main engines.

"The weather here is very good with calm conditions 90% of the time, so when we reach the oilrig and tie up, we will stop our engines but still record the fuel consumption as though they were continuously running at a reduced speed."

I said, "Harry, how come the oil companies don't know this?"

He said, "Of course they do but believe me, and you will see it as you spend more time here, they also have their scams."

He then told me that nobody liked to come and work in Nigeria but the money they made from 'fuel deals' eased the burden and for those who saved all or some of their ill-gotten gains, they could in effect take home a considerable 'bonus' at the end of a six-month contract. A lot of the married guys did this, but what about the single men?

It was a little dangerous to go into the town at night by yourself, so usually we would go as a group, and then with a taxi driver we knew and who we would pay to stay with us for the entire night no matter where we might end up. There was a lively casino, run by and probably owned by Lebanese and a lot of the fuel money would go over the roulette or blackjack tables.

There were hookers and plenty of them. Every country had its share of beautiful women and Nigeria was certainly no exception. They were attractive in their long national dresses and head gear and when they decided to go western, well, they had the long legs, firm bosoms and fine features that would be the envy of many women in Europe and the USA.

In short, for many of the large number of expatriate oil field workers, the 'extra' money gained illegally would end up being ploughed back into the economy.

For those who took the trouble and were interested, beautiful wooden carvings were readily available, brought down by the Muslim traders from the north of the country. They were carved out of hardwood and were heavy. Carvings of men's and women's heads and some much more intricate of traditional tribal masks.

Our manager was smart and through local contacts, had assembled a collection of genuine tribal carvings from the Benin region of Nigeria and somehow, as it was illegal to do so, he managed to get them back to the UK. To a collector, they would be extremely valuable and no doubt, he stood to make a lot of money if indeed he chose to sell.

With three months remaining on my contract, I was transferred to another Zapata vessel, the *Marine Service*. Not only was it a change of ship but it was a change of country. We were to depart Nigeria for Pointe Noire/Congo Brazzaville.

My new Captain and Chief Engineer were from Louisiana and Mississippi respectively and they were good people to work with. I was allowed to get on with my job and basically, they were content to sit in one or others' cabin, drink beer or whisky and listen to country music on a very expensive stereo set. As the day progressed, the music got steadily louder.

When we were in Pointe Noire, my first job each day was to go to the duty-free outlet inside the port gate and buy a case of beer and a bottle of Johnny Walker Red Label. Once I had this valuable cargo back on board, I would set about my work.

The local manager did not like their carry-on but was smart enough not to interfere as both had been with company forever and were good buddies with the senior office staff back in Houston.

The chief engineer had some tales to tell. Before coming to sea, he made his living operating moonshine stills in his home county in Mississippi. I told him of my experience being shown how to test the quality of moonshine in Charleston, South Carolina and he said that it was true, if it burnt with a clear blue flame, it was a good brew.

His name was Herbie, and he came to sea after serving a jail sentence for being caught transporting moonshine across the state line. He described at length his pick-up truck that had specially modified suspension to carry heavy loads. He said he had made many trips before getting caught. Herbie was a bottle of whisky a day man and yet never seemed to get really drunk, he would just go to sleep, and the country music would carry on until he came to again.

He had a photo of a very attractive blonde woman on his desk, and I asked him if she was his wife. He said she was his daughter, and the photo was taken just after she had been crowned Miss Mississippi, wow that's a mouthful!

He was serious when he went on to tell me his wife was a wonderful person but unfortunately, she had a drinking problem! She had a drinking problem, come on Herbie, what a couple they must have been!

There was a new bar just outside the port gate and after work, I would stop by for a couple of beers and then head back to the ship. The bar was owned by a Corsican and to bring in the customers, he had a very attractive young barmaid, a French woman born in Algeria.

At no time did he seem to show any concern with her flirting with the customers and I was really hitting it off with her. One night after a few drinks, I left and headed back to the port. I remember nothing more until the following morning when I was woken up by Polish crew members and the Port Gendarmes on a Polish Cargo ship.

At daybreak, when they began opening the ship's hatches, they saw me laying still at the bottom of the cargo hold, thought I must have somehow fallen down during the night and for sure was dead. On this ship, it was a twelve to fifteen metre drop from the deck to the bottom of the hold.

Maybe I should have been dead but instead I was fast asleep and alive. I had somehow managed to climb down a steel rung ladder from the top to the bottom. It was amazing that in my condition I had not fallen. One of the Poles said sorry, but we had to call the police.

I was arrested and taken to the port lock-up. I was being questioned in French and it was not going too well because I simply could not remember anything. I gave them the name of our agent who turned up, money was passed over, and half an hour later, I was back on my ship.

That afternoon, I was talking to a German on a neighbouring tugboat and telling him my story. He then told me the barmaid was in fact the owner's wife and in all probability, some kind of drug had been slipped into my glass and I was very lucky to get off unharmed.

By this time, my contract was up and I was getting ready to leave the ship. I stopped by the country music cabin to say farewell to Herbie and the Captain. I was wearing jeans, which were clean but a little torn. Herbie went to his wardrobe and took out a suit.

He said, "Jake, you can't go all the way to Paris looking like a bum, please take this old suit of mine, it will fit you." I tried hard to thank him and at the same time say no, but he was insistent.

In the end I put it on, and his face lit up. The suit may well have been fashionable at one time, but that was surely a long time ago. I wore it to the airport and changed out again in the toilet.

The Herbie saga had a sad ending. Shortly after I left the ship, he also completed his contract and went back to the USA. Company office staff wanted to get with him to discuss the Congo operation and they put him up in a hotel near the office.

During the night, he woke up to find an intruder in his room, Herbie tried to grab him and was shot dead. As far as I am aware, the culprit has never been apprehended.

A Spell as Relief Manager

My flight back to Paris with Air Afrique was routine and then a connection to London. To my surprise, my next assignment was to relieve Charles in the London office for a short time while he took leave, and as a bonus I could use his membership to the Playboy Club.

I felt like saying, have a good leave, there's no need to hurry back. The handover from Charles was brilliant. "Don't worry about anything, she knows it all and does everything, just keep my desk clear until I get back."

By 'she', he was of course referring to the same secretary I had phoned from Israel and then met six months previously. She was the first person I had ever met who came from the British possession of Gibraltar.

Tall, very good looking and married to a successful lawyer, one had to wonder how and why she came to work for Charles. He made the company big decisions, and she did all the routine work. She had a very posh accent, which was maybe how they all spoke in Gibraltar, and there was a wonderful story going around about her which did sound so like her.

It concerned a job applicant from the north of England, Hull, I think. He had contacted her to see if there were any vacancies. As she did with me, she said he should come to London for an interview. We had several people with his background in that they had come off the British deep sea fishing trawlers when that industry very much died for a number of reasons.

They were amongst the best employees we had as they were used to hard physical work over long periods and found our boats a holiday after what they had been used to fishing in the freezing cold, rough Icelandic and White Sea waters.

They were at home in the fisherman's pubs in their neighbourhoods; however, walking into an upmarket office in the west end of London was a situation in which they did not feel comfortable. The particular applicant is supposed to have entered and stood temporarily tongue tied when this beautiful secretary greeted him by saying, "and who in the fuck are you?"

If she did say this, and the applicant who was later hired by Charles swore she did, I would think it was just her idea of getting back at some of our employees who could not complete a single sentence without at least one swear word, and you know what that word would have been.

Charles came back, my tenure as a big shot behind the manager's desk was over and I was to be reassigned to North Brazil. I knew and liked Brazil, there could have been any number of far worse assignments. Air tickets were provided to Madrid and then onto Rio de Janeiro/Belem, so it was goodbye to London and off I went.

My place of birth was now to cause a problem in Rio de Janeiro with the immigration at the airport. I was born in Wales, a part of the UK and our travel agent had naturally assumed I was British. I was not, I was an Australian arriving in Brazil on an Australian Passport. Now UK citizens did not require a prior visa to enter Brazil while Australians did.

To complicate matters further, I had arrived in the evening of the day before Brazil's annual carnival was to commence. The country shut down for four or five days during this much awaited festival. Very few people work and those that must work, do so very reluctantly and with little interest.

The immigration officers were not a happy lot. They told me, "You will have to go back with Iberian Airlines as they brought you here and they should have checked you had the correct entry visa. Their next flight is in two days, and you cannot leave the airport."

I blatantly lied to the immigration, showing them my onwards ticket to Belem and telling them that Petrobras, the national oil company was expecting me. Petrobras had never heard of me!

No that did not work, immigration said I must get someone to guarantee my stay in Brazil or wait for the return flight. I asked them if they would call the Australian Consulate in Rio as they might guarantee me. I was surprised when they agreed to do this.

I expected the Consulate to be closed for the start of carnival but, halleluiah, the Consul was in but just about to leave his office. I explained my predicament thinking he would say, "Sorry mate, you're on your own for this one," when much to my surprise, he said, "I'll come to the airport and see if we can sort things out." True to his word, an hour or so later he bowled up.

To this day, I can see his face. He was an elderly man, and his opening words were, "let's get a beer and you can tell me what's going on." We finished the beer and he said, "Now, let's sort these blokes out."

A guarantee I needed, a guarantee I got. By this time, it was mid-afternoon and my flight to Belem did not leave until seven in the evening and the Consul said, "how about another beer?" Too good, this was just too good!

It turned out that he was having problems of his own and I think just wanted a shoulder to cry on. He told me he had been in Rio by himself for six months as his wife had hated the city and had returned to Australia. In the meantime, he had fallen madly in love with a Brazilian woman. Now his wife had decided to come back. He did not know what to do.

He said his marriage had been dead for years, the two children were grown up, had completed university and were beginning careers. He said maybe the only way out was a divorce and even though that would financially ruin him, it might be the best solution.

What did I think? I was, to use that familiar English expression, 'gob smacked'. This was a sad and worried man. Well, he asked for an opinion so I had better say something. I suggested he tell his wife the city she so disliked had not changed any and she should reconsider returning. He should tell her he still really enjoyed living in Rio and if she did come back, he asked her to please not bring up all the arguments they had previously had.

He liked the beach, he liked going to the football, and he still had the same friends she previously did not like. I suggested he get a small rental apartment for his girlfriend and restrict her coming to his place, which was paid for by the Australian Consulate. He should visit his wife in Australia as his job allowed and try and give his new relationship in Brazil time to either work out or fail.

I said divorce would not be a good option and he should work towards an amicable separation. I steered clear of asking him the most important question, "How old is your girlfriend?" I did not want to hear that she was in her twenties while he was obviously in his fifties.

We parted, he back to his girlfriend and carnival celebrations and me on my four-hour flight to Belem. My role as a marriage councillor completed. Touched down in Belem, which was right on the equator, de-planed, entered the terminal and looked around for a driver holding up my name. No luck. Brazilians are so often late. I sat down to wait.

It was now midnight. Half an hour later, it was apparent my company had not been given my flight information. What to do, the airport was practically deserted. Well, taxi into the centre of town, an area I knew previously and find a hotel. Looked for something cheap and found a hotel down at the bottom of President Vargas, the main street. In better days, the hotel might have enjoyed a two-star rating.

Carnival had just kicked off and the streets were filled with people. In the background, the endless sound of Samba music throbbed away. Checked into the hotel but there was no way I was going to bed just yet, carnival was calling. I wandered down the street, just soaking up the atmosphere until eventually, next door to a luxury hotel, I saw the entrance to what looked a smart night club with a uniformed flunky on the door.

Went in and the place was packed. It seemed like all the tables were full, the only empty seats had drink glasses in front of them indicating the occupants were on the dance floor. Well, I would just have to look and wait when a woman motioned me over. She indicated an empty chair next to her and I grabbed it.

She spoke a little English and when the waiter came to the table, she was more than happy to accept a drink. She was small and looked Chinese. She asked my name and told me she was Sonja. OK at least we now had the basic introductions out of the way.

Of course, she wanted to dance, a painful exercise for me but the dance floor was so crowded, dancing meant little more than holding each other closely and shuffling around. She only just came up to my shoulder and the perfume she had in her long black hair was very sensual.

I ordered another round of drinks and told the waiter the Chinese woman wanted a vodka lime. He said she is 'Nisei' not Chinese and then in reasonable English, he explained she was Japanese not Chinese, her parents' Japanese immigrants and that their children born in Brazil were called 'Nisei', which was apparently not a derogative term.

I was enjoying the club but was starting to get tired and in my mind, I was trying to rustle up some basic Portuguese words to ask her if she would like to meet me tomorrow when she suddenly lifted up her blouse.

No bra, of course she was a hooker, and I had no idea. She started laughing, put one hand on the side of her head and closed her eyes for a second. Message received; I did the same, so I was going to have company on the first night of carnival.

And so back to the hotel. Without really understanding what either of us was saying, we were hitting it off and entering the room. I leapt onto the double bed. A bad move, as one of the legs promptly gave way. Turned the bed frame on its side and propped it up against the wall, mattress on the floor and our honeymoon suite was ready.

The following morning, I told her I would have to try and find my company's office as I did have their address. She said she knew where it was and would come with me. Meanwhile, carnival was in full swing. Those like us who had had some sleep had now woken up and were ready to continue partying. I was to find out this was to continue unabated for the next three days.

We found the office which was closed, a sign on the door in both Portuguese and English telling anyone that was interested that it was closed for carnival and would reopen in a further three days. Told her I would go to Petrobras, the national oil company to see if they could help out as I would be indirectly working for them. They could call my manager as they must have his home phone number.

Their office was open, only just open, with a skeleton staff and the desk guys comment I guess was typical, "It's carnival, go and enjoy and come back in three days."

Now I had to pay this young lady for services rendered and see how much was left for the next three days. Showed her my wallet and told her I still had some dollars in the hotel, but this would have to last the next three days. She was not worried, she said, "you can give me some money after carnival, can you pay the hotel until then?" Did this and she said, "You give me some money and I will pay for our food and drinks as they won't cheat me."

OK, but handing over much of my remaining money, I thought if she disappeared, I'm in big trouble. I shouldn't have worried, she was as good as her word and when our office finally re-opened, I was able to pay her. And I now had a girlfriend, no doubt shared with many other guys, but who cared, so she was a hooker, she was also a nice person and she had taught me some more Portuguese.

Our company manager was apologetic, telling me that it was only when he opened the office, he realised that he had a new crew member and one who had now been in town for four days. I told him I had enjoyed carnival and he relaxed and became friendly.

My marine qualifications were British and I had been sent to Brazil to join one of our British flag vessels as they required officers with national licences. And so, I was sent to the 'Paramount Service'.

My new Captain was a youngish guy sitting on his swivel chair with his right foot raised on to the settee. "A touch of gout, excuse me if I don't get up," were his opening words. I thought to myself, hello here's another drunk!

He was a very good Captain, but I was only to do one trip with him as his gout flared up worse than ever and he had to get off. Apparently, it can be a very painful affliction. To add to this, the ship had developed a major engine problem and would require a technician to fly out from the UK. Meanwhile, the charterer temporarily put the ship off hire until repairs could be carried out.

Also, we now needed another Captain. Due to our British flag, the Captain had to be either British or from a Commonwealth country and hold a licence accordingly. They were few and far between and our London office was having trouble finding a suitable applicant. And Captain Truman turned up.

The manager brought him down to the ship and the officers gathered in their mess room to meet him and hear a bit about him. The London office must have been desperate as he had never been on board an oilfield vessel before. These ships were different in so many ways from standard commercial vessels.

With everybody listening, Captain Truman began by saying that he had been on a large tug before, in fact it was his last command. Then he should have kept his mouth shut, but no, he had a story to tell, and he was going to tell it. His tug had been hired to tow a ship from Singapore to a shipyard in India.

He continued, "Had a bit of bad luck, my tow wire broke and when I tried to reconnect it, I 'bumped' the ship I had been towing and unfortunately, it sank. However, we managed to pick up their crew from a life raft just after she sank so no lives were lost."

You could see disbelief on the faces of our guys. Our manager then said, "if you have any problems handling this vessel, get Jake on the bridge he can assist you as he is familiar with this ship."

As he was leaving, the manager motioned for me to follow him and once out on deck, he told me he was going to call London, request an immediate replacement for Captain Truman and that if he had to manoeuvre the ship at all, I was to be on the bridge with him at all times. Our repairs were dragging out and our ship stayed at anchor off the Petrobras company wharf.

Captain Truman was sent back to the UK and his relief arrived. In fact, he arrived in some style. The chief engineer and I were sitting in the mess room one evening around eight o'clock when the door to the outside deck opened and this voice from the darkness said, "I say, could someone please come and help me with my butterfly net?"

Captain Thistlethwaite had arrived on board. A small launch had brought him from the wharf to the ship. I went to the door and sure enough was handed a butterfly net attached to a long handle. As the door opened onto the main deck, the step into the mess room was a high one to avoid sea water coming in during bad weather.

I had turned around and moved away from the door when there was a sickening crash. Captain Thistlethwaite had now entered the ship. He had tripped and fell face forward onto the mess room deck. It was a two-point landing, right arm and nose, the nose now gushing blood.

Went to assist him to his feet, when he said, "Don't touch my arm, I think it is broken." He had got that almost right, it was his wrist that was broken, not his arm. The odd angle of his nose indicated that it too was broken. The chief engineer called the manager and then passed the phone to me. The manager's name was Danny and I told him we had a hospital case on our hands.

If he agreed, I would have our crew call the Petrobras launch so we could take him back to the wharf. He said, "Go ahead. I'll be down in a few minutes and will run him to hospital as I'll have to post a deposit before they will admit him. Send his belongings with him and make out the incident report for me by tomorrow morning."

Told him OK and said, "Danny, when you get this incident report, you are going to want to frame it."

And again, now we were going to need another Captain! This being the third time in as many weeks; surely this time, we would strike it lucky. It was not to be. Captain 'Red' Russell had arrived. He was a Canadian from Vancouver Island.

He immediately took charge, telling the assembled crew, "I run a tight ship and expect you all to do your best. Apparently, this ship has a bad name with management and with our charterer, so working together we are going to change this."

It was an impressive address and after he had departed, one of the engineers said, "I thought of saying Rah, Rah, Rah at the end of it but thought better not."

A few days later, the technician had completed his work and our main engines were back online. We pulled up our anchor and did an engine trial, running up and down the river for an hour or so. Our Manager Danny was advised, and he passed the news onto the Charterer Petrobras. We returned to anchor and the technician got off.

It was around two o'clock in the afternoon when Danny called back and told the Captain he should berth alongside the wharf. We would load fresh water overnight and in the morning, Petrobras would load deck cargo and we would sail.

Once our ship's anchor was up, I went to the bridge which was normal, only to be told that my place was on deck with the seamen not on the bridge, so go down on deck! The chief engineer had also come to the bridge and the Captain told him, "what are you doing here, we have just had repairs, and you should be in the engine room when we are tying up, so please go to the engine room."

Our ship was 78 metres long and the wharf we were to tie up to was 110 metres long. Plenty of space for these types of vessels, which by their very nature were highly manoeuvrable providing the operator knew what he was doing. The berthing operation should take no more than 10 minutes.

An hour and a half later, Red called me to the bridge. So far, the closest he had got to the wharf was 15 meters off. He was manoeuvring very carefully, very slowly and going nowhere.

He said, "The current is very strong and I'm having problems. I want you to watch the wharf and keep giving me distance off as I move in."

I could see he had no idea and although likely that it would probably upset him worse, I said, "Red, I have driven boats like this many times; if you like I will show you, it is not difficult, and you are going about it completely in the wrong way. You are fighting the current when you should be using it to assist you."

I thought he would really get mad but instead he said, "Go ahead, but you are aware that if you do any damage, it will come back on me."

I told him, "not to worry, just watch me so next time, you will know what to do."

We tied up. Not so much as a thank you or get fucked from Red, he told me to go and start loading the fresh water. The next day, Petrobras loaded our deck to the maximum and set our sailing time for 9 o'clock that evening. I would normally go to the bridge an hour prior to sailing to test all the equipment and stand by to accept control of the various engines when the duty engineer phoned to tell me he was ready.

Once again, 'Red' was in a grumpy mood and asked me why I was on the bridge. I told him and he said he would do this and that I should go down with the crew, let go and then come to the bridge to watch the radar while he took the ship down the river.

I was on the bow or front of the ship as we let go. I had a VHF radio for communication with 'Red'. We let go the mooring ropes and with a few bumps against the wharf, we were off. Ahead of us, though with plenty of clearance room were several small Petrobras craft and a large barge with a big crane on it. There was ample space for us to manoeuvre.

Red was going too fast, and I called him, requesting we slow down until clear of the anchored vessels. No response. I asked the bridge for a radio check in case my handset was out. No response from Red but the Brazilian Second Officer who was on the stern of the ship confirmed my radio was OK.

Called the bridge urgently to tell Red to alter course to port (left) as he was going too close to the crane barge. Again, no reply. Called the bridge to request engines to full astern as the crane barge was now ahead of us and advised that I was ready with our ship's anchor. No response but the ship did start to swing to port. Too little, too late and he had not slowed down at all, collision with the barge now inevitable. Crash!

This barge was almost as big as our ship. I had already sent the crew quickly off the bow. We careered down the side of the barge when unfortunately, our ship's forward anchor hooked into one of the very heavy wire stays that supported the barge big crane.

Repeated calls to the bridge to stop the ship but to no avail. I ran for cover to the lower deck. With the crane barge 'secured' alongside us, we then cut a swath through the small, anchored boats, I knew we hit at least two of them and their crews sleep on these small craft.

Twang!

The heavy wire stay on the crane barge had parted, and now finally Captain Red stopped the ship. I headed up to the bridge. He said, "We will continue out to the oilrig."

I told him, "no way Captain, there will be a massive inquest into this incident and if you continue, you will face arrest and possibly prison."

The chief engineer was now on the bridge and heard what I had said. I continued, "Captain, we must return to the wharf immediately, shall I berth the vessel?" He said nothing but motioned me to do so.

I could see a number of lights on the small boats and the crane barge and was just praying nobody had been hurt. We tied up and I asked the Captain if he would please come with me to check on any damage to our vessel. He replied, "No, you go ahead."

There was a gash in the steel plating on the hull some two meters above the water. It was some 6 meters long and it looked like some giant had attacked the ship with a huge can opener. I reported back to 'Red' and asked him if he had called the manager. He said no and he would wait until morning.

I said, "Sorry Captain, but if you won't call him, then I will as for sure the charterer will also call him if they have not already done so." He did not answer.

By this time, it was after midnight. A sleepy Danny answered the phone. Told him better pour a stiff drink as my news was all bad. Told him quickly what had happened and the damage to us and that the ship in its present condition was not seaworthy.

Assured him there would be big claims from Petrobras and our only concern was for any injuries or worse to any of the Petrobras crews on the small craft. He asked to speak to 'Red'. I told him he did not want to come to the phone and would see you first thing in the morning.

Danny asked if 'Red' had been drinking, I told him I did not believe so. Danny asked what he was doing now. I said, "He told me he would go to his cabin and pack his bags, so guess that is what he's about."

Danny said I should tell all the crew not to say anything to Petrobras. Told him OK but for sure, the Brazilians would no doubt ignore this. Went down to 'Red's' cabin to inform him I had spoken to the manager. He was not packing his bags but was putting on his dress clothes. He said, "Don't you guys go to a little bar just outside the gate if you want a beer?"

I told him, "Yes, it's open around the clock, and I'm going there right now with one of the engineers for quiet beer."

Red asked if he could come with us. Told him, "Sure, but no need to get dressed up as it's kind of a rough dive."

As it turned out, we three were the only customers. 'Red' was a completely different man, he said, "I know I will be fired tomorrow so at least I can enjoy a beer or two in Brazil before I have to leave." It was as though the events of the past few hours had simply not happened.

He then wanted us to go with him to the whorehouses in the nearby village of Icoraci, he was determined to party. I told him, "No way. I will have a very busy day tomorrow," but the engineer said he would keep him company and off they went.

Managers in oilfield related companies had considerable responsibility but generally an easy life. They received a reasonable salary and if they were smart, and a 'tiny' bit dishonest, they could forward their complete monthly pay cheques straight into their bank accounts with no need to dig into their 'hard earned'.

Good or even high standard accommodation was provided, a quality car was a part of the package and if they had children of school age then all the educational expenses were taken care of. Every month, they must supply substantial food orders to the boats operating in their area of management and invariably they would have the supplier, or ship chandler as they were known, deliver their home needs, which of course were charged off to the fleet. Home needs, I should add included alcohol and cigarettes. Just some of the 'perks' of being a manager.

However, there were days when they really had to earn their wages, and when our manager Danny came on the boat early next morning, he knew that this was going to be one of those days.

I had been to the Petrobras workers canteen first thing in the morning, and they told me that one small un-crewed boat had been sunk and there had been damage to other vessels but not a single crew member had been injured. That was the only good news I had for Danny as he headed off for the confrontation meeting with our charterer Petrobras.

He lied, telling them one of the engines that had been repaired had failed resulting in the Captain losing control of the ship. It was probably about the only thing he could say though the incident report to our company would tell a very different story.

Danny told us the results of the meeting. To start with, they did not like the ship due to the engine problems and this was really 'the last straw'. There was a small island in the river about half a mile from the wharf. Their marine manager told Danny to anchor the ship behind the island so it could not even be seen from the office and keep it there until it was either 100% operational or was replaced by another vessel, which he was now actively searching.

Danny told me to prepare the two reports, charterer and our company, and give them to him. I said that 'Red' should do this and was told that 'Red' when asked, had said, "I'm fired, by contract terms, I now must pay my ticket home, so fuck the reports!"

Now the ship had to be taken from the wharf to the 'hidden' anchorage. Danny told me to do this. I told him this was not a problem, but I would have to talk to the British Engineers first to see if it was OK by them as my licence was not as a Captain, the ship was British and the engineers English. They gave me the OK and we returned to anchor.

Zapata had a small Panama flag ship working out of Belem and the Captain there had just resigned. My licence could be 'stretched' to cover this, and I asked Danny could I have a transfer. He said he would think about it but really, he needed my British licence for the two British flagships he was managing.

The engineers had told Danny that according to their contract agreements, he would have to supply a launch daily at 6pm, midnight and again at 7am while the vessel stayed at anchor. He checked and sure enough, they were right.

All in all, our trips to the bars were now even better than when we were at the wharf. There at the client's base it was forbidden to bring girls through the gates as security would not let them in. But the launch service operated from their own small jetty, no security, no problems, girls welcome.

We were coming back one night. I was still with my 'Nisei' girl, and we would go to the bar where she worked. There two of our engineers had picked up a couple of girls and with six of us in a cab intended for just four persons, we were on our way back to the launch jetty.

The second engineer had picked up a real honey, she was absolutely beautiful. Now what transpired in a packed taxi was scary. Halfway back to the jetty, the pretty girl had an epileptic attack, leaned over the driver's seat and bit him on the neck. Not only bit him but would not let go. Fortunately, he did not crash and brought the taxi to a stop. We all piled out and by this time, although only seconds had elapsed, she had slumped over the seat.

We sat her on the ground, the other girls watching her, and we discussed what to do. First, we had to deal with an irate driver. This not a problem in Brazil as a few extra banknotes would quieten him down and his neck had only bled a little. As for the girl who had now come to, the second engineer would take her back to the bar with my girl as an escort, drop her and they would then come back, pick us up and continue to the jetty.

By this time, we had a good understanding with the launch drivers and for a very small extra payment, they would pick us up or drop us at any time after midnight, only the 6pm/7am trips remained as scheduled.

My girl Sonja asked her did she have any medicine, as although we thought she had had an epileptic fit, we were still a bit unsure as it might been some sort of a drug overdose. She produced the medicine and showed Sonja. Apparently for epilepsy, these pills must be taken at regular intervals, and she had forgotten.

We had all chipped in a few bucks for her so her night's earnings would be OK. The now pacified driver headed off and the taxi was back in less than half an hour.

Next morning, Danny called on the radio and said I should get packed as he was sending me to the small boat as Captain, with no increase in salary, and he just laughed when I told him, "Danny that's kind of mean, come on!"

A typical manager's reply, "now if you're not happy, you can stay on the 'Paramount Service'."

My short reply. "I'm good Danny, thank you."

The Territory of Amapa
A Jungle Wilderness

The boat I had requested to join was a fast crew boat. These boats were used to transfer crews to and from the oilrig being serviced. It was fast and in calm seas, sped along easily at something like 40 kph. It could carry 72 passengers who sat in reclining aircraft seats in one large main cabin. However, we normally would carry 32 persons, a mix of both foreigners and Brazilians.

The boat was constructed from aluminium, which is enormously strong and being comparatively light was an essential factor contributing to our speed. It also meant that if we were pushing into any sort of head sea, the boat could be thrown around quite violently.

All the passengers had aircraft seat belts, which as a part of our safety briefing, we told them, "Unless you are going to the WC, please keep your seatbelt on at all times." They soon learnt to do this. Driving the boat from the small wheelhouse, I had full harness like those worn by racing car drivers.

My crew were all locals from Brazil and their leader Mario, I was later to find out, was a big shot in the local mafia, it was always handy to know someone 'connected'.

We were scheduled to make one trip a month in and out of Belem. It was 432 nautical miles to the rig (700 km) and depending on the weather, it could take us up to thirty hours. Full of fuel, we had a 20% safety factor so better not to get lost! As mentioned, it was at best long rough ride for the rig workers and the seasick bags in the pockets in front of the seats were certainly in demand.

The seasickness however provided us with a real bonus. Before leaving Belem, the oil company would provide us with properly packed pre-cooked meals for the passengers. These only had to be heated up and 'voila' a tasty meal ready to go. If we served 10% of these meals that would be all, the remainder neatly stashed in our fridge would supplement our diet for days.

Arriving at the rig, the passengers would be offloaded into a 'Billy Pugh' personnel basket named after its designer. It was a cone shaped basket connected to one of the rig crane wires. From the deck of the boat, the basket was lifted some thirty metres into the air before being swung over the rig and set down.

Three passengers at a time would cling to the outside rope netting on the basket with their luggage stowed in the centre. Now some of these guys had been chronically seasick since leaving Belem.

If I had not seen it with my own eyes, I would never have believed that a person's face could go a grey green colour as a result of seasickness. It could. We had to tie some of the worst cases into the centre of the basket; they were physically so exhausted, and these were tough oil field workers.

For the remainder of the month, we then had to make regular trips into the Amapa River, which was a twelve-hour run from the rig. The charterers had secured an old barge to trees at the edge of the jungle, and we would tie up alongside this barge to discharge our passengers.

They would then send a Hughes 500 helicopter, which could land on the barge and take three passengers at a time for a ten-minute run into the township of Amapa. In World War II, the Americans had built a long runway in Amapa for military use and now decades later, it was still very usable.

Full rig crew changes took place every 28 days but there were many smaller crew changes in between. When not running back and forth to the rig, we would stay tied up to the barge. Petrobras had a man permanently based in Amapa Town and he quickly came up with the idea that every Friday morning, he would like us to leave the barge and head up the narrow river into the town. It was a six-hour run and as the Amapa River was shallow in places, we had to make the trip at high tide.

With the small helicopters set up to make the trip from the barge to the Amapa airstrip, I could not understand why he now wanted the boat to make this trip into the township. I was soon to find out. It was nothing to do with his operational duties; he wanted us in Amapa on Friday so we could pump off diesel fuel to supply a small generator in the town square. This to provide the power and lighting for the Friday night weekly dance.

Our first trip into the town was uneventful and quite exciting as the river was very narrow in places with no more than a few metres clearance on either side from the dense undergrowth along the river banks. Our client was on the tiny rickety town wharf when we arrived and turned out to be a really nice guy.

We became good friends and several trips later, I asked him if his transfer to a remote jungle base, Amapa, was simply a step-up in the promotional ladder with his company. He laughed and told me it was the opposite. He had been stationed in South Brazil as a deputy manager, 'learning the ropes', when he had been caught screwing his boss's wife. An immediate transfer followed, and he said he was lucky not to have lost his job.

The dance was the social event of the week in the small township and girls from the surrounding jungle came into town for the big night. Some beautiful young women among them, many with very indigenous Indian features. Small in stature, skin colour varying from very light 'creamy' complexions to dark golden brown, wearing vividly coloured dresses, poor make up lavishly applied, and literally bathed in cheap perfume, they were shy, sexy and in a word, totally desirable

As the night progressed and the beer and cachaca flowed, couples would disappear for intimate moments. We had a big advantage in that we had an air-conditioned boat at our disposal just a short walk away from the action.

Cachaca, Brazil's national drink was made from freshly fermented sugarcane juice and with a 40% proof alcohol content could be a very potent drop. Being cheaper than beer it was very popular, either drunk straight in shot glasses or mixed with ice, lemon and some soft drinks. It came in numerous brands and prices depending on quality. The best cachaca was smooth on the throat.

'Caipirinha', the best-known mixed drink was made up of crushed limes, brown sugar, ice, cachaca added to suit and was hugely popular. The cheapest varieties were as 'rough as guts' and popular opinion said that in a real emergency, it could be used in place of petrol in your car. Maybe, although I had never heard of anyone who had done this!

The dance would carry on into the early hours of the morning, when those sober enough would wend their way unsteadily homewards while some of the more serious drinkers would sleep where they had passed out. For a couple of days after, the smell of the girls' perfume would linger throughout our boat.

Our Friday night in town became a complete weekend unless the oilrig called us out. We got to know the townspeople who were very friendly. The kids made a point of coming to the boat when their school for the day was over and most often accompanied by their teacher. He was originally from the far south of Brazil and had found his way to Amapa due to a highly unusual and indeed lucrative pastime. He was the only teacher in the school with students from ages 6 through to 16.

His hobby was collecting venom from poisonous snakes which he then sent to Sao Paulo where it was used to make antivenin to treat snake bite victims. He explained most of the snakes he sought were nocturnal and invited me to go along with him on one of his outings.

When I heard these snakes were out at night, I asked him if they ever came into the township itself and he told me it was not unusual for them to do so. What he was looking for were basically three types. Coral Snakes, Bushmasters and Fer de Lance. All were very poisonous with both the Bushmaster and Fer-de Lance having nasty reputations for being aggressive.

Although he carried phials of antivenin with him, I declined his invitation, there was just something about snakes that scared the shit out of me! He told me of a time that a Fer-de Lance had come into a house in town, chased one of the occupants inside her own living room and then without biting her, disappeared into a drain on her balcony.

He had been called and came ready to catch the offender, but a delegation of townsfolk would not let him do so. They had mixed up cement and blocked off the drain, trapping the snake inside. When he argued with them, they told him if he caught and released the snake, it might return to the house again.

I asked him if that made any sense as it might take quite some time before the snake died in the drain. Surprisingly, he told me it was indeed possible. He said the snake had come into the house, seeking rats or mice and could well return if assisted to escape.

So much for that snake story but there were two more coming out of our sojourn in Amapa. One Saturday morning, when we were still at the rickety town wharf, I got an urgent wakeup call from an old villager. I could not fully understand him, just the word 'cobra', which in Portuguese means snake. My crew were jabbering nonstop, and I understood that somebody had been bitten. I sent one of the crew to get the schoolteacher and the charterer representative.

By this time, the man had been recovered from the water and was stretched out on the back deck of the boat. He had not been bitten, at least not by a venomous snake but had suffered a broken collarbone when an anaconda had overturned his fishing canoe and grabbed him. His right arm had some nasty lacerations where the snake had attempted to sink its teeth in.

The school teacher arrived and told me what had probably happened. He said that it was certainly the work of an Anaconda or smaller Boa Constrictor and probably not a fully grown one. He confirmed that there were plenty of Anacondas in the area, but they were rarely sighted and although he had heard of attacks on humans, this was the first time he had seen evidence of this.

These snakes kill their prey by wrapping their coils around their target and squeezing them to death. However, to get leverage to begin constricting or squeezing, they fasten their teeth into their victim. Both Anacondas and Boa Constrictors have rows of long, sharp hook-shaped teeth angled backwards down their jaw so that once they sink their teeth into whatever it is they are attacking, it was very difficult for this unfortunate to escape.

The fisherman confirmed that the moment he managed to shake loose from the snake's bite, it simply released him and vanished back into the water. He was a very lucky man. His canoe, still upside down had drifted into the riverbank and was laying in the mud.

When we were back on station at the barge, we would shine our searchlight into the thick undergrowth and protruding trees, looking for wild geese or ducks. They would always roost for the night high up in the trees. Many were a very bright pink colour; I was later to find out that these were flamingos. There was always the chance we might see some animal life, small deer, wild pigs, and if exceptionally lucky, perhaps sight a jaguar or ocelot. We never saw an animal one!

There were always lots of fireflies around and huge swarms of mosquitoes, and moths. One night, I commented to one of the seamen who was with me that there were two very stationary, tiny bright red lights in undergrowth close to the side of the barge. The sailor told me they were snake's eyes and that he and the others had quite often seen the same in the glare of the searchlight.

We had a single barrel shotgun on the boat, which we had bought to shoot ducks. Now with a supposed snake just metres from our boat, I loaded up and 'bang'. The red eyes disappeared. We were using cartridges for ducks which should have been fine for snakes.

When daylight came, we walked across the barge and sure enough, here was a yellowish-brown snake, about a meter long draped across a prickly bush. We prodded it with a long pole, and it was dead alright. We scooped it onto the barge.

We had no idea what kind of snake it was, and it wasn't until a very close examination that we found out a single shotgun pellet had hit it almost between the eyes, apparently instantly killing it.

We wrapped it up in plastic and put in the fridge to show the teacher in Amapa so he could identify it. This he did after scolding us for killing it unnecessarily as it was a member of the python family and non-venomous.

I always felt guilty shooting flamingos as they were such beautiful birds, but in our defence, they did make a welcome variation to our diet.

Jaguars and Ocelots

I had always been fascinated by big cats. Siberian tigers probably my favourite.

As a youngster, one of our neighbours in Sydney was from South Africa. When I was just six years old, her grandmother came on an extended visit and when she learnt this little pest of a boy living next door was interested in wildlife, she was more than happy to sit me down and tell me stories of the Africa she loved so much.

Her husband, long passed away, had been a big game hunter operating safari for the very wealthy and as a young wife, she had travelled with him until her children came along.

I was asking her about lions one day, and how they were the kings of the jungle, when she abruptly interrupted me and told me that was nothing more than a myth. The king of the African Jungle was the leopard; never the lion, never.

She went on to tell me that for the big game hunters in the past, a leopard was the ultimate prize as being solitary animals, they were difficult to find, and then get close enough for their client to shoot and claim his trophy. She said some of these clients, despite having the best guns money could buy, were sometimes not the best shots and would end up wounding the animal. A wounded animal could never be left, and it was then up to the safari leader to track and finish off the beast.

Old Granny told me this was not a big deal with wounded lions but was extremely dangerous with a wounded leopard. She told of one such instance when a wounded leopard being followed was able to lose his trackers, double back and attack them, killing one of the trackers and seriously wounding the safari leader himself, before perhaps sadly, it was killed.

Brazil had just the one species of big cats and they were magnificent animals. The English name was the Jaguar while in Brazil, they were called Oncas. They could grow up to two metres in length and weigh well over 100 kilos. They were very similar to the African leopards but had a slightly 'chunkier' appearance rather than the very sleek look of their African counterparts.

They were excellent climbers and swimmers. There were three colour variations, buff colour like the American mountain lions, 'painted' or pintada as they were known in Brazil, which had the almost identical markings to the leopard and black or preta to give them their Brazilian name.

As far as I know, a jaguar female could give birth to cubs of any of the three colours as they were the one species. The painted/pintada variety were the most common, the most attractive and featured on Brazilian currency banknotes.

My favourites were the black jaguars who with their amber-green coloured eyes had a definite menacing appearance. When seen in bright sunlight with black jaguars, it was possible to see feint painted markings beneath the glossy black coat. Truly superb animals.

There was also quite a common, much smaller wild cat known in the western world as an ocelot and in Brazil as a 'Gato Maracaja'. They were about the size of a medium size dog and had almost identical markings as leopards. If obtained when they were very young, they were easily domesticated. They were well known in the Amapa region, and I asked the locals if they came across any young ones, I would very much like to buy one.

They had a couple of fully grown ones in the town, which were very tame. These animals were illegally hunted for their skins and that was how the locals got the young ones after their mother had been shot by poachers.

Just a few weeks later, one of the townsfolk came onto the boat and told me they had not one but two of these cats for sale and would I like to look at them. I was excited and with one of my seamen, I rushed off with them to a hut at the edge of the village. They had two cats alright, but they were not ocelots but half-grown jaguars.

They were in a heavily constructed wooden cage with reinforced steel bars in front. When we neared the cage, they growled and snarled angrily, baring their teeth. My seaman gave me a very worried look and said, "Captain, not a good idea to take on the boat."

They were a male and a female and the owners were asking an equivalent of 500 US dollars for the pair. Had to tell them I wanted a young ocelot not semi matured jaguars, so they dropped their asking price further. Although there was no way I could keep them, I was wondering how I could get them onto the boat, take them down to the barge and then release them back into the wild.

They were already being fed fish and meat offal. I could have raised the money, but two things stopped me. My crew totally vetoed having them on the boat no matter how good their cage was and the owners told me that if released back into the jungle, they would almost certainly starve to death as they had never learnt how to hunt for their food.

The school teacher knew of them and was trying to have them legally sold either to Sao Paulo where, through his snake venom business, he had good contacts, or to a zoo in the USA. I do hope he succeeded as apparently, they were in the money discussion stage with Sao Paulo, and with a zoo in California.

On our next long voyage down to Belem, I was given an assistant or second Captain in the form of Jimmy Rogers from Texas. My crew of five Brazilians was reduced to four, but it was nice to have another person I could converse with in English.

Jimmy was a good friend with one of the Houston office staff and had just retired after twenty years' service in the US navy where he had been a submariner. The transition from the military to the offshore oilfield was a big step as in many instances, the only thing we had in common was that we were all seafarers. Jimmy had been in communications in the navy, was eager to learn his new job and was good to work with, plus a very talkative person.

He told me lots of navy tales, some of which I think he should have kept quiet about whatever! We returned to our barge in the river and life carried on as previously, the Friday trips into Amapa had now become a routine event. Approaching the township of Amapa, the last few kilometres of the river were very shallow in places to where we had to pass over these areas only at high tide.

Transiting small shallow rivers in the Amazon region has one very common hazard, hitting sunken logs. Logging was a big industry, both legal and increasingly illegal and the logs cut down in the jungle were then dragged to the nearest river and floated down to a point where they could then be loaded onto cargo vessels.

The more valuable logs were hardwood, which would not float unless supported. Special rafts were constructed to ferry these logs downstream, but inevitably some rafts would break up and the heavy logs would sink to the bottom, and there they would stay.

On what was to be our final trip up the river, we hit a submerged log or logs. The impact damaged both of our ship's propellers, bending the blades out of true and breaking off the tip of one of the blades. The effect of this was that instead of the ship running smoothly through the water, the damaged propellers now caused excessive vibration on the stern of the vessel.

We could now only run at very slow speed to minimise the vibration and we got orders to go back to Belem and dry-dock for repairs. A big farewell party in Amapa so with the usual hangovers and the final sweet smell of the girls' perfume throughout the boat, we said goodbye to this quaint little river port.

It was not to be a simple navigation exercise. Our ever-reliable GPS navigation system, which normally pinpointed our position every few seconds chose this precise moment to fail.

Called our office in Belem, found that our manager was conveniently not available and was told by our lovely secretary to call back in a few days. Asked her to arrange a technician and a replacement GPS unit and send both urgently to Amapa and I would head back and wait for them to show up.

Her classic answer was, "I cannot do that, only the manager can authorise this."

I replied, "Then please contact the manager immediately."

And her so Brazilian answer, "his phone is off, and I don't know where he is." For sure, he had picked up a bar girl and had gone into hiding. What to do?

I got with my back-up Jimmy and told him we would just have to go without the GPS being operational. He, being a communications expert had looked at it with no success. He was not happy but as the saying goes, 'we were stuck between a rock and a hard place'.

So the voyage began, fortunately in good weather. Where the mighty Amazon River reached the sea, the outward flow of water was immense. In fact, for two hundred miles out to sea, the normally salt water was still partly fresh. The volume of water now posed a problem to us as with our very slow speed, it would push us sideways and out into the Atlantic.

Instead of steering our normal course, we had to allow for this. It was partly guesswork and without GPS, we had no real position available until such time we would pick up land after crossing the mouth of the Amazon.

After three days while sailing slowly along but I was becoming increasingly worried about Jimmy. At the best of times, navigation was a bit of a mystery to him, and what we were now doing had him totally confused. One of the seamen called me and said, "Captain, Jimmy is sitting in the passenger's area wearing his lifejacket."

I went down to see him and found him praying. He said, "We are lost, and we are all going to die, I'll never see my family again."

What could I say? Lost well kind of, as I certainly did not know exactly where we were, but it was time for a good 'white' lie. I told him, "Jimmy, come to the bridge and I'll show you on the chart where we are within a few miles." As for an exact position, I had no fucking idea!

He seemed a bit relieved, and I told him the plan was to head south for the next two days and then head due west until we would come into the Brazilian coast and from there would work out where we were. He cheered up a bit but would not remove his life jacket.

We were lucky and when we did eventually alter course and head directly into towards the coast, I found out that we had gone some 30 miles too far. No big deal and after following the coast for a few hours, we visually sighted a lighthouse we recognised and began our trip up the river into Belem.

Arriving and immediately going into the dry dock, Jimmy and I got a bonus in the form of a three day stay in a good hotel as thanks for making the trip. Jimmy had stopped praying, his life jacket was safely packed away and it was now time for wine, women and song, and Belem was as good a place as any for these diversions.

I was long overdue for leave, which I had dodged in order to continue working in Brazil but now I was told I would have to take the days due to me or lose them. Leave days were paid, so it would have been crazy to throw them away. I would fly out to the UK once my three-day bonus hotel stay was up.

Same Job but with a New Employer

And then a chance encounter changed everything. As far as personnel were concerned, employment in the oilfield in some ways was a kind of a closed shop. Although a very high-cost industry in the sense that huge amounts of money were spent on the exploration side, the returns on investment when oil was found were astronomical.

The number of oilrigs in operation was not excessive, and consequently the number of persons required to work them was relatively small. As wages tended to be very good, despite hard work but with generous leave breaks, very few people quit.

This in turn meant there were very few job openings for inexperienced, or to use the industry term, 'green' hands. As such, the number of new entry personnel were very limited. After a few years in the industry, it was quite common to bump into guys you had worked with at some point in time. This was generally in hotel bars, whorehouses or most commonly, in airports.

It was in the hotel bar on my second last day in Belem that I bumped into Arthur, last seen in Ashdod Port in Israel where he was a diving superintendent. He was doing the same job in Belem and the company he worked for also had several oilfield tugs. We chatted, he told me the kind of money they were paying, told me who to call when my leave (or money) ran out, and that was that.

They were paying nearly double my present wages. Again, not so long ago, it was the custom, particularly in the USA, when applying for a change of company to simply say, "You know 'so-and-so', you worked with him in 'wherever'. He said I should drop by as maybe you are looking for hands." It was standard procedure and almost always worked.

The interview would be spent talking about guys you both knew, where they were now and on and on. Yes, your documentation would be checked, but unless you later failed the mandatory medical, the job was yours and had been from the moment you entered the interviewer's door.

Unfair practice, perhaps, but nobody I knew ever recommended anyone who was not good in their job. It was very unusual to go to a boat or oilrig literally anywhere in the world and not know somebody working there. Most of my fellow workers were from the southern states of the USA. Hands from Texas, Louisiana, Mississippi and Alabama would normally have made up at least 70% of most crews.

My friend Arthur had spoken with the personnel department and when I first rang, I was put through to a Mr 'Red' Clifton. He said he had expected a call and could I go to Gabon/West Africa at short notice. Yes was my answer and just two days later, visa received in London, I was sitting in an Air Afrique jet on my way from Paris to Libreville/Gabon.

From Libreville to the operation base in Port Gentil by helicopter with a French crew change headed for one of the rigs there. The ship I was to join was in port but the charterer Elf Petroleum had booked a room for me in their company staff house and I was asked to report to their office the following morning before going to the port and joining my new vessel. A very unusual start to a contract, so I was somewhat puzzled.

I am a very early riser and next morning could well have been my last on the planet. The staff house had one long central corridor with some eight guest rooms on either side. It was just daylight and, in a T-shirt, shorts and thongs, I decided to go for a walk around the neighbourhood before taking breakfast or at least a wake-up coffee.

I was just about to step out of the doorway when an African guy shouted really loudly and held his hands in the air. He rushed towards me, motioning for me to retreat back into the corridor. He then came over, pointing at the step outside the door and telling me in French to go out the door at the other end of the corridor. I did this and then slowly made my way around to where he was still standing and shouting, by this time several other African people had arrived.

The cause of the excitement was a large snake coiled up on the step. It did not seem unduly worried about the people and the noise, but had I stepped out that door, one foot would have landed right on top of it. It was certainly more than a meter long, was quite fat and with a beautifully patterned skin. The guesthouse manager, a Lebanese had come and had told his staff to get rid of the snake, presumably to kill it and he asked me to join him for breakfast.

At breakfast, he apologised but instead I asked him to thank the staff member who had certainly saved me from probably being bitten. He said the snake was a

Gabon Viper and extremely poisonous. I thought he was simply covering his ass when he went on to say he had never seen this type of snake in Port Gentil and certainly never in the staff house area, which was neat and tidy.

However, it turned out that he was probably telling the truth. Apparently, this snake rarely leaves the floor of the dense jungle where it hides in dead leaves and low undergrowth alongside game trails, waiting motionless for hours until prey comes along.

It strikes extremely quickly and has the largest fangs of any of the viper family. The fangs do not retract after biting its victim but continue to pump in venom. I saw all this in the Elf Petroleum Office when one of their staff showed me and translated a brochure they had prepared for their workers who spend time in the jungle.

It concluded by saying the snake despite its venomous capability was normally very docile and unlikely to strike unless inadvertently handled, or no doubt in my case, stepped on! Now I found out the reason I had been 'overnighted' in the staff house and brought to the office before going to my ship.

There had been an accident on the ship on its last trip while tied up alongside one of the oilrigs. A wire had snapped under load and had whipped back and struck the leg of the chief engineer, who was standing nearby. His leg just below the knee had been almost completely severed. There was always qualified medic on the oilrig, and he attended the man until an emergency helicopter arrived and transported him to hospital in Port Gentil.

The German Captain on the boat was very distressed, blaming himself for what had happened by allowing the engineer to be where he was. The ship returned to port and tied up at the wharf. A little later, an ambulance stopped at the gangway and two African hospital staff in white uniforms came onto the ship carrying a package for the Captain.

He thanked them, they left, and he opened the package to find the chief engineer's severed leg. Fortunately, the Chief Mate was there at the time as the Captain passed out. When he regained conscientious, he was mumbling incoherently, and the Mate phoned the charterer's office to request medical assistance.

A few minutes later, the ambulance returned this time taking the Captain off to hospital. He had suffered a complete mental breakdown. This left just the Mate and a handful of African crews on board. Charterer Elf were great and told me the ship would remain in port until investigations were carried out and a new chief engineer came in.

So with this introduction I was dropped at the gangway of my new command. It was practically a ghost ship. I went right through the vessel from top to bottom, looking for the Chief Mate, crew members, or people of any description.

There was one African seaman on the boat and he in African French, my knowledge of which was at best very limited, told me that the rest of the crew were at a cafe outside the main gate, taking their morning coffee break.

Off the boat, out the main gate and sure enough, fifty meters down a side street was a cafe with some Africans drinking what looked to be coffee. No Mate evident. How to speak to them? I simple repeated the name of the ship several times and was rewarded by smiles, yep these seemed to be my crew, or at least some of them.

At this point, a skinny white man rushed out from an alleyway, hot in pursuit of a chicken. My new African crew pointed at him, shouting, "Colin, Colin." He looked up, saw me, gave up chasing the chicken and came back to my table.

He was my Chief Mate. No good morning or how are you, his first words were, "I just bought that chicken, now it's gone." I thought, better not ask, it will only complicate things further.

I told him, "I'm Jake Smith and it looks like I'm going to be your new Captain."

He said, "I'm Colin and I'm the Mate. I'm a bit new in the job, previously I was a taxi driver in Belfast in Ireland." The situation was getting better by the minute.

I told him what the client Elf had told me, and he said, "Yes that's what happened. The chief engineer is being repatriated as soon as he is well enough to travel, and the German Captain is completely 'gaga'."

I asked him how the crew were in their duties, and he laughed and said, "They're fucking hopeless, but they are good men and I'm teaching them."

I said, "You speak a little French then."

Which generated another laugh and the response, "not a fucking word, Cap."

I was soon to learn that the 'f' word occurred in every sentence Colin uttered, but it was hard not to like the man. As Irish as they come, a hellish sense of humour and as good as his word, he achieved wonders with the crew who, to quote his first words, really were hopeless.

But with dogged determination, he was determined to make seamen out of them despite his own scanty seamanship skills and the language barrier. I was later to find out he had obtained his professional licence through dubious means.

Three days in port was proving to be expensive as even a few beers in Port Gentil cost 'a bomb'. The supermarket shelves held almost all products, which could be found back in France, but the cost was France plus, plus, plus.

I went to the local market one morning with Colin as he wanted to show me live monkeys for sale but unfortunately, he did not tell me the full story until we were in the market.

There were monkeys, two or three different types but all small monkeys. They were arrayed on a table with just their little heads protruding through holes in plywood sheets. When Colin told me what the idea was, I walked away. I loved most animals, not particularly monkeys, but I didn't like to see any form of cruelty towards any.

A Gabonese belief, at least by some, was that monkeys' brains were beneficial for any number of reasons and best eaten when just removed from their owners' skulls. Sickening, but it was for real. These little 'men' (they looked almost like little kids) were going to have their brains removed and eaten while still warm. YUK, the headless bodies would also not be wasted but would end up later on the table.

In the oil company office, I saw a large photo of the late legendary Dr Albert Schweitzer with an attached summary of his life. After a brilliant academic youth studying theology, music and in his late twenties, medicine; he decided to devote the remaining years of his life as a Christian medical missionary in Africa.

He chose Gabon, which at the time was called French Equatorial Guinea, one of many countries which made up France's vast colonial possessions in west and central Africa.

He chose to move to a remote township, Lambarene, in the jungle some 200 miles upriver from Port Gentil and Libreville, then the only cities with a significant French or European populations.

A small basic hospital was built under the supervision of both him and his wife, and although considered somewhat primitive even by the standards of the time, he was, for the first time able to offer medical assistance to the local people.

Schweitzer won a Nobel Peace Prize for his work and although he passed away decades ago, his hospital had gone from strength to strength. He was buried in the grounds of the hospital he created. These days Lambarene is a small city, capital of one of the Gabonese States and the now modern hospital is recognised worldwide for research into malaria.

He was an outspoken critic of colonialism his entire life, a fact which did not endear him to the authorities, and towards the end of his life, he became a fierce opponent of nuclear armament.

The summary in the oil company office concluded with a quote attributed to him. 'Do something wonderful, people may imitate it'. Makes a lot of sense in this troubled world! Meanwhile, the Captain I had replaced had been sent back to Germany as had the injured chief engineer.

A new engineer had arrived from Scotland. He reported on board drunk, and sadly it was a condition that turned out to be pretty much on going. The Chief Mate helped him up the gangway, carried his suitcase and then came to tell me that it seemed like he had bottles in it.

We sailed on a twelve-hour run out to the first rig we were to supply. The engineer was ok but reeked of whisky. After finishing the discharge of our cargo, the rig sent us to anchor to wait for them to prepare items for shipment back to Port Gentil.

Time spent standing by at anchor varies according to the oilrig requirements and we were still at anchor three days later. By which time, my new engineer had made several appearances on the bridge demanding to know when we would be released to go back to port, claiming he was sick. Quite simply he had run out of booze and was in a bad shape.

The Mate and I were having our supper when the ship's engines started up, followed shortly after by the sound of our ship's anchor being retrieved. Rushed forward to find the engineer driving the anchor winch, having told our seamen to 'piss off'.

He told me he had to see a doctor as soon as possible and that the ship had to go to port now. I told him I would contact the rig immediately and he could go up and see their medic. He did not want this, but I told him this was procedure, and this was what would happen.

The rig medic immediately diagnosed the problem, gave him some medication and told him to go back to the boat. He point blank refused, demanding instead to be medically evacuated by helicopter into Port Gentil. The rig called me and asked if we could do without an engineer for a few days. Told them OK and that was the last we saw of our Scottish friend, but not the end of his mischief making.

His medivac helicopter arrived in Port Gentil late afternoon, the agent picked him up, took him to his house and from there to the hospital where he was admitted. Around midnight he walked out of the hospital, somehow without being seen and headed back to the private home of the agent.

Again, undetected he managed to enter the house, went to the main bedroom where the agent was asleep with his wife and shook him awake, demanding some local money. The agent pacified him while his wife called the cops.

Port Gentil was not a big city and shortly after the gendarmes arrived, had to physically restrain him, cuff him and take him to jail. He was deported the next morning, apparently after he had been allowed to buy a small bottle of whisky to settle him for the flight.

A couple of days later, we returned to Port Gentil and found a new American Chief Engineer waiting on the wharf. It turned out our crew troubles were over as he was a top-notch hand. Our life became routinely pleasant and boring in and out of Port Gentil on a weekly schedule.

Each time we were out in the oilfield, we were able to catch plenty of fish, the best being Dorado. It is a surface fish growing up to a meter in length, the male being distinguished by a big 'bull' head. The female smaller and most often you would see them swimming together, maybe they paired up for life, and I was never able to find out.

For bait, we used tiny squid bought in Port Gentil and when the Dorado were around, they could not resist the offer, hard striking at high speed almost hooking themselves with little effort on our part. When you pulled in one, the other of the pair would often follow and end up being caught with next throw of the line.

In the water, the fish were brilliantly coloured with a mixture of almost luminescent shades of blue, green and yellow topped off with a long, big blue dorsal fin running down the entire back.

Once landed, it was sad to see the dazzling colours rapidly fade as the fish died. So why catch these beautiful fish, one reason only, freshly caught they were an excellent table fish. In Hawaii, they go under the local name of Mahi-Mahi and were a prime restaurant fish.

On the boat, we would both grill and deep fry the fillets, either way made for an excellent feed. My leave was now overdue and back to Libreville, onto Paris as I was planning a month's holiday in North Europe. After three months of Africa, I was ready for some cooler weather and exposure to some of these beautiful Scandinavian blondes, hopefully with morals to match those of the stars in the porno movies we had on the ship. Well, no harm in dreaming!

So farewell 'adieu' Gabon, or so I thought. An intended two days in Paris turned into a week after finding a wild discotheque in Saint Denis. I met up with a girl, OK to be honest a good time girl, and we had a great time but my carefully hoarded savings were disappearing by the minute.

St Dennis was a fascinating suburb, lots of cheap, clean places to stay, any number of excellent places to eat, and to fill in the daylight hours away from the temptations of bars and clubs, plenty of historic sites to visit. On the down side, parts of St Denis contained blocks of what were low income apartments, which for the most part were tenanted by people of North African Arab descent. They were almost all Muslim.

In these communities' youth crime and unemployment were big problems. Drug abuse was an ever-increasing issue and prostitution was rife. My new girlfriend had been born in St Denis though her Mum and Dad had come to France as immigrants from Morocco.

One morning, she asked me to come with her to visit her Mum. I tried to back out and she said, "Jake, I believe you're scared."

My answer, "You bet I am, where you want to take me is no place for a white European with blue eyes and blonde hair who can hardly speak French much less Arabic!"

Of course, I went with her and am so glad I did. I saw a part of France I would never have believed existed. These housing blocks were light years away from the France of the tourist brochures. Spoken Arabic (or similar) everywhere, Arabic music emanating from the apartments and groups of young people hanging around on street corners no doubt dodging school, the law, or maybe both.

The whole area was surprisingly clean though very run down and the word that flashed through my mind was 'ghetto', I'm in a mini ghetto! No 'Vive La France' here! The visit to her Mum was to give her some money, of course some of my money, but after all she was a working girl and was looking after Mum, so all in a good cause, her dad having passed away.

We left and as we got back to the Metro station, I told her I was glad I had come with her. She brought me down to earth when she replied, "don't ever come there alone at night Jake, even the cops come in numbers to this estate, some of the guys you saw this morning are bad."

There was something about French women which almost makes them distinct from their sisters in other countries. Regardless of whether they were wearing outfits from a local department store or the latest designs from one of the up-market fashion houses, they instinctively seem to know just what to buy and how to dress in a way that was both chic, sexy and totally in accordance with their character.

It didn't seem to matter whether they were shop assistants, students, secretaries or hookers on the streets of St Denis, they just had this certain 'je ne sais quoi'.

A great way to spend a sunny morning was to sit for hours sipping endless coffees or enjoying a beer in anyone of the many city sidewalk cafes simply admiring the women walk by, a continually changing 'catwalk parade' and totally free.

I did all the things a visitor to Paris was supposed to do, mentally clicking them off my memory bank. Yes, the Louvre-done, yes, the Eiffel Tower-done, yes, Montmartre-done. Everybody had favourite places to visit, visit again or perhaps decide to settle permanently.

I don't think I would ever want to live in Paris, I'm just not a big city person, but if ever I had enough money to just buy an air ticket and 'go anywhere for a few days', then Paris was certainly high up on the list.

Wonderful Copenhagen

It was now time to head for Scandinavia and the starting point was to be the Danish capital, Copenhagen. My mental vision of Copenhagen was straight out of a TV travel documentary.

I remembered scenes taken on a sailboat cruising the city waterways, tourists drinking beer and shooting innumerable photos, while the guide portrayed it as the city of Hans Christian Anderson, the author of so many magical tales for the very young. Throughout, discretely in the background, the lilting melody 'Wonderful, Wonderful Copenhagen' played over and over.

Yep! I was ready for the touristy thing. A short flight and we landed in Denmark. Found the Metro train office and a friendly lady speaking impeccable English, told me which station to alight nearest to the Nyhavn Canal. First stop was to line up a bed, the cheaper the better. I was starting to realise that Denmark, or perhaps it was just Copenhagen was turning out to be a lot more expensive than St Denis.

Room found, it was now time for a beer or two as it was late afternoon, but still pleasantly warm. A Danish woman I had met in Israel had told me if I ever made it to Copenhagen I should head for, and stay in the old downtown port area, by name 'Nyhavn'. Well, I'd made it!

She also told me that in Denmark it was within the law to buy beer in a supermarket and then quite legally drink it in the street. I remember asking her why you would do this, and she laughed and told me that bar prices were high, and most people would have a few 'cheap' drinks, get a slight buzz on before hitting the bars or clubs. She being Danish and from Copenhagen would have to be right, so following her advice had to be the way to go.

Bought a couple of cold beers in a supermarket, walked no more than a kilometre and found myself at the Nyhavn Canal. A string of colourful two-story houses lined the Canal and beneath them at ground level were numerous pubs, restaurants and bars. A lot of old wooden boats were tied up along the Canal, many of them double berthed. Without exception, they looked in immaculate condition.

I sat on the harbour wall and nervously opened a beer. I had never been in a city or country where, without being in a sidewalk cafe, you could drink openly in the street. Sure, many a time I had seen 'winos' in alleyways, drinking from a bottle concealed in a paper bag, and the law, knowing who they were, generally would leave them alone if they stayed out of trouble.

But here it was open and above board for everybody, though I suppose an age limit came in somewhere. The street was crowded, and nobody paid the slightest attention to me, this was great, I was really starting to love Danish customs.

I asked a passing guy if some of the tied-up boats were commercial fishing boats. He told me they were at one time, but government catch quotas had hit their income hard. Many had sold out, somewhat of a tragedy where fishing had been a family livelihood for generations, while others had been able to enter the booming tourist trade. He told me that some of the houses along the Canal were 200 years old, looking at them you would never have known.

My two bottles gone, time for a meal and some more excellent Tuborg beer. I spent half an hour just wandering down the Canal 'casing' the many different restaurants, one thing they had in common was high prices across the board. There were plenty of fast-food joints around but as much as I loved pizza and McDonald's hamburgers, I wanted something better for my first meal in Copenhagen.

I picked out a little seafood restaurant with nice decor and ordered good old fish and chips. It took forever for the food to come but knocking back beers and crowd watching kept the hunger pains at bay. When the meal arrived, it was excellent and worth the wait.

Now time for the dreaded bill and it was high, but Tuborg had worked its magic so just shrugged my shoulders and threw in a good tip. Tomorrow, it would be back to breakfast and a budget evening meal, but that was tomorrow and there was still tonight beckoning.

Made a move to a pub, as it turned out not a good move. I had had enough to drink in the restaurant and was drunker than I realised when I entered the pub. Ordered a beer, drank it slowly, ordered another and clumsily knocked it over. Over the bar, over me and over a guy sitting next to me, chatting to his girlfriend.

He was extremely understanding, even refusing to let me buy him a drink. I really was starting to like these, Danes. Had he been aggressive, he could have floored me in an instant, but then again, his slim girlfriend could probably have done the same.

The barman was giving me dirty looks, time to pay and go and back to the hotel which was, oh shit, where? All's well, made it back courtesy of a couple in the street and a business card from the hotel, which fortunately I had not lost. Finally, to bed; crash!

Day two Copenhagen kick started with a super hangover, would have to watch this Tuborg beer! There were many and varied ways of getting rid of last night's overindulgence and I guess in time I had tried most of them.

The 'cold turkey' approach, don your sneakers, T-shirt, shorts and then walk, walk, walk, popping a Panadol before beginning. Others say a 'bloody Mary' with a dash of Worcestershire sauce works, and some swear by a couple of mini bottles of Red Bull for a quick fix.

But my favourite remains the tried and true 'hair of the dog that bit you'; quite simply, start your cure with an ice-cold bottle of beer. It does work though sometimes a second bottle helps to speed up the process. The obvious danger of this was the temptation to take a third bottle and before you knew it, you were half pissed again!

According to a brochure I picked up in the hotel lobby, any trip to Copenhagen was not complete without a visit to the famous Tivoli Gardens Amusement Park. First the waterfront Nyhavn Canal and then the Tivoli. Well, the Nyhavn experience had happened but after last night, the thought of an amusement park and roller coaster rides was definitely not on, I needed a quieter recovery day.

Where better for a quiet day than a museum. The National Museum of Denmark was no more than a short walk from the hotel. It was a large impressive light brownstone three story building with typical high sloping roofs, no doubt to cope with snow in the winter. And it was free entry.

There were several separate pavilions, and I chose to concentrate on the exhibition which focussed on the Viking era covering the years 850-1050 AD. During this period, the seafaring raiders or Vikings in their fleets of long ships raided far and wide throughout Western Europe, plundering towns, churches and monasteries.

Archaeological records now show they visited Iceland, Greenland and the eastern shores of Newfoundland in Canada some four centuries before Christopher Columbus's discovery of America.

In their own language, the word 'Viking' translated as 'pirate' and now centuries later, there was a certain romanticism attached to the word, but in that era for a villager living in a peaceful hamlet in East Anglia or Ireland, the arrival of these savage hordes from the north must have been a terrifying experience. Anyone, including monks, who offered resistance were summarily killed while the fittest of the others were taken as slaves.

Their sometimes-long sea voyages were made in their longboats. Built out of oak, they had a single tall mast carrying a relatively large square sail. On each side of the boat, long oars were mounted in ports. As many as sixty men, fellow Vikings or preferably slaves did the hard work of rowing presumably when the wind had died.

On the voyages, the warriors' shields were secured along the sides of the boat above the oar ports, serving the dual purpose of saving valuable space and preventing the entry of sea spray.

I stopped off at the museum shop, just for a browse and but for an elderly lady attendant, it was empty. She greeted me and we started to chat. Her parents had lived in Copenhagen all their lives including the period when Nazi Germany occupied Denmark from 1940 until 1945. I asked her if she had any stories from her parents about this period. She did, she liked to talk, and I was a rapt listener.

She told me that when Germany attacked Denmark in 1940, the Danish Military resisted, but quickly realised that it was futile and surrendered 'with honour' was how she put it. The idea being to avoid the destruction of their beautiful country by a vastly superior war machine.

A deal was reached between the conquering Nazis and the Danish Government, allowing the country to continue to run normally; however, under the strict watchful eyes of the Germans. The first dissention occurred when the Nazi headquarters informed the Danish people that any Jews among them would have to wear a yellow armband inscribed with a Jewish Star of David.

The Danish King Christian X responded by saying that all Danes were the same and he would wear such an armband when he went for his daily ride through the city on his white horse. He further would expect every loyal Dane to wear such an armband.

I asked the lady if she had any photos of the King, on his horse, wearing the armband. She said she did not, and suspected he was never obliged to carry out his threat as the new Nazi Administration rescinded the order the next day. She did say that now many decades after WW2 had passed into history, the story of the King's action had become a legend that Danish people were proud to recount.

She then went on to tell me of another instance coming out of WW2, which the Danish people at the time were ashamed of. As in most of the countries annexed, conquered, overrun by Germany at the start of the war, the invaders found active sympathisers amongst the local population. Denmark was no exception.

She then showed me a photo taken in the Copenhagen Central Railway Station in 1940 of a train departing for Germany with Danish volunteers for the Waffen SS Viking Division. They were leaning out the windows of the carriages waving, smiling and obviously shouting.

She seemed a bit embarrassed and went on to explain that most of these Danish volunteers came from the south of Denmark near the German border, and that when the war was over, those that survived and came back to Denmark were arrested, tried and served jail sentences.

Feeling much better after the museum venture, it was back to the hotel, checked my emails, only to find my employer wanted me to call urgently. Calls from the 'Boss' were rarely good news and this was no exception.

"I've been trying to contact you for two days, please call me on this number as soon as you can," blah, blah, blah.

What to do? They were a good company and had treated me well. Really, I had no choice if I wished to keep working for them.

"Can you fly back to Gabon as soon as possible as the guy who relieved you has family problems back in the States and wants off?"

"Hi Mr C, no problems. I'm in Copenhagen right now, can you arrange a ticket from here?"

"You'll have it tomorrow, Jake, is that OK?"

Oh well, it had been a short leave but a good one and let me think, Gabon again!

Gabon, Port Gentil Take 2

Two days later, the ship was alongside the wharf, and I walked up the gangway. Entering the accommodation, I came across three African women doing their laundry in the ship's washing machines. Strange, but no problem, and no seamen around. I went up the staircase to where the officers had their cabins and was greeted by a tall Italian guy who introduced himself as the Chief Mate.

The obvious 'what's going on' brought the news that the ship had completed its contract and would be leaving Gabon in the next days for South Africa. However, there were crew problems. Our Gabonese seamen had decided they would not sign off the ship, would not work, and had gone ashore, leaving their wives on board to ensure we did not slip out of port. These were the ladies I had encountered as I passed the laundry.

The seamen had gone to their union and were demanding six months' salary in hand before they and their wives would leave the vessel. Within minutes, the ship's agent came on board and told me he was in contact with our head office and was negotiating a deal with the Union as regards the sailors' demands. He said this would be resolved the next day, but a bigger problem remained.

The Union advised that as the seamen were being terminated, where were their replacements? The Union representative told the agent that he would not allow any non-Gabonese seamen to come onto the ship while it was in Port Gentil. He wanted the local seamen to stay until South Africa, but the agent said this was not a good idea due to the time required to get visas for our crew to sign off in South Africa.

Nothing was happening fast! The agent finally agreed to pay the seamen two additional months' salary, providing they left the ship. Big, noisy argument in African French followed with the sailors sticking to their original cash demand. I was out of this mess, I knew the seaman's pay was not a lot, so I said why not give them what they were demanding, and we could leave port. This idea was quickly rejected, the agent saying that if we did this, all other companies operating locally would face serious wage demand problems.

The agent then showed me the crew work agreements, which clearly indicated they were only entitled to one month's additional pay in event of termination at short notice. By this time, after only a few hours on board, I was about ready to quit. My first trip had been chaotic and now the second trip was heading down the same sad path.

And then the shit really hit the fan. A posse of the local gendarmes stormed on board, brandishing their truncheons. The agent informed the seamen and their wives that he would pay them two months wages immediately after which they were to peacefully leave the ship. Failure to do this and they would be arrested. The union man advised them to leave as soon as they had been paid.

An hour later, only we three Europeans remained on the ship. Legally, I could not sail the ship out of port. Each vessel had what they call a Manning Certificate, showing the minimum number of crew that must be on the ship in order to put to sea. As crew numbers went, we were short, and short, big time!

If I sailed and some unexpected incident occurred then as Captain, I would have to go to court, could lose my licence and if there was a serious disaster, I could end up in jail.

On the other hand, if we stayed alongside in Port Gentil, we would have to have a police guard, would not be able to go off the ship at all, until such time as money changed hands and a new crew appeared from somewhere. We three put our heads together and I asked for their thoughts, namely what the fuck were we going to do?

No response so I said I would go with the agent (and gendarme) to his office, phone the USA and ask them if they were ok with it, then I would sail shorthanded with just a chief mate and chief engineer as my crew. The instant reply from head office was, "Ok with us Jake, if you're confident the three of you can manage the trip, then go." Not a mention about the legality of such action.

Actually, I was pleased, we wanted out, and it was not the first time I had 'bent the rules' and would probably not be the last. However, my fine Gabonese crew in a way had the last laugh. All the ship's food stores were gone as were all the bed linen and hygiene materials. In a way, can't blame them. In any African country, jobs were hard to come by and it could be some time before these guys were back on a payroll.

In the meantime, they had plenty of food in the house and soap and toilet paper for months! We had to remain an extra day just to replace the 'borrowed' items. Departing Port Gentil, our destination was Cape Town in the Republic of South Africa.

Basic navigation in that once clear of Port Gentil, turn to port, or left as the Americans would say, and then follow a southerly course down the west coast of Africa, in turn passing the coastlines of the two Congo's, Angola, Namibia until finally South Africa.

Too easy, but things rarely follow the simplest prepared plans. With just our crew of three, we had to keep the navigation bridge always manned. Our engineer had directed all the engine room alarms to the bridge so we could get by with a just a walk through the machinery spaces hourly to visibly check all was OK, presuming of course no alarms had activated.

Two of us would be always up except between midnight and 4 am when just the Chief Mate would be on the bridge and every hour, he would call either myself or the engineer for our engine room visual check.

We Run Aground

The two Congo's and the long Angolan coastline slipped by with no dramas, and it was not until we were off Namibia that our 'luck' changed. The ship was maintaining course using an autopilot, which operated off the ship's magnetic compass, the preferred mechanical gyro compass being out of commission and waiting on spare parts.

The coast off Northern Namibia, renowned for dense fog at times, was known as the skeleton coast, and it very nearly ended up as exactly that. The Mate was on bridge watch, comfortably reclining in the Captain's chair when he drifted off to sleep.

There had been patchy fog around but after he had nodded off, the fog closed right in, reducing visibility to meters only. He must have sleepily adjusted his feet for comfort and inadvertently hit the magnetic compass, damaging it.

His slumbers continued as the ship, no longer with a working compass, headed directly into a remote sandy beach, finally coming to such a gentle stop that all on board, including the erstwhile officer of the watch continued their slumber.

Twenty minutes later, the Mate came to, puzzled that although the main engines were throbbing away, the ship appeared to be stationary in the water. He called me, I rushed to the bridge, by which time the Mate had realised we were aground. The fog was so thick I could only just see the bow of the ship. The sea was dead calm and with the fog, there was no wind.

I made a snap decision not to attempt to refloat until daylight when hopefully the visibility would improve, so we could at least see our predicament and plan a way out. The engineer had also appeared on the bridge, and I asked him to shut down the main engines.

The Mate went right around the ship, dipping a small weighted line into the sea to get an idea of how deep the water was surrounding us. It appeared we were aground from the bow of the ship back at least some 25 meters towards the bridge and stern. Further inspection revealed no apparent damage to the hull and no entry of water into the ship. Our radar was still working fine, but of course ineffective when the operator was in dreamland!

Morning came and the fog lifted. Miraculously, we had run into the beach at right angles. I breathed an immediate sigh of relief when I saw this. Now we had a reasonable chance of using our engines to retreat into deeper water.

Waited until an hour before high tide conditions, had the engines started and slowly put both in the astern mode. We gracefully slid astern, the water very slowly getting deeper as we progressed. Opportunely we had 'chosen' a very gently sloping approach over sand to the beach, which explained the smooth and unnoticed grounding when we 'collided' with Africa.

We had beer on board and instead of waiting for our appointed 'happy hour' in the evening, we immediately cracked open a couple of bottles. We had been unbelievably lucky, in an area notorious for shipwrecks, we were once again under way and back on course. Somebody up there just had to be keeping an eye on us.

Now with our magnetic compass broken, our auto pilot steering was useless as it no longer had a compass reference to work by. Magnetic compasses were a mandatory part of the ship's equipment and basically short of being intentionally sabotaged, they never failed. Unintentional human error had caused our compass to fail.

A small needle supporting the actual visible compass direction card had broken. We had no spare needle, so with no functioning compass, the only option was to use our radar to keep a safe distance off the coast and head for the nearest available port, which was Luderitz in Namibia.

Radioed the company in the USA, told them of our latest failure 'forgetting' to mention the 'not recorded grounding', why make things worse, and told them to alert Luderitz for our arrival in 48 hours.

Luderitz, Namibia

Bright sunny day as we steamed into Luderitz harbour to be greeted on arrival by the Harbour Master who had apparently told our company that for a rather spectacular fee, he would repair our compass, to which they had agreed. The Harbour Master told us he would take our compass off and work on it in his office, but in the meantime, he would like to show us around the town.

He told us that the original town site had been purchased by a German businessman, who not surprisingly had named the new purchase Luderitz in honour of his family name. In typical colonial tradition, he allegedly bought the land from a local Tribal Chieftain for a mere pittance.

All this took place in 1884 and at the same time, the vast area of territory stretching from Angola in the north to South Africa in the south was seized by Germany and called German South-West Africa. It was to be Germany's only colonial possession on the west coast of the African continent.

Shortly afterwards, work began on the construction of the port, which took some years and the wharf facilities with basic modifications were still in use today for small cargo vessels and a booming rock lobster fishery. German rule in their new colony was extremely harsh and several rebellions broke out with the local tribes. These outbreaks were ruthlessly suppressed by German troops at a cost of thousands of African lives.

The colony of German Southwest Africa was short lived as in 1915, with World War 1 raging in Europe, it was seized by South Africa who easily defeated the small German garrison. South Africa maintained control over the country until 1990 when it was handed over to the UN who renamed it Namibia.

Namibia was largely desert and despite its vast land area, it remained sparsely settled with a total population of just over two million persons. There were several main African tribal groups, each with their own language though everybody we saw spoke Afrikaans as a common tongue.

Luderitz still boasted several fine old colonial buildings built during the German times more than a century ago. We were able to go inside several and were impressed by how well they were maintained. The most interesting was a mechanical workshop, which was still using lathes and drill presses which had originally come out from Germany just prior to World War 1.

So why did the Germans settle in what was then a remote and isolated desert region? What was the attraction? Quite simply, it was rumours of mineral wealth. Small finds of copper, lead, zinc, silver and tungsten had reportedly been found in some areas but with no estimates of quantity or quality. However, this was enough for the German Government to show interest and soon new settlers began to arrive from the motherland.

The rumours surrounding the minerals did turn out to be true and mining operations commenced on a small scale. And then came the discovery that was to change everything and really put German South-West Africa on the map. Diamonds were found literally laying on the beaches just south of Luderitz.

Shortly after this, further diamonds were discovered in the desert sands just a few kilometres inland from Luderitz in what would soon become the town of Kolmanskop. A number of mining companies entered the scene to exploit the new found wealth and basically from that time on, diamonds became the economic foundation of the colony, then SW Africa and finally until today, Namibia.

Gradually, all of the smaller diamond mining outfits were bought out by the South African giant De Beers, who up until recently had a virtual monopoly on the world diamond trade. The Harbour Master told us that while occasional diamonds could still be found on isolated beaches around Luderitz or in the hinterland, it was no longer a common occurrence as all probable 'find' areas had been fenced off by De Beers.

There were frequent signs warning potential trespassers from intruding. Armed security patrolled these secured areas which in some cases covered huge areas of land or beachfront.

Nevertheless, such diamonds were still being found, and if it was outside a secure area, it was legal to pick them up, providing the finder did not attempt to keep them. Legally, any such stones had to be sold back to De Beers at their office in Luderitz.

Confiscation of the stone, fine and or a jail sentence awaited anyone not doing this or getting caught trying to smuggle the diamonds out of the country.

Our tour of the town completed, we all adjourned to the local pub for a few excellent 'Windhoek' thirst quenching beers.

In the pub, I asked the Harbour Master how in the past large numbers of diamonds had been found lying on the beaches. He told us they had originally been washed down rivers after rare heavy rains ending up in the sea. Wave action of the sea had in turn washed the diamonds back onto the beaches. In time, these diamonds would settle deep into the sand and now De Beers were processing the sand down to bedrock to recover these stones.

He also told us that diamonds were classified as being either rough or gemstone quality stones. Gem quality being worth any amount of money per carat, depending on size and colour of the stone. Rough stones, while in demand for a multitude of industrial uses were worth a more standard value, way less than any gemstone.

Further as a market guide, he said the best gemstone, a brilliant cut blue/white flawless one carat stone, would at the present time be valued at a cool twenty thousand US dollars or more. The afternoon was becoming more and more educational when he told us a 'carat' was a measurement of weight and not an indication of size as many people, us included, thought. A one carat stone would weigh just $1/5^{th}$ of a gram, possibly worth $20,000. Wow!

The Harbour Master, who was getting on in years and had been drinking two beers to every one of ours, was starting to slur his words and said he had better go home before he fell over. He thanked us for a great afternoon, no doubt the words of a lonely old timer just glad to have new faces in his small town, but he certainly knew all about diamonds.

However before leaving, he asked us if we would like to visit a former diamond mining town, Kolmanskop which was a half hour drive out of town. Of course, we said yes and he promised he would send down his driver next morning to take us there as first we would have to get passes to enter a secure De Beers area.

We were not sure the following morning whether he would remember the car and driver but both turned up. He had the De Beers' passes and 30 minutes later, we arrived in the ghost town of Kolmanskop. We were really in luck as the driver who was an Ovambo tribesman had heard numerous stories from his forbears who had worked as labourers for the Germans when the diamond boom was in full swing.

He told us he would start from the beginning and said it all began in 1908 when a passing local African, working for a railroad surveying company had picked up a diamond from the sand and shown it to his German boss. The German passed it on for successful appraisal and in no time, other Germans had taken out mining licences and the new town of Kolmanskop came into being.

The town was founded in an area of low hills and sand dunes interspersed with flat areas of windswept rocky plains. It was on one of these plains that the first diamond was found. Miners, many with their families flooded in until by the early 1920s, over 300 families had settled in the new town.

In the first few years, there were so many diamonds in the sand and adjacent windswept areas that on full moon night's, prospectors would sift through the sand on their hands and knees, picking out stones by their bright reflection in the moonlight.

Some of the miners quickly became rich. Family homes following German architectural designs and built of stone were soon constructed, the more successful wealthier settlers building virtual mansions complete with all the latest and best furnishings brought in from Germany.

This was all in the period from 1908-1914 prior to the First World War by which time more than an incredible five million carats had been shipped out of Kolmanskop. With typical Germanic efficiency, exact records were kept of the diamond output and showed that in the early 1920s, production peaked at 30,000 carats per day.

As our informative driver was quick to tell us, the small German community became very wealthy while his ancestors who did the lion's share of the work received very little. A school was set up with teachers from Germany, shops, casino and even a bowling alley to cater for the small white community.

A new hospital was built and had the first X-ray machine on the African continent. I commented to the driver that there must have been lots of injuries amongst the miners to justify this and he laughed, saying the X-ray machines primary use was to detect miners smuggling out diamonds concealed in their bodies.

Kolmanskop went through a real boom to bust cycle. First settlers in 1908 and the last family to leave the town was in 1956 by which time mining was no longer considered economical and many of the townsfolk had moved on to a new boom area to the south of Luderitz.

So, this was the town that greeted us. A ghost town devoid of inhabitants for more than 50 years. Remarkably, many of the town's original buildings were still in a reasonable state of repair, no doubt due firstly to the quality of the German workmanship nigh on a century ago coupled with the extremely dry desert climate.

Many of the glass windows had long since broken and wooden doors were mostly damaged, ajar and open to the weather. The windblown sands of the Namid Desert had gradually encroached on the town to where sometimes more than a metre of sand would be banked up inside most, if not all the buildings.

DeBeers now had put the ghost town on the tourist map and had renovated some of the old buildings. There was a large sign posted at the site, advising that tours were only possible between 8:00am and 1pm on selected days. Again, this was a secured area under the joint control of DeBeers and the Namibian Government. All visitors must have the entry permit and nobody was permitted to stay in the town outside the stated hours.

Not that it was likely that anybody would want to stay after dark as many of the ghost town buildings were, appropriately enough, reported to be haunted. Our Ovambo friend assured us that these stories were true and that in the past, people staying overnight had seen disembodied figures, awoken to find an unseen body whispering in their ear, and heard footsteps as the tortured souls moved around their domain of so long ago.

I was not overly superstitious, call me 'chickenshit' if you will but there was no way I would stay in such a place just in case the rumours were not merely rumours. We ended up giving the driver a generous tip as it really had been a day to remember and his accounts of Kolmanskop so interesting.

He dropped us back at the ship to find the Harbour Master had repaired our compass and suggested we go for a short trial tomorrow morning before leaving for South Africa. Meanwhile, he wanted us to adjourn to the same pub as yesterday, why not, any excuse for a few beers had to be good.

Thanked him for the use of his driver and he told us DeBeers wanted the man to be a tourist guide as he spoke not only his Ovambo language, his everyday language Afrikaans and fluent English as well. He had turned down the offer, happy to remain as the Harbour Master's driver and handyman until such time as he retired.

It was so nice and increasingly uncommon to find men and women who were happy, contented and simply enjoying life with the job they had, not continually wishing for something better. Next morning, the sea trial around the harbour with our repaired compass was successful.

I signed the HarbourMaster's invoice, we received our Port Clearance from Luderitz, and departed—next destination: Cape Town, Republic of South Africa.

Just before departing from Luderitz, I had received a forwarded message from a marine agency, asking me to contact them soon. Apparently, a former employer was looking for a manager for a new start-up operation in Russia. Would I be interested; if so, contact them and an interview could be arranged.

First, a safe arrival in South Africa after which contact the agency, Russia, never been there before, sounded interesting, but interviews could be tricky.